Safety Law
A Legal Reference for the Safety Professional

Edited by Dr. George A. Peters, Esq.
Santa Monica, California
Co-Editor: Dwight B. Esau
Director of Society Services, ASSE

A collection of essays on legal issues and problems facing safety professionals, by some of the nation's foremost technical and legal authorities

Published by
American Society of Safety Engineers
Park Ridge, Illinois

Safety Law

A Legal Reference for the Safety Professional

Ed. George A. Peters, J.D.

ISBN: 0-939874-55-5
Library of Congress Information in Publication Data

Printed in the United States of America

Table of Contents

Appendices

Preface

This book is intended to be an educational and reference document covering one important area relating to the knowledge, skill, and activities of the safety professional. It presents a comprehensive introduction to the basic legal considerations that should be understood by the safety specialist. If read and studied, it will serve to sensitize and alert the safety practitioner to possible legal problems, so that he or she will know when and where to seek legal advice from a licensed attorney. Without a basic understanding of "safety law," a well meaning and properly motivated safety professional could inadvertently violate some legal obligations or requirement and create difficulty for himself and an employer or client. Thus, reading this book could constitute an essential phase in the professional development and a key element in the training of prospective safety professionals.

This book reflects and describes the increasing overlap between occupational safety and product safety. Product liability has vigorously entered the workplace by means of the legal concepts of third party liability, the dual capacity doctrine, the aggravated tort, new interpretations of intentional torts and the increasing allegations of fraud, deceit, and concealment of matters relating to occupational health and safety. This broadening of responsibility for the safety professional has been accompanied by an increasing reliance on the common law in situations where, in the past, compliance with standards and regulations seemed to be the paramount consideration. The regulatory law has also broadened and become more complex. Therefore, the safety professional cannot avoid almost constant interaction with the broadened legal requirements that increasingly govern the profession.

The law should not remain a mystique, a mystery nor a misunderstood set of concepts and requirements for the safety professional. Some basic understanding of the law that pertains to the activities of safety engineers, safety scientists, and safety managers is absolutely essential. This does not mean that the safety professional should become a "jailhouse lawyer" or pseudo-lawyer. What it does mean is that he should gain enough understanding to know when to consult a lawyer, an ability to communicate and coordinate with attorneys, and sufficient comprehension to follow or carry out the legal advice rendered to him, his employer or his client. The old adage "ignorance of the law is no excuse" is still valid and this book is an attempt to dispel ignorance of the fundamental concepts of the law as they pertain to the safety profession. This is the first step in a gradual learning process.

This book illustrates several other legal principles. First, that other countries may have laws quite different from ours, but some apply to overseas employees of American companies and some apply to American products used in a foreign workplace. So the safety professional in a company that has overseas activities or sales should not overlook this potential source of liability.

Second, that the specific law varies in each state or jurisdiction, so the safety specialist should either become aware of the most stringent local requirements that might apply to his work or, better yet, attempt to use the "worst case" (most restrictive) law as a general guide.

Third, that the law seems to be in a constant state of flux or change, with considerable argument and a strong measure of political ideology appearing in the logic underlying enforcement and proposed legal concepts, so the safety specialist should "err on the side of safety" rather than rely upon some current "legal technicality" that might change tomorrow.

Therefore, what is required of the safety professional is a general understanding of the basic principles of law and their social objectives; not a lawyer's precise knowledge of specific cases, exact legal procedure, and legal technicalities. The lawyer is a specialist and fellow professional who stands available to help the safety professional, but it is the safety professional who must know enough to ask the first question.

Hopefully, this book will improve the relationship between two interacting independent professions: the law and safety.

George A. Peters, J. D.
March, 1983

Disclaimer

The material contained in this book is intended as a preliminary source of information and understanding of those elementary legal concepts and requirements that have or should have some influence on the activities of the safety professional. Such basic understanding should alert the safety professional to possible legal implications in his work activities and serve as a "signal" as to when to contact an appropriate legal specialist (lawyer) or other specialist (such as a design engineer, human factors engineer, or occupational physician).

In particular, the safety professional should not attempt to render opinions or act, in any manner, as would a licensed attorney.

In addition, the interpretations and conclusions expressed in this book do not necessarily reflect the views of the editors, officers, members or staff of the American Society of Safety Engineers. They do not reflect any ASSE policy, but are intended solely as a means for stimulating independent thought on controversial matters or problems that may be of concern to the safety profession. The ASSE cannot and will not assume any liability for the contents of this book, in part or in whole, nor for any interpretations of the legal concepts embodied herein. However, there is a hope that conscientious readers will become sensitized and more aware of the possible legal ramifications of their work which, previously, they may not have fully comprehended nor understood.

The objective of this book is to provide a means for a better informed safety specialist acting within the legal constraints of his profession. This, of course, is the hallmark of any professional specialist.

George A. Peters J. D.—Editor

Dwight B. Esau, Co-editor

George A. Peters is an engineer-lawyer who has served as a long-time member and national Vice President-Divisions of the American Society of Safety Engineers, as President of the System Safety Society, a Vice President of the World Safety Organization, a Director of the Board of Certified Product Safety Managers, and as a Director of the Board of Certified Safety Professionals of the Americas. Dr. Peters is the author of several books, numerous articles and is a frequent lecturer on safety related matters. He is authorized to practice law at the state and federal trial court level and before the United States Supreme Court. He is a Registered Professional Engineer and a Certified Safety Professional.

Editing of the manuscript and supervision of the production of this book were carried out by Dwight B. Esau, Director of Society Services for the American Society of Safety Engineers.

Judicial Assessment of Technology (Stare Decisis)*

Honorable Howard T. Markey

Judge Markey is Chief Judge of the U.S. Court of Customs and Patent Appeals in Washington D.C. This philosophical discussion of the relationship between engineering, technology and the law was originally delivered to the American Association for the Advancement of Science in February, 1978. It is reprinted here, with permission, as an introduction to the subject of safety law. It was published by ASSE originally in the March 1979 issue of Professional Safety Magazine.

In the movie Star Wars, the technology was impressive indeed. But it was courage, self-sacrifice, and belief in the Force, something greater than themselves, that enabled the good guys to win. It was not superior weaponry. The theme accords with history. Never has a higher standard of living, or superior technology alone, been able to preserve freedom and justice for a society that abandoned its ideals.

We speak here, not of science, but of technology. I hope and trust that the judiciary will never be asked, or consent, to assess science. Indeed, there should be a Constitutional provision, "Congress shall make no law abridging the freedom to learn." Knowledge never hurts; only the use, or abuse, of knowledge, i.e., technology, including the technology of learning, can injure. Only technology, therefore, should be subject to assessment.

Judicial assessment of technology is a fancy way of saying "evaluation of technical evidence by judges." And that's a function that judges have been performing since the first robed creature mounted a raised bench and a baliff said, "God save the King and this Honourable Court." Many of the early nuisance cases of the common law involved the technology of a new sulfur-spitting factory built near a residential area. Patent infringement cases have been with us in the United States for over 150 years.

The reason people give speeches and write articles on the judicial assessment of technology is not because the subject is new, but because our modern technological flood has flowed into the courts. When over 90% of all the scientists and engineers who ever lived are living today, it is not surprising that the technological juggernaut has invaded the court room.

Technology comes into the courthouse in different guises. Criminal cases may involve ballistics, lie detectors, or chemical analysis of a poison or a drug. There are some civil cases in which the technical facts may either control or influence the ultimate decision, like some product liability and patent cases. Then there is a new and separate kind of case, of which I shall say a good deal later, which might be called the technological risk/benefit case. This latter type of case has brought to judges much, if not most, of the so-called "social engineering" or "judicial legislation" activities of which we have, often rightly, been accused. The risk/benefit analysis cases have also brought into the judicial process the "social scientists" whom some have described as neither social nor scientific. With them has come the use of statistics, epidemiological studies, probability exercises, and suggestions that juries and judges be instructed in Boolean algebra and Bayesian analysis.

Congress has in recent years been the major conduit to the courts for the risk/benefit, social-engineering, group-interest-balancing, type case. A close second to the Congress is the growth and proliferation of regulatory agency actions dictating the technology of our eating; our wearing; our driving; our riding of motorcycles; of our wording on our labels; of how we must protect ourselves from ourselves with helmets, seat belts, and air bags; of protection from seeing cigarette ads on television; of how we must not take saccharin because it may have an effect and of how we must not take laetrile because it may not. One result of the scientific revolution is the technologically dependent, bureaucracy-regulated state.

It seems to me that judicial assessment of technology involves at least five broad elements. First, there is the need to recognize the essential difference between the judicial process and the scientific-technological process. The second requirement is similar, the need to avoid scientizing the law. Third, there must be created a judicial welcome for technology. Fourth, the special differentness in the risk/benefit type case must be recognized. And last, consideration might well be given a set of rules, known perhaps as the Federal Rules of Technological Adjudication.

---

*to stand by decided matters.

The differences between the judicial and scientific-technological processes are profound and pervasive. Failure to recognize that difference has led to judicial expressions of frustration and an unfortunate tendency to rest judicial decisions on current, and often transient, "truths" and "facts" of science and technology.

The purpose and function of law is to resolve disputes and to facilitate a structure for the organization of a just society — in a word, to provide justice.

Science normally evolves a new, general, physical principle from hypotheses proven by numerous specific experiments. The normal judicial process is precisely the reverse, for, when properly conducted, it applies an existing, generally accepted moral or social value — an ethical principle — a rule of law — to a specific problem.

When understood as the source of the just society, law, to remain law, must be humanistic. When understood as the search for facts, science, to remain science, must never be humanistic.

Judges must approach with great care, the idea that their decisions can be justified solely on the findings of science, lest the quest for justice be lost along the way.

For the particular "scientific truth" relied upon may prove transient indeed. The Supreme Court relied on eugenics in approving the involuntary sterilization of imbeciles. About 12 years later, it reversed itself when the earlier eugenic findings were found to have been incorrect.

To rest a judicial decision on "social science" is to mire the law in even deeper quicksand. The conflicting and changing opinions of psychiatrists and sociologists regarding the question of whether a book, movie, or TV show is "harmful," as Forer believes, may have led to judicial interpretation of the First Amendment as reading, "Congress shall make no law abridging the freedom of speech, except when the experts say the speech has no redeeming social value." Yet the First Amendment exists precisely to protect that speech which the majority consider valueless! Speech considered valuable needs no protection.

The first need is to view technological evidence as merely one evidentiary element in the judicial matrix of decision and not necessarily as the sole justification for the judge's legal decision. After all, Federal Rule of Evidence 702 permits expert testimony to "assist" the trier of fact. In a particular case, as I have said, such as in deciding whether a product infringes a patent, the technological facts may dictate the decision, but the important thing is to distinguish between those rare cases when science and technology do, and the more common cases when they do not and should not, control the outcome.

The second problem is to avoid "scientizing" the law. Typical of the confusion is the common remark — "If we can land on the moon," we should be able to solve the problems of the urban ghetto, or our crime problem, or whatever!

Thus has arisen a failure to distinguish between scientific facts and what man does with them — to distinguish between physical facts and moral values. But to the law, values are its very life. To science, though certainly not to scientists as people, values are non-existent.

Law is not a science. The judicial process cannot become a mechanical, technical, value-free, process and remain judicial. The philosophy of the law is jurisprudence, not "juriscience."

That is not to say that law, anymore than science, can solve all of man's problems. Our people are now turning to the Law as Mecca, with 172,000 cases filed in the district courts last year. But there is a growing paradox. While rushing to the law, like the ancients to Olympus, people are simultaneously disregarding the civil and criminal law in droves. Thus even the limited power of the law to solve some of man's problems is diminished. For if the basic law — that man shall respect and honor and obey the law — be disregarded, all law is rendered ineffective.

The problems of man are not legal primarily — nor primarily scientific. They are moral. To the extent that the law abandons moral values in favor of science, man will find solutions not in his lawbooks or in his laboratory, but in his soul. Darth Vader, the villain of "Star Wars," was defeated, not by science or law, but only by a young man's faith in the "Force." The law, like the Force in Star Wars, must be honored, respected, and believed in, not just used.

The *business* of the law is justice — not truth, not law per se, not the Federal Rules of Civil Procedure, not science, not technology, not economics, not social policy.

Law is designed to solve only one "problem." The problem of justice, or, to use our definition, the problem of affording equal treatment to all persons similarly situated. There are attempts today to make the law only a scientific tool, for solving broad social problems, for achieving a goal in current vogue, for promoting a modern "societal good," for "compensating" or "adjusting" the status of whole classes of people.

The third problem is to encourage a judicial welcome for technology. Judges are, and will for a long time continue to be, confronted with a requirement that they engage in some form of technology assessment in many cases. Because science and technology are strange mysteries to judges, and because judges, some without knowing just why, sense that in many technologically oriented cases they are not dealing in law, *qua law*, the tendency is to cry "let this cup pass."

Many judges have spoken and written of their felt inadequacies to decide such cases. Some have suggested a need for new and trained tribunals, designed to supply reliable answers to technological and scientific questions. Many judges seem to sense the fundamental differences in science and law, even though few would recognize the term "dialectic" as describing their traditional, judicial method of decision, and the term "empiric" as describing the scientific method. But abandoning to others all assessment of technology is a solution not currently open to the judiciary. That is why I say there must be a judicial welcome for technology, in full replacement for the judicial abhorrence now so prevalent.

Technology has nothing to fear from the judicial mind open to receive it. One cannot welcome the unknown, but the judicial mind has nothing to fear from technology properly understood.

Judges cannot all become scientists or engineers — nor should they if they could, As earlier said, that switch in roles would destroy the law and produce a cold, hard society, governed solely by cold, hard facts — without compassion, mercy, equality, and, most important, without justice. But judges can learn to know the methodology of science, the place of science in history and society. Judges can't learn science, but they can learn about science and about scientists. With that background, judges can assess the credibility of conflicting technical or expert witnesses.

Judges can then be freed of the frustration some have expressed with the inability of the "experts" to give them answers, judges may be freed of the felt need to "find an answer" where none exists, and a judge may be freed of the fear of reliance on false answers in a case where he now knows there may be no scientific answer. For example, "Do aerosols destroy the ozone layer?" Science simply doesn't know. After a theory was publicized, the government convened a large number of top experts, who decided that further studies were needed over the next few years, before a reliable answer could be given.

Assessing testimony

A judge who has assessed daily the cover-ups, the stratagems, the dark complex of concealed motives of that inscrutable entity — man — should have little difficulty in assessing the expert testimony of *man qua*-expert. He should have even less difficulty in assessing the best technical witness, a mechanical or electrical or chemical exhibit, which presents no frowns, no tears, no smiles, no sexual vibes, no body language — which never dissembles, or lies, or conflicts with itself.

As in all his judging, the judge in a technologically oriented case must confront certain human frailties. He must be willing to admit he doesn't know. He must avoid a parrotting of sci-tech jargon not understood. He must be neither awed and intimidated by science, nor scornful as a cover for his fear of the unknown.

Technology is in court and is likely to stay there. It cannot be shunned. But it can be welcomed by judges made happier by the welcoming.

Now for the fourth element. Judges must recognize that some technologically oriented cases are different — fundamentally, essentially, different — from the traditional case or controversy which our courts and the judicial process are designed to resolve.

A case involving a decision based on a risk/benefit analysis, for example, of building a dam, or a nuclear plant, is entirely distinct from the decisional process employed in determining the legal liability of A to B, or in assessing the damages sought by C, or in determining the guilt or innocence of D. Part of the problem evidenced by judicial dislike of technology stems from an effort to force these risk/benefit cases into the traditional judicial process, where they simply don't fit. The judicial process as it has developed over the centuries, has dealt primarily with past events; even injunctions which did look to the future, dealt only with the parties to the case — but the risk/benefit case involves a broad policy, future-direction-of-large-segments-of-society type question, the very thing legislatures were designed to decide.

We judges cannot, apparently, escape the risk/benefit case. Not in years has a court said, "This is a political, non-justiciable question." Rules on standing relate to who, not what, may enter the courtroom. Congress in the last few years has passed 47 statutes, establishing broad new rights and social goals and ending with "For details take this to the nearest court." So, if we must be resigned to hearing and determining the risk/benefit case, we had best learn to recognize its true and different nature and we had best study how our new found responsibilities can be met. If, as Lawrance has pointed out, the real question in these cases is "what risk is acceptable to society?" I am not sure that one judge, or three judges, or even nine justices, should be deciding that question, but at least for a time we will be.

And that leads to the last element. A set of new rules. We have now the Federal Rules of Civil Procedure, the Federal Rules of Criminal Procedure, the Federal Rules of Appellate Procedure, and the Federal Rules of Evidence — all designed to resolve a traditional dispute between A & B concerning a past event or events.

We have no rules specifically designed to help judges understand the testimony of conflicting experts, to help him decide between them, or to help resolve a dispute over whether a proposed new activity, or continuance of a present activity, will be so technologically or sociologically injurious to society or to certain groups as to warrant its prohibition or modification. Perhaps what is needed are the Federal Rules of Technological-Sociological Adjudication.

Of course it is the lawyers' job to educate the court and aid the decisional process. A Rule on Jurisdiction, requiring some prior showing that the science-technology questions involved are in fact capable of answer, might be useful. There might be Rules of Technical Evidence — not perhaps what can be shown, but how, by whom, upon what and when such technical evidence may be presented. The rules might include a rule forbidding *ex parte* technical tests, or permitting such tests only under specific provisions defining the conditions under which they may be conducted and recorded, and the results submitted in evidence. Perhaps the rules should state that the courts will not attempt to decide "scientific truth," but will confine themselves to determining whether the law requires or permits a change in the status quo. The rules might well assign the burden of proof. For example, one who desires to introduce a new technology may be assigned the burden of proving its efficacy, safety, etc. Perhaps he who desires to force a change in established technology (established, say, for five years, with an investment of over a set amount, etc.) should have the burden of proving a present injury sufficient to require a change in the status quo.

Perhaps there should be a rule requiring the parties to agree on a simplified statement of any and all technological questions in the case, or to submit their own simplified statements. Perhaps a rule could require submission of statements analogizing the technology to commonly understood, everyday phenomena experienced by judges — like analogizing an electrical circuit to the plumbing in the judge's home. Perhaps a rule should require submission of an agreed glossary of technical terms — with clear definitions — so the court can understand the jargon of the expert witness and the lexicon of the technical publication exhibits. Perhaps a rule should structure the expert conflict, so that they meet on the same ground along the way and do not simply argue "past" each other. Finally it may be both possible and useful to develop clear metes and bounds governing the scope of judicial review.

I know the good lawyer will do much of this without rules, and the wise judge will instruct each set of lawyers along some of these lines at the first pre-trial conference in each technologically oriented case. I also know that some of all this should follow from some of our present rules, particularly those in Article VII of the Federal Rules of Evidence. But I suggest that things might be easier all around — on judges — on lawyers — on the parties — and on the Lady Justice — if law and technology played out their courtroom roles under a special set of rules designed for this special type of game.

In the risk/benefit type case, it must be remembered that plaintiff desires to change the status quo, through the courts. He is not willing to submit the proposed change to the elected legislative representatives of the people, or he has submitted it to them and has been rebuffed.

Unless judges in risk/benefit cases are to become only policymakers — and not judges — unless the courts are not to be courts of law in these cases, but are to become courts of policy — there must be rules which permit and require the courts to look to the law — to find the values recognized and accepted by society — and require the courts to look only thereafter to see how the technological facts before them affect those established values. The rules should not stop with merely looking to see that a correct procedure was followed and correct rules of evidence applied. To stop there — to disregard the values of the centuries — is to slam the door in the face of law.

Among the values which must remain in court, is the philosophy of Government expressed in the Constitution. It is just not enough — if judges would remain judges — to submit evidence that x number of motorcycle riders receive head injuries when they fall — the deeper question is whether the government owns the rider, whether laws to protect me from me are constitutional, whether the risk that a government ambulance may be called makes me a ward of society — the same questions apply to the $600 million cost of seatbelts forced on the 97% of drivers who never wear them, or the $320 per car cost of air bags presently legislated to protect car riders from self injury. The point is not whether Orwellian regulation of every aspect of life, when everything in life is either ordered or forbidden, is good or bad. The point is that courts cannot remain courts of law if they look only to the technical facts in the case before them, and ignore the underlying constitutional principles and values of a free society affected by those facts and by the regulation or proposed change in status quo engendered by those facts.

In summary, the courts have always dealt with technical evidence — the difference now is the complexity of technology, the pressure of a vastly increased judicial workload, and, principally, the demand, in risk/benefit cases, that judges determine whether technological fact predictions require an injunction against otherwise perfectly legal action. In facing up to technologically oriented cases, judges must recognize the fundamental differences in science and law; must avoid, whenever possible, resting their decision solely on technological fact, or scientific "truth"; must avoid the substitution of science for law; must welcome technology, and must recognize that the risk/benefit case is *sui-generis* and not amenable in all respect to traditional judicial processes. Finally, it may be that we need a set of Federal Rules of Technological Adjudication, to govern at least those cases which do not fit within the traditional judicial process.

Courts will continue to make the best possible decisions, while seeking new means toward perfect decisions. But Utopia is unlikely. It may be wise to remember that in almost every decision some social values win and lose — that we are unlikely to devise a decision-making system that lets us have our cake and eat it too.

Whatever we do, it had better be soon. "Coming events cast their shadow." Law is already falling under the shadow of the technological juggernaut, a juggernaut moving too fast for man to absorb or understand or handle. Like man impressed, law is snuggling up to science and is in danger of being herself "scientized." If that process continues unabated, we will have Star Wars without the saving influence of the "Force." We had best rescue law and stand her once more on her sovereign pedestal — lest we one day find that we live no longer under a rule of law — or even under the rule of men—or even under the rule of nice, friendly robots like R_2 D_2 and C_3 PO—but under the harsh, cruel, cold, hard, despotic, but scientifically brilliant, rule of Darth Vader.

Human Factors Considerations in Lawsuits

Julien M. Christensen, Ph.d.

Editor's Note — A long-time Professional Member of ASSE, Dr. Christensen is Chief Scientist-Human Factors, General Physics Corp., Columbia, Md. He is a veteran educator, consultant, lecturer and practitioner in the field of ergonomics, or human factors engineering, as it relates to safety and personnel management.

INTRODUCTION

Rapid advancements in technology have brought incredible benefits to mankind. However, a price has been paid for them. In the United States alone, for example, more than 50,000 people are killed annually in transportation accidents, approximately 14,000 are killed annually in manufacturing industries, and nearly twice that number are killed in the home. An undue proportion of the latter are the very young and the very old — the first group will never have a chance to enjoy the benefits of high technology; the second will not enjoy those few years of leisure that they have earned. Add the cost of hundreds of thousands of injuries every year, and *personal injury and accidental death become our largest single industry!*

Psychologists tell us that human behavior is a function of heredity and environment. The environment in a society like ours is determined principally by scientists and engineers and their supporting staffs. **(Should you doubt this, when you arise tomorrow vow that you will not use or interact in any way with a manufactured product. You will quickly become convinced that those who design, manufacture and distribute products have a lot to do with determining your behavior.)**

It is fair to say, however, that those who produce the artifacts of our society have rather limited knowledge of the capabilities and limitations of those who will use them. Universities and colleges have been slow to include human factors courses in their engineering and design curricula. Thus, the typical designer uses the model of human behavior that is most readily available to him — himself. However, in terms of technical knowledge, personal habits, attitudes, etc., the designer is hardly representative of the population that will use the products. As a result, products are frequently quite incompatible with the knowledge, habits, training and expectations of their users. These incompatibilities often lead to accidents.

Harry Philo, past president of the Association of Trial Lawyers of America, put it succinctly and well when he said, "**Any risk of serious injury or death is totally unreasonable and unacceptable if reasonable accident prevention methods could eliminate or reduce that risk.**" Juries are daily deciding in the courts of our country what is "reasonable." The legal profession has assumed responsibility for righting the wrongs, serious injuries and deaths that have resulted from products that were designed and distributed without adequate consideration of the *human factors* involved. *In virtually every personal injury accident, investigation will disclose human factors considerations that are central to the issues of the trial.*

DEFINITION OF HUMAN FACTORS ENGINEERING

Human factors engineering may be defined as the application of information (data and principles) from the biological and behavioral sciences to the design of equipment, products and systems. One product liability suit after another has demonstrated that ignoring this information frequently results in serious injury, death or significant economic loss.

A MODEL FOR THE REDUCTION OF HAZARDOUS PRODUCTS

Although its origins are obscure, the model below appears to be a modification of an earlier systems safety model developed by the military services. It consists of only five words:

Design
Remove
Guard
Warn
Train

These five elements are listed essentially in order of precedence. Thus, if *reasonable* (there's that key word again!) to do so, safety *designed* into a product is preferable to the attachment of *warnings*.

Design. The preferred method of achieving a safe product is to design it as free of hazards as possible. This can be done in a number of ways. Examples include the use of redundancy on components whose failure presents an unacceptable risk (e.g., automobile brakes), fail-safe designs, interlocks, forgiving designs, etc. Some light aircraft, for example, are so inherently stable that if the controls are left alone the craft will usually assume a posture of straight and level flight. They are "forgiving."

The designer should design for the intended user and, if the product is to be made generally available to the public, for the unintended (foreseeable) user. No one expects an aeronautical engineer to design a jet fighter so that anyone can fly it. However, it is expected that automobile designers will design their products so that any qualified driver (presumably one who has a current license) can handle the vehicle safely and effectively. If this is not so, the vendor should restrict the sale of such vehicles or, as a minimum, offer instruction in their handling. Too frequently in the past, designers, being unaware of the information that is available on human capabilities and limitations, have designed with themselves in mind or some mythical "average user" in mind. This, of course, ignores the vast individual differences among users: a ratio of *at least* 3:1 for most skills. Further, there is no assurance that the rationality of the user will be at all like that of the designer. "The foolish consumer," the "nut behind the wheel," etc, are no longer effective defenses. Even if there was such a thing as an average user, (which there definitely is not), design for this mythical creature would often automatically eliminate 50 percent of the distribution.

Further, while a designer may find averages for any single characteristic (e.g., height, weight, intelligence, etc.), the intercorrelations among most variables are such that most of his distribution has disappeared after consideration of the first four or five characteristics and abilities. In the military services, for example, this has usually meant, at least with respect to physical characteristics, design for the middle 90 percent of the distribution and, where feasible, personal design for the remaining ten percent.

While it is now economically practical only to a limited extent (e.g., eyeglasses, dentures, etc.), in the future we expect to see more and more products designed to "fit" the physical and mental characteristics of a single individual. Adjustment factors may still be required to accommodate changes that take place in the individual because of learning, fatigue and other factors.

Finally, no one expects a completely safe design; however, the courts of our land are making it increasingly clear that they expect the designer to do all that he *reasonably* can to present the user with a safe product.

Remove. We understand that since the early 1900's there has never been a collision between a train and an automobile in New York City. This is because city officials decreed that train tracks and automobile pavements would never cross at the same level — *the dangerous interface was removed.* Another example of the "remove" principle is the handling of hazardous materials (e.g., radioactive) with remote manipulators. Also, robots show promise of *removing* man from many jobs that are unduly hazardous.

Guard. If residual hazards still exist after the designer has done all that he can reasonably do in the areas of *design* and *remove*, he has an obligation to develop *guards*, if appropriate, that will prevent the user from inadvertently contacting a danger point. However, guards must be convenient and obviously essential, and must not impair operations. Otherwise, they are almost certain to be removed or defeated. Some safety experts have cautioned against *undue* reliance on guards. They suggest that guards may often induce a false sense of security and may reduce general alertness, awareness and competence.

Warn. If hazards exist after the designer has done all that he can reasonably do with respect to *design, remove,* and *guard*, then he has an obligation to warn the user. Many product liability suits center around the adequacy of warning labels. Below is a set of rules for warning labels which, if followed, will generally result in adequate warnings:

> *Don't try to correct poor design with labels.*
>
> *Tell* what *to expect,* why *it is a hazard, and* what *to do about it.*
>
> *Be clear, comprehensive and complete for* all *potential users, regardless of degree of literacy or native language.*
>
> *Warn against hazards of both use and foreseeable misuse.*
>
> *Make them conspicuous, attention-demanding, urgent and* emphatic.
>
> *Make them durable and legible; affix to product as well as to case or container*
>
> *Conform to standards but consider standards* minimum *requirements.*
>
> *Pictures, symbols and diagrams are acceptable* if *universally understood and adequate.*
>
> *Current — must reflect latest design and user experience.*
>
> *Use redundancy.*
>
> *Test effectiveness* on representative *sample of potential users.*

See related article on p. 95

Unfortunately, after all of these characteristics have been designed into warning labels, one still cannot specify precisely how effective a particular label will be. Even though the device or label may be perceived by the individual, there is no assurance that this perception will be followed by appropriate action. At the cognitive level, the cues provided by devices and labels must interact with such factors as past experience, attitudes, perceived urgency, and so on. Therefore, it is always recommended that warnings be tested under representative conditions with representative users.

Training. It is assumed that adequate training will be provided. While training can sometimes compensate for poor design, this is a poor basis for the establishment of training requirements. Ideally, both design and training requirements should be considered together during the development of a product. Training should be the responsibility of the designer/manufacturer since they are often the only ones who understand the product thoroughly enough (1) to say whether or not a special training program is needed to assure safe operation, and, if "yes", (2) to specify the requirements and details of the training program. The training expert, like the human factors specialist and safety engineer, should participate in product design early and throughout development. The design engineer may wish to enhance his ability to understand and employ these specialists by taking short courses in human factors engineering and in safety engineering.

CONCLUSION

Investigations have shown that those who use products are generally quite poor at assessing the hazards associated with them. More and more, legislatures and courts are looking to those who design, manufacture, and distribute products to assure that they are reasonably safe and do not contain hidden hazards and unreasonable risks.

The responsible designer should become familiar with the disciplines of human factors and safety engineering and, when indicated, include their representatives early and continuously during product design, development and distribution.

Investigation of Industrial Deaths

Zoyd R. Luce
R. H. Wilson, M.D.

Zoyd Luce

Dr. R. H. Wilson

Both authors have had extensive experience, in their professional careers, with investigation of industrial accidents. Mr. Luce is Director of Industrial Relations for the Bermite Division of Whittaker Corp., Saugus, California. Dr. Wilson is Assistant Coroner for Los Angeles County, California.

Editor's Note — Athough this discussion deals specifically with fatalities, the procedures and recommendations apply equally well to investigations of serious injury or property damage, and even to relatively minor incidents if there is injury or damage. It provides helpful insight relating to the gathering of evidence, dealing with witnesses, and improving the validity of accident analysis conclusions.

This discussion is based upon the authors' experience in the industrial setting and in the Department of the Chief Medical Examiner-Coroner for the County of Los Angeles, California. It should serve as a warning to safety professionals that a careful and systematic investigation of an industrial death may well be the only thing that keeps them and their employer out of court. *One of the most serious mistakes a safety professional can make in investigating an industrial death, within his organization, is to abdicate his responsibility to "proper authorities."*

BACKGROUND

In an age of increasing federal and state legislation regarding industrial deaths, the safety professional must not only ask, "Did I do everything possible prior to this accident to prevent it, to protect the interests of my company"; but, he must also ask, "Have I done everything possible to protect my own interests?"

Ideally, the law seeks justice, independent of the hopes, fears, wishes, and aspirations of all parties concerned. However, in reality, *legal procedures rule supreme.* As a consequence, today's safety professional must not only do everything possible to prevent industrial deaths, he must conspicuously protect his professional integrity, his career, and his legal rights. It is a reality, in the world of industry, that accident prevention, professional integrity, career needs, industry goals and production needs and demands do not always seem compatible. An industrial death, therefore, demands that all of the skills, knowledge and professional judgment of the safety professional be applied to the investigation of that death. A proper investigation also requires that the investigator be intimately familiar with applicable laws in the geographic locale in which he is employed.

AN ILLUSTRATIVE STATE REQUIREMENT

In California, deaths occurring in industrial and other job related facilities are processed by the coroner the same as any other accidental death. There is no special law applicable to industrial deaths. Such incidents are covered by the various provisions of state law that govern overall coroner responsibilities. Sections 5706 and 5707 of the California Labor Code do provide, however, that when an application is presented to the State Workers Compensation Appeals Board that an employee has died as the result of injuries sustained in the course of his employment, the Appeals Board may require an autopsy. Prior to passage of the controversial Proposition 13, the well known "Jarvis" amendment (that significantly reduced funding for all local government agencies), it was the policy of the Los Angeles County Coroner to hold an inquest (an official hearing or examination into the cause of death) on all industrial accident deaths. Following passage of Proposition 13, such cases are now only inquested if there are allegations, or a probability, of serious neglect concerning safety or management practices of the company, or the possibility of criminal activity or neglect.

Although economics may inhibit the investigative activities of California County Coroners, industrial accidents are automatically subject to investigation by the Bureau of Investigations of the California Department of Occupational Safety and Health. An employer can be fined up to $10,000 and/or given six months in jail if convicted of a violation of a safety or health standard resulting in the death of an employee. For a second offense, the employer may be fined up to $20,000 and/or be imprisoned for one year. Such fines may, in the light of a death, may seem insufficient, but the response toward his safety professional by an employer who has to defend himself in court may well be imagined.

It should be noted that these regulations are rarely enforced at the present time. However, there have been instances of enforcement and it should be recognized that the intensity of enforcement of any set of government regulations is contingent upon the particular government administration in power at any given time. Thus, it is a wise safety practitioner who operates under the assumption that any law or regulation (federal, state, or local) must be complied with while they are "on the books."

DEPTH OF INVESTIGATION

A safety professional should make every effort to properly prepare data required by his organization's legal staff. It is the responsibility of the safety professional to acquire all information necessary on an industrial death to not only prevent a re-occurrence but also provide his employer with sufficient data for court defense. That data requires more than just the traditional information derived from accident investigation.

An effective death investigation should encompass the same information which will be developed by official investigating agencies. These agencies may include the police or sheriff, the coroner, Federal or local OSHA representatives, etc. The key factor is that these agencies will frequently lack the expertise necessary to evaluate an injury, especially when the death occurs in unique industries dealing with chemicals, munitions, or other specialized products. It is highly possible that the industrial safety professional will develop a more detailed and accurate report than the investigating agencies because of his specialized knowledge of the work environment.

Herein lies an important fact. Official agencies may occasionally perform inadequate investigations. Therefore, failure to properly and completely perform your own investigation could well leave your company open to unnecessary legal action and expense. The authors' analysis of several prominent industrial deaths in California revealed poor investigative practices by some of the aforementioned agencies. As an example, in some instances official investigators freely accepted second hand information as fact. *Do not fall into the trap of assuming official agencies will perform a competent or even adequate investigation.* The fairness of any subsequent hearing or injury into an industrial death involving your company may well hinge upon the quality of your own work.

EXAMPLES

The primary requirement of an adequate industrial death investigation is thoroughness. Assumptions can be made from the beginning, but one should be prepared to discard them immediately once evidence suggests a contrary interpretation. In visiting the scene of an industrial death, several years ago, the cause of the accident appeared clear enough at first. A construction worker had fallen fourteen feet to his death when a 2′ × 4′ plank he was using as a walkway between two building walls split apart. He had broken his skull and suffered brain injuries. The details began to paint a different picture. He wasn't wearing a hard hat, was an illegal alien totally unfamiliar with any form of safety procedures on the job, and the fatal error was that the 2′ × 4′ that he and his co-workers had been using as a walkway had actually been broken previously and the pieces glued together. In other words, his death could be directly attributable to the lack of enforcement of common sense, as well as OSHA-required safety procedures at the work site.

A similar case occurred when an employee of one of the cities in California was killed at a dump site. He had been standing behind his truck when the driver drove the vehicle backward over him. The key to the accident was that the back-up bell on the truck was not working. Had it been, he probably would not have been killed.

In both these instances, the patched 2′ × 4′ and the inoperative warning device, the actual causes of the accidents had been initially overlooked. In the first instance, a coroner's investigator was sufficiently alert to examine the broken beam carefully. In the second instance, the coroner's investigator acquired the information through his own investigative efforts.

Conversely, another accident investigation carried out by a coroner's investigator contained enough erroneous information to make it almost valueless.

Conclusion: Official investigations vary in thoroughness and may often, in their incompleteness, ignore the role of the employer or incriminate him (because of the investigation shortcomings, independent of the real cause of the industrial death). In essence, allowing official agencies to do your investigation for you may be opening you and your company to extensive personal and organizational liability.

BASIC REQUIREMENTS

The mandatory ingredients of an effective investigation include:

(1) Photographing the body or bodies and the accident scene.

(2) Taking measurements to establish physical interrelationships of material, equipment, and the body within the geographic locale of the accident scene.

(3) Any pertinent material which may ultimately relate to the accident must be collected, tagged, and its supposed relationship to the accident indicated on that tag.

(4) Where multiple casualties occur, stakes (markers) should be posted indicating the location of the body (ies) for future research. (NOTE: If at all possible the outline of the body (ies) should be indicated on the ground by chalk or string and photographed or otherwise recorded.

(5) Witnesses should be interviewed immediately following the accident while the incident is still fresh in their minds. However, this should be viewed as a preliminary interview, preparatory to a more intensive in-depth consultation later. It is important to follow up the first interview so that any contradictions in testimony can be discovered and resolved.

There should be careful photographing of the body, including full field shots showing its relationship to the environment. Pictures should be taken from four sides (where applicable) North, South, East and West. Secondly, the wounds on the body should be photographed; although it is important to keep in mind that in nearly all states the body must not be moved until the police and/or coroner arrive. The source of the injury, established or estimated, should be photographed as well as any other real or imagined factors in the environment which may have contributed to the industrial accident. Stakes should be driven into the ground indicating location for future reference. Where a body (ies) were dismembered, the location of various parts should be identified either by stakes driven into the ground or by making chalk marks. It is incredible how important determining the exact location of a body may become in subsequent follow-up investigations and analyses.

The significance of measurement will vary. Consider, for example, a death resulting from an explosion of unknown origin in an ordnance factory. By establishing the location and distance of the deceased from the origin or source of the explosion, it is often possible to determine, through analyses, the magnitude and direction of the force of the explosion.

After photographing the accident scene and after the area has been released for cleanup by the proper authorities, further collection and tracking of evidence can be carried out. Proper collection of evidence is just as valuable to a safety professional employed by a private company as it is to the examination of an air crash by government officials.

Witnesses, when available, offer both a blessing and a curse to the investigator. Properly questioned, they can offer a clear insight and sometimes the most positive evidence for establishing the cause of the accident. It is necessary to keep in mind one critical truth about witnesses; that is, *a witness' observations must be based on his frame of reference.* The frame of reference consists of two factors, perspective and reality. Reality is the world as it is, the event as it occurred. However, as investigators know from experience, frequently three people see three separate realities. What is observed does not change. What does change is the frame of reference (perspective). The frame of reference is the perspective from which a given individual views things and that can become complex. Examples of how a frame of reference works:

(1) First, personal prejudices may color the way in which an individual perceives reality. A witness who is racially prejudiced may well view an accident negatively in terms of the victims if they are a member of a race the witness dislikes. Example: A black forklift driver was involved in an accident in which a forklift turned over. A witness commented and believed that the driver was driving recklessly when, in fact, he was not. The reason for such a harsh conclusion on the part of the witness was predicated on an intense dislike for blacks.

(2) In another instance, an employee who harbored ill feelings towards a member of management in charge of a particular project, stated frankly that the project manager was responsible for a death caused by an explosion. There were no apparent reasons for the employee to have this opinion other than a dislike for the manager, who, it was claimed, "had failed to take adequate safety measures to insure the welfare of employees working on his project."

(3) Three people seeing the same accident from three separate perspectives, from a scaffold, from the north side of the accident and the south side, will most assuredly see it from a different perspective and conceivably misinterpret the cause and effect of the accident because of their different views of it.

There are a variety of ways to approach witnesses to an accident. There is never a specific right way because circumstances vary so widely. However certain rules of thumb do exist and should be kept in mind by the investigator of an industrial death.

The responsible investigator, or if necessary someone he delegates the task to, should take statements from accident witnesses as soon after the accident as possible. Witnesses have a way of seeking each other out after an industrial accident and, through discussion, their stories often blend together. The more dominant and persistent observer usually influences his less certain counterpart into "correcting" his perspective on what took place. Reality frequently becomes distorted in the process.

After taking down the brief initial statements, it is advisable to request that the witnesses provide more detailed statements at their and your earliest possible convenience. These formal statements should be made in a relaxed atmosphere with a single witness, a trained safety professional, and someone to take notes. Keep in mind that it is better to have someone else, preferably a secretary who takes shorthand, take notes so that the interviewer is free to listen and ask pertinent questions. It is perfectly alright to record an accident witness interview, if the witness is willing. If the witness tends to freeze up or appear extremely uncomfortable, it is better not to record the statements. Very cooperative witnesses frequently become uncomfortable when they know that they are being tape recorded.

One rule that all accident investigators should follow is, never interview more than one witness at a time. Witnesses should be interviewed separately to insure the integrity of their stories.

In interviewing witnesses, it is better to start out by asking them to describe what happened in their own words. After they make their statements, it is time to begin asking questions about details to clarify obscure or confusing portions of their statements. However, always question, don't interrogate. Witnesses are volunteers until under subpoena in a legal proceeding. Consideration and kindness may well make the difference between a witness willing to spend his time stating the facts and someone who becomes uncooperative and anxious to leave.

The investigator must be prepared to correlate the statements of several witnesses and, in consideration of their frame of reference and the physical evidence he has gathered, prepare a more accurate picture of the accident by isolating cause and effect relationships.

CONCLUSION

In the final analysis, the safety professional has no choice but to be his own investigator of industrial deaths occurring within his own jurisdiction. And he must do it with precision and professionalism.

State Workers Compensation — Past, Present, Does it Have a Future?

John C. Vocke, Esq.

This introduction to the philosophy and purpose of workers compensation was originally presented at the 1979 ASSE Professional Development Conference in San Francisco. It is reprinted here from the Annual Volume of Proceedings of that conference, pp. 149–153, with permission of the author. Mr. Vocke is an attorney for Pacific Gas and Electric Co., San Francisco, specializing in workers compensation and occupational safety litigation.

Historical Background

In order to evaluate some of the problems that we are facing today in the area of workers compensation, we have to take a look at the history and background of it. I will take you through a thumbnail sketch of the workers compensation statutes with which we deal today.

The earliest reference to workers compensation comes in the Code of Hammurubi. This code, which was enacted about 5,000 years ago in Babylon, indicated "that *the employer* is obligated to care for the employee by providing sufficient shelter, food and clothing and *is liable for any accident* that might befall him in the course of his labor." In this context, I don't know if the employer faced only monetary damages or was more extensively liable.

In historical perspective, the development of modern workers compensation laws is recent.

There are a variety of reasons for this very slow development of the law from 5,000 years ago. First, for a number of centuries the predominent form of labor was agriculture. Most people were farmers. What trade and industry that existed was generally family or small town industry, people knew each other on a family basis or neighborly basis and there was no concern for providing a formal workers compensation system.

Second, those civilizations such as the Egyptian — which relied on slave labor as their pool for heavy labor — would obviously have no concern for workers compensation. Third, the Middle Ages saw the development of the guild system of long apprenticeship, and membership in the guild protected its members should they be injured. Again the exposure to injury or disability in those days was far less than it is now.

Finally, the system of law that we are dealing with is the English Common Law. The Common Law reflects the needs and the customs of the societies in which it was enacted. Until the Industrial Revolution, there was no need for a formal system of rights and liabilities dealing with industrial injury. However, the Industrial Revolution, with its great change in technology, created this need. The long apprenticeships were ended, membership in the guild essentially died out. Family industry gave way to the development of the steam engine and we saw an unskilled, untrained pool of men, women and in many cases children working in an atmosphere of heavy industry, heavy equipment and exposure to new and complex hazards. The whole series of horrors that we read about in the Dickens novels (Oliver Twist, David Copperfield) the unsafe, poorly lit, ill-ventilated mines and factories, the long sweat shop hours and the use of child labor, created the first need for a system of workers compensation. This developed in Europe during the latter part of the 1800's.

Clearly, *workers compensation is social legislation*. It meets a social need. The first formal statute was developed in Bismark's Germany. By the early 1900's, the reform movement had reached the U.S. The first workers compensation statute was put into the hopper in New York in 1898. It did not get out of Committee. The economic ethics of the time did not support a workers compensation system. Maryland adopted the first American statute in 1902, Montana in 1909 and New York in 1910. However, subsequently, the Supreme Courts of those states declared them all unconstitutional in that they were compulsory. It was not a volunteer situation. So, the legislature went back to the drawing board and many legislatures amended their constitutions.

Here's what occurred in California: We adopted a constitutional amendment in 1910 which permitted the development of a workers compensation system. In 1911 we adopted a voluntary, elective system to avoid the criticisms that the courts had leveled at the other state statutes. In 1914, we adopted a formal compulsory workers compensation system. The main reform of that system was the Workers Compensation Act of 1917, which created major amendments to our basic workers compensation statute. In every state legislative session since 1917 there have been amendments made to the 1917 compensation law in California.

That basically is a thumbnail sketch of some 5,000 years of legal history, but it can be done very quickly: *for about 4,800 years nothing happened!*

Modern Workers Compensation

What does the workers compensation system attempt to do? We have to look at the aims and the goals of the workers compensation statute before we can deal with some of the problems that are presented. Generally, workers compensation is a system that attempts to assure the employee of an expeditious remedy which is both adequate and certain. The remedy is certain and independent of the fault of the employee. At the same time, it provides the employer with a liability that is determinable and within defined limits. Essentially, *it is a no-fault system.* The negligence of the employee does not affect the determination of liability.

Basically, the compromise that is reached in a workers compensation system is that the employees have given up their right to proceed against the employer for unlimited damages for pain and suffering. On the other hand, the employers gave up their defenses to the third party civil suit and at the turn of the century, these defenses were very substantial. Besides there were strong social pressures against suing your own employer, the employers had the "fellow-servant" rule available to them, which meant that if the injury was caused as a result of a co-employee, there would be no recovery by the injured employee against the employer. A second defense was simply the "assumption of the risk," which meant, if you go to work in the mornings with knowledge of the hazards of your job, you have assumed the risk of injury and you cannot recover against your employer. And the final and the major defense would be that of "contributory negligence." Under this theory, the plaintiff, if negligent in any manner, was barred totally against recovery from the negligent defendant.

So this is the balance that was reached in workers compensation: that the liability would be ascertained, it would be determinable, but it would be a no-fault system. Compensation would be paid regardless of the employee's fault. All of the 50 states now have a workers compensation statute. My comments regarding the present law will mainly be drawn from California, because that reflects my experience, but I will attempt to indicate those aspects in California law that I think are unique to the area of workers compensation. If anyone has a question regarding a jurisdiction outside California, I would refer them to their corporate counsel or to a legal consultant.

Most, if not all, of the workers compensation statutes that have been drafted are directed to indemnify an employee for the result of an industrial accident. Many of the states still maintain an Industrial Accident Commission. In California we had an Industrial Accident Commission until the late 40's, when it became the Workers Compensation Appeals Board. The concept of "accident," the sudden traumatic event, has been keyed to the American Workers Compensation Statutes. The other basis of workers compensation law is that of rehabilitation of the industrially injured employee. I believe these two concepts are basic to the majority of workers compensation statutes.

Workers compensation is a very structured system. The liability is *structured* and it can be *predicted.*

We should distinguish the delivery systems that we have for compensating an industrially injured employee or an injured employee in general. Workers compensation, I believe, is unique in that it is a no-fault system: it is not based on the concept of damages. We should try to distinguish workers compensation benefits from health and accident insurance benefits and disability insurance. Society security benefits which are available in many cases to the prematurely disabled employee should also be distinguished. The main thrusts of workers compensation benefits are to rehabilitate the employee and indemnify the employee for his reduced ability to compete in the labor market.

Cumulative Injury

Being geared toward the industrial "accident," the concept of occupational disease and cumulative trauma has posed conceptual problems for the state industrial accident commissions as well as the courts that have been called upon to render decisions in this area. Many states, to avoid the inequitable result of denying an occupationally injured employee benefits because he suffers from a disease, have developed this concept so that they can stay within their conceptual framework of "accident." In these states we now look at each individual chemical or physical insult to the body as being an injury, the cumulative effect of which causes disability.

New York has carried this even further, there the courts perceive of occupational disease as having a sudden impact: suddenly one day you wake up and you have cancer. You have, therefore, experienced an accident. You didn't have it yesterday; you have it today. You have had a sudden traumatic event; therefore you are not compensated for the disease, but under New York law you have had an "accident" and you are indemnified for it.

The concept of cumulative diseases or cumulative injury is not new. In England, in 1921 the case of *Bunnel & Sons Limited* vs. *Selvage*[3] was decided based on the idea of a cumulative or repetitive trauma. In that case, an employee over a short period of time sustained cuts and abrasions in the course of her work. Suddenly an infection set in and the claim was contested on the grounds that there was no injury. There had been no sudden accident that caused this problem. The court, however, affirmed the decision of the two lower courts and awarded compensation, saying that "the accident is no less accidental because it occurred on a series of occasions instead of one." Based upon this case, we can read "repetitive" or "successive" as synonoms for cumulative.

Although the concept of cumulative injury is not new to the law, what *is* new is the increased utilization being made of that term today. The California Workers Compensation Institute, in a 1977 report, noted that the "evidence shows incidents of cumulative injury claims are increasing — conservatively this increase is 20 to 25 percent a year with no signs of abating." The PG & E experience would reflect this: in 1978, we had 301 applications filed, 95 of which alleged a cumulative injury (fully 30%). Our experience in 1979 is much the same. About 38% of our cases involve a cumulative injury allegation.

One of the difficulties associated with the concept of cumulative injury stems from the fact that the disability is usually in the form of a disease rather than a traumatic wound. Thus, we are confronted with the usual degenerative process that affects all of us, because of age. Disorders such as cardiovascular discrepancies, arteriosclerotic heart disease, emphysema, peripheral vascular disease, degenerative disc disease and osteoarthritis involving the joints are symptoms of age, but they can also be symptoms of an occupational exposure. So the workers compensation appeals boards are presented with a very difficult problem of attempting to distinguish the part of the disability related to the occupational exposure from that which would normally be experienced as a condition of aging.

California, as early as 1920, recognized the doctrine of cumulative injury and is one of the few states that has codified the concept by adoption into a statute. In *Beveridge* vs. *Industrial accident Committee*,[4] the California Supreme Court said "The proposition is irrefutable, that while a succession of slight injuries in the course of employment may not in themselves be disabling, their cumulative effect in work effort may become a destructive force." About 10 years after that decision was handed down, the California legislature acted to amend the definition of injury present in our Labor Code so that it can be specific or cumulative. A cumulative injury is defined as: "occurring as repetitive mentally or physically traumatic activities extending over a period of time, the combined effect of which causes any disability or need for medical treatment."[5]

A portion of the solution to the problem presented by the cumulative injury case rests with the safety and the health professional. It is crucial that the medical examiner in these cases be provided with a good history and data which reflects the conditions present in a workplace. From my experience, any time I'm going to litigate a cumulative injury case, I want to have a complete file on what the employee was exposed to, what his length of exposure was as well as his complete medical history. Any trial attorney would want to have that type of information before attempting to contest an allegation of cumulative injury.

Conclusion

In the area of occupational disease, from a litigation point of view, the opinion of the treating physician or the examining physicians is crucial. In California, one has the option, or the Board has the power to order that there be an independent medical exam by a doctor. Many of these cases will be resolved through the use of an independent medical examiner. But *it's vital that a close liasion be maintained by the safety and health professional with the attorney and the physician involved in the cumulative case.*

A good working relationship with the medical professionals in a cumulative case is crucial. PG & E maintains a panel of physicians. We don't employ a staff physician or a medical director. We utilize expert medical practitioners from around the state and I believe that the success of any compensation program depends in large measure on the skill of the treating physician. According to the late L.J. Henderson, a professor of biochemistry, modern medicine began about 400 years ago and by 1910, when workers compensation was just getting underway, the medical art had progressed to the point that "a randomly selected patient who consulted a randomly selected physician enjoyed a better-than-average chance of benefiting by the encounter".[6] As the compensation laws have been amended over the years to meet society's needs, the medical profession has increased its knowledge and abilities to cope with the injuries and diseases which are coming now within scope of this law. To meet the challenge we are facing in the area of cumulative injury, a close working relationship must be developed among physicians, attorneys, workers compensation administrators and safety and health professionals. I believe it is incumbent on the physicians who are called upon to render opinions in an occupational disease case and on the courts who may eventually analyse the medical record, to keep in mind the basic tenets of workers compensation which are the rehabilitation and the compensation of industrially injured employees.

I also believe it is the duty of corporate counsel to work closely with the safety and health professionals within his own organization so that he can fully prepare and develop a defense appropriate to the cumulative injury case.

References

1. *Hanna, Warren L. — California Law of Employee Injuries and Workmen's Compensation (1953) Matthew Bender Publishing, Inc.*
2. *Herlick, Stanford D. — California Workers' Compensation Law Handbook (1978) Parker & Son Publications, Inc.*
3. *Volume 27 King's Bench Decisions 357*
4. *Volume 175 California Appellate Reports 2d 529, Vol 346 Pacific Reports 2d 545, Vol. 24 California Compensation Cases 274*
5. *California Labor Core Section 3208.1*
6. *Morrison, R.S. — An Outcome of Man's Knowledge of the Modern World (1960) Nelson Doubleday, Inc.*

Workers Compensation Safety Programs

Jack R. Fenton, J.D.

Dr. Fenton is Chairman of the Workers Compensation Appeals Board in the State of California. He was Chairman of the California Assembly Judiciary Committee and a member of the Judicial Council, the Commission on Uniform State Laws and the Commission on California State Government Organization and Economy. He is well known for his investigative and legislative activities relating to occupational safety.

For the United States in 1980, about one industrial injury or illness occurred for every 12 workers in the private sector.[1] The total number of job-related injuries was 5.5 million with 2.5 million of those injuries resulting in about 40.9 million lost workdays.[2]

In California, *during the decade of the seventies, work injuries increased 6 percent per year while the average year-to-year gain in employment was 3½ percent.*[3] Industrial disabilities numbered 213,262 in 1970 as compared with 382,227 in 1979; disabling injuries per 1,000 workers increased 27 percent. Incurred losses for insured employers increased from $414,000,000 to $1.45 billion. Premiums increased from $616 million to $2.8 billion per year. *Average annual premiums increased from $1.89 per $100 of payroll to $3.22 per $100 of payroll.*[4] *These California figures are reflective of benefits paid out for workers compensation injuries nationally.*

Part of the bargain for the exclusive remedy of a no-fault workers compensation system was that the employer paid a limited recovery, i.e., workers compensation benefits and indemnity, while the injured worker gave up the right to sue for damages in civil court.

There is a trend in recent court decisions toward diminishing the exclusive remedy provisions of workers compensation acts. In *Bell v. Industrial Vangas, Inc. (1981) 30 Cal. 3d 268, 277,* the California Supreme Court held that if an additional concurrent duty flowed from an "extra" employer status or a relationship that was distinct from the employer-employee relationship and invoked a different set of obligations, a second capacity arose and the employer status was coincidental. This so-called *dual capacity doctrine* allows the employer to be sued in civil court because he or she was considered a person other than the employer.

In *Johns-Manville Products Corp. v. Superior Court* (1980) 27 Cal.3d 465, the California Supreme Court again broke new ground, upholding a civil action against an employer where the employee alleged that his employer *fraudulently concealed* from the employee, his doctors and the State, that he was suffering from a disease caused by ingestion of asbestos, thereby preventing the employee from receiving treatment for the disease and inducing him to continue to work under hazardous conditions. Those allegations were held to be sufficient to state a cause of action for *aggravation of the disease* as distinct from the hazards of the employment causing him to *contract* the disease.

Escalating costs of workers compensation liability plus potential new civil litigation should furnish the incentive for employers to implement workers compensation liability programs.

The two main features of any workers compensation liability program are *accident prevention* and *loss control.* The minimum acceptable elements for an accident prevention program are (1) a training program designed to instruct employees in general safety work practices plus specific instructions on uniquely hazardous jobs; and (2) scheduled periodic inspections to identify and correct unsafe conditions and work practices. Statistics and research have shown that a high percentage of occupational accidents and illnesses can be prevented through effective education and training, together with periodic inspections of the workplace.

These minimal elements can be voluntarily expanded by an employer into a total accident and illness prevention program by establishing a workplace program which includes management leadership, assignment of responsibility, identification and control of hazards, employee and supervisor training, safety and health recordkeeping, first aid and medical assistance, and employee awareness, acceptance and participation.

The boss's attitude toward job safety and health will be reflected by the employees. If the boss is not interested in preventing accidents, the employees are not likely to be interested. Management might consider meeting with all employees to discuss job safety and explain the mutual responsibilities under local or state law and federal OSHA. Employers should issue written policy statements indicating that they are serious about safety and health and these statements should be posted where all employees can see them.

A code of safe practices and operating procedures should be established setting forth specific instructions and rules to keep the workplace safe and healthful. Job safety and health items should be included at all meetings whether involving top management supervisory personnel or other employees. Employers or management should personally review all inspection and accident reports to insure followup where needed. Above all, employees and members of management should set a good example by complying with safety rules when they are on job sites.

The details for carrying out the basic safety policy of a company can be delegated to those persons in charge of operating and production details. Plant managers, supervisors, group leaders, or other key people can be assigned specific responsibility for safety and health and held accountable for getting the job done. Each employee should have training and responsibility for safety and health procedures.

To maintain a safe and healthful workplace, the employer needs to identify existing workplace hazards as well as those which could develop. The employer should use local and federal health and safety standards to help recognize the hazards and institute procedures to control and eliminate them. If the employer is insured, the insurance carrier can provide information on how to set up a periodic inspection program. The local industrial safety and health government organization and federal and state OSHA should be contacted for additional information.

Employee and supervisor training is a very important part of any accident prevention program. Each employee needs to know that he or she is not expected to undertake a job until he or she is instructed on how to do the job properly and has been authorized to perform that particular job. *No employee should undertake a job that appears to be unsafe or use chemicals without understanding their toxic properties.* Mechanical safeguards must be kept in place at all times. Every employee should be expected to report any and all unsafe conditions encountered during work. Any injury or illness suffered by an employee — even a slight one — should be reported at once. *Employees should know that the employer has only started a safety and health program and is willing to go further as necessary when new methods are discovered.*

Supervisors should know how to train employees in the proper way of doing their jobs and know the special training requirements for federal and state OSHA standards with particular attention given to new employees. However, regular employees including "old timers" should be continually instructed as to safe procedures.

Records of sales costs, profits and losses are essential to all successful businesses. They enable the owner and manager to learn from past experience and to improve future operations. Records of accidents, related injuries, illnesses and property losses serve the same purpose if they are used in the same way.

Under the laws of most states, recordkeeping requirements exist and information concerning accidents is gathered and stored. When facts have been determined, causes can often be identified and control procedures instituted to prevent similar illnesses or injuries from recurring. Many states require a report on every injury or illness requiring medical treatment.

During the year, it would be helpful for the employer or manager to review these records to learn where injuries and illnesses have occurred and in what numbers. Patterns of repeat situations provide valuable insight into helping identify causes of accidents. Accident and illness records can help employers identify high risk areas so they can be given immediate attention.

Not only injuries and illnesses which produce a need for treatment should be reported, but also *all incidents* — even those where no injury or illness has resulted — especially if such information would assist in pinpointing unsafe conditions or procedures. The illness/injury records may not be the only records required to be maintained. Some states require toxic substances and hazardous exposure records for employees exposed to these substances and sources together with physical examination reports, employment reports, etc. Employers using any regulated carcinogens may have additional reporting/recordkeeping requirements.

Essential records, including those legally required for workers compensation insurance audits and government inspections, should be maintained for as long as the actual need exists. Employers are encouraged to keep records of their activities, such as policy statements, training sessions for management and employees, safety and health meetings held, information distributed to employees, medical arrangements made, etc. Maintaining essential records will demonstrate sound business management and will provide supporting proof for credit applications and afford the employer an efficient means to review his current safety and health activities for better control of his operations and planning future improvements. *Records should not be looked upon as a burden but rather as a tool to be used in more effective management of accident prevention programs.*

Many states have varying standards requiring medical services and first aid to protect employees. It is necessary that employers contact the appropriate local agency to determine exactly what protective measures are required for different types and sizes of businesses. In many cases, effective first aid and medical assistance on the job will prevent lost time injuries and enable the employee to return to work in a short time.

Employee awareness, acceptance and participation in accident prevention programs is a must if such programs are to work. As indicated before, if the employer or manager is sincerely dedicated to a safe and healthful place to work, the employees will also sense it. It is important to get some activity started with employees so that they become aware that something is being done about safety on the job. Displaying safety and health pamphlets on workplace bulletins and using safety-related and health-related posters and information devices will keep employees aware of constant concerns for safety.

Remember, it is necessary to get all employees

involved in inspecting, detecting, and correcting to make a safe and healthy workplace. Employees should be included in management's plans and asked for suggestions and assistance.

Compliment employees when they are doing a good job and when their work in the safety area is acceptable. *Many plants have formed joint labor management safety and health committees — an excellent means of communicating safety and health information.* A small employer who has few employees might consider rotating employees to take an active part in the safety and health program of the workplace.

The second part of a workers compensation liability program is loss control. Although loss control generally relates to events after the occurrence of an industrial injury, preemployment and ongoing physical examinations are essential elements of any loss control program. Applications for employment should contain previous employment information and a complete medical history questionnaire covering all previous nonindustrial or industrial diseases, illnesses or injuries. Pre-employment physical examinations should be created or modified to fit job requirements as needed and there should be an annual physical examination program for specific jobs identified as being hazardous and usually strenuous.

An *accident response system* should be established outlining the chain of events to take place after an industrial accident occurs. This should include first aid; i.e., training and identification of personnel to administer; transportation of injured workers to the physician or hospital; posting of emergency phone numbers and notification of the proper supervisor.

It is imperative that strict procedures be set up for reporting industrial injuries. Supervisors should be instructed on how to deal with employees who have suffered industrial injuries — these include referral of the employee for medical treatment. It is essential that the proper forms be filled out detailing how the accident occurred. In large companies, there should be coordination between the Personnel Department, the safety officer, and supervisors and foremen on the reporting of industrial accidents. Detailed information concerning industrial accidents will enable the employer to evaluate federal safety precautions which must be taken and to insure prompt handling of the claim by the insurance carrier.

If the employer is insured, prompt reporting of any industrial accident to the insurance carrier, the adjusting agency or persons designated by the employer to adjust industrial injury claims will insure that the injured worker is provided benefits promptly. Delay in reporting can increase claims cost. Though an injury may appear small, delay may aggravate it and require costlier treatment. The sooner an injury is reported, the sooner its validity can be investigated and cost kept under control.

Failure to provide benefits may be grounds for penalty in some jurisdictions. Delay causes the employee to be uncertain as to who will pay the medical bills and compensation for lost wages and this uncertainty can lead to litigation which further increases claims costs. Maintaining good relations with workers who have been injured is essential to preventing increased losses. However, good working relationships with employees can be jeopardized by the delayed filing of injury reports. An employee who feels he or she has been treated properly and received all the benefits due will usually be anxious to return to work as soon as possible, thus saving not only benefit costs, but other economic loss which may be incurred by the employer when the employee is unable to work.

Wherever possible, employers should develop an inventory of temporary light work assignments to encourage early return to work. In most cases this will speed up the injured employee's recovery and reduce liability for temporary disability indemnity or wage loss payments.

The suggestions set forth above are *by no means intended to be a comprehensive treatment of all elements of a workers compensation liability program,* but are only intended to serve as a guide. While cost savings engendered by workers compensation liability programs is of high importance, it is more important that workers continue to be, and if injured, again become productive and socially participating members of society, whose health and welfare are clearly related to the needs of our society.

References

1. *United States Department of Labor News,* Bureau of Labor Statistics, Washington, D.C., November 18, 1981
2. Ibid.
3. *California Work Injuries and Illnesses, 1979,* California Department of Industrial Relations, Division of Labor Statistics and Research, January, 1982
4. Ibid.

EDITOR'S NOTES — Workers Compensation and Dual Capacity

1. One good source of information on workers compensation laws, in all 50 states, is the annual "Analysis of Workers Compensation Laws," published by the U. S. Chamber of Commerce. (It is available from the Chamber at 1615 H Street, Washington, DC 20062).
2. The dual capacity doctrine received a major endorsement in 1981 by an Illinois appellate court, which ruled (Sharp vs. Gallagher) that an employer, when operating as both employer and landowner, could be sued for damages by an injured worker (even though the worker had received maximum workers compensation benefits). An appeal to the Illinois Supreme Court is pending.

   Businessmen predict economic disaster if employers can be held responsible for all occupational injuries just because they own or lease land on which the injuries occur. Much of this fear may be based on the fact that employers may not be adequately insured against claims brought by workers, unless they carry both workers compensation coverage and some form of insurance that protects against common law actions. Insurance costs, as a result, could skyrocket if direct action lawsuits against employers become commonplace and are not controlled by the courts or the legislatures.

   By way of contrast, many employee groups, unions, and some attorneys seem to agree that the *exclusive remedies* (of workers compensation) often do not provide sufficient compensation for injuries and illnesses, citing an inflationary economy and sharply rising costs of medical care. The direct action common law has long-prevailed for the employer who is uninsured,commits an intentional tort, or is guilty of something similar to gross negligence in some jurisdictions. However, the courts have not been uniform in their interpretations of concepts involving direct action against employers. In some decisions, they have ruled that the dual capacity doctrine is not applicable to the employer/landowner or the employer in control of the worksite. Other decisions have said that the "exclusive remedy" concept will always shield an employer from common law liability for an unsafe workplace, a defective product, or a toxic chemical exposure. This is an area of law that is in transition, but of vital concern to the safety professional.
3. In another opinion an appellate court described an employer's contentions that its employee, who was "injured while engaged in his employer's work, has already received a workers compensation award and therefore is precluded from suing his employer for tort damages as a matter of law...the workers compensation is the exclusive remedy...a Pandora's box will be opened, if the employee is permitted to sue, and there is a recognized statutory 'tradeoff' embodied in the workers compensation scheme and to whittle away at one side of that equation is to upset a delicately struck balance."

   But the same court held that "The 37-year history of California legal precedents — buttressed by an analysis of the Workers Compensation Act and its constitutional foundations and underlying public policy considerations — contradicts the employer's over-broad statement of the scope of the exclusive remedy doctrine. "This court, as well as appellate courts of this state, has authored many opinions recognizing employees' rights to recover damages from the employer for injuries sustained in a jobsite setting in addition to those allowed by workers compensation law."

   In explaining its opinion the court said, "What has come to be known as the 'dual capacity' doctrine was first recognized and applied in the landmark case of Duprey v. Shane (1952) 39 Cal. 2d 781 (249 P.2d 8), where Duprey, a nurse, sustained an industrial injury while employed by Shane, a chiropractor. Although he carried workers compensation insurance, Shane and another chiropractor employed by him undertook personally to treat Duprey for the injury and, as it was found, did so negligently. This court upheld a recovery in an action for malpractice, reasoning that in treating Duprey, Shane was acting as an attending doctor rather than as an employer and that "the employer-doctor is a "person other than the employer" within the meaning of section 3852 of the Labor Code...." (Id., at p. 793.) This court reasoned: "It is true that the law is opposed to the creation of a dual personality, where to do so is unrealistic and purely legalistic. But where, as here, it is perfectly apparent that the person involved — Dr. Shane — bore towards his employee two relationships — that of employer and that of a doctor — there should be no hesitancy in recognizing this fact as a fact. Such a conclusion, in this case, is in precise accord with the facts and is realistic and not legalistic." (Ibid.) Since Duprey, California courts have applied the dual capacity concept in a variety of factual situations. The *dual capacity doctrine* has been recognized and applied where the *employer in one capacity — proprietor of a dairy produce business — supplied defective products from a separate legal entity of which the employer was also a general partner.*" (Dorado v. Knudsen Corp. (1980) 103 Cal. App. 3d 605, 612 (163 Cal. Rptr. 4771.)

And in Shook v. Jacuzzi (1976) 59 Cal.App.3d 978, 981-982 (129 Cal.Rptr.496), the court recognized the dual capacity doctrine and its application to an employer guilty of faulty design or manufacture, etc., of equipment which caused the employee injuries but held the principle non-applicable, stating: "We note, also, that products liability rules do not apply in the circumstances here shown. International created the machine exclusively for its own use in its own plant and premises. It did not sell the machine or in any way place it in the stream of commerce. Rather, it was but an occasional or casual manufacturer, and thus not subject to strict liability (see Rest.2d Torts, & 402-A, com. f."

The court further reasoned, "Closest in point of factual application are the recent California appellate court cases in which the *dual capacity doctrine* has been applied to a defendant who occupied the *dual positions of employer and manufacturer of a defective product* sold to the public. In Douglas v. E. & J. Gallo Winery (1977) 69 Cal.App.3d 103, 107 (137 Cal.Rptr. 797), the defendant — both an employer and a manufacturer of scaffolds sold to the general public — was held liable for damages in the latter role to an employee injured while using one of the scaffolds. And in Moreno v. Leslie's Pool Mart (1980) 110 Cal.App.3d 179 (167 Cal. Rptr. 747), an employer engaged in the selling of pools also was a "manufacturer-distributor to the public of swimming pool maintenance products. The Court of Appeal reversed a summary judgment in favor of the employer where the employees' suit for damages was based on strict liability for a defective product."

Most recently, this court (D'Angona v. County of Los Angeles (1980) 27 Cal.3d 661, 666-667 (166 Cal.Rptr. 177, 613 P.2d 238) applied the dual capacity concept, saying: "Underlying Duprey is the rationale that *if an injury arises from a relationship which is distinct from that of employer and employee and invokes a different set of obligations than the employer's duties to its employee, there is no justification for shielding the employer from liability at common law.*"

The majority of the court held that "The imperative of public safety, the deterrence of manufacture of shoddy products, was a powerful force motivating the establishment of product liability law. The manufacturer is held strictly liable because it "is in a peculiarly strategic position to promote the safety of (its) products....*(T)he pressure of strict liability could scarcely be exerted at a better point if accident prevention is to be furthered by tort law.*" (James, General Products — Should Manufacturers Be Liable Without Negligence? (1957) 24 Tenn.L.Rev. 923.). Vangas, as a "manufacturer" who sells its products to the public, continues to be strictly liable to nonemployee consumers: There is naught to commend a rule of the law which would encourage manufacturers to do less in the area of product safety if by chance the product is to be used by their own employees. The inherent deterrent aspect of a manufacturer's strict liability law is thwarted if the manufacterer has no responsibility to its employees (or the third party joint tortfeasors) beyond a workers compensation award. The obligations Vangas owed as a manufacturer-designer-seller of equipment to all users was entirely independent of those obligations imposed upon him as an employer. (Cf.2A Larson, Workmen's Compensation Law, & 72.80) "Manufacturer" Vangas owed a duty to all foreseeable users of its product not to introduce a defective product into the stream of commerce. (Rest.2d Torts, & 402A.) Neither law nor right reason excludes employees of a manufacturer from this broad rule."

Finally, in justification for its opinion, the court said that "Perhaps the clearest, most authoritative (outside California) exposition of the dual capacity concept is to be found in the United States Supreme Court decision of Reed v. The Yaka (1963) (373 U.S.410 (10 L.Ed.2d 448, 83 S.Ct. 1349). There plaintiff's employer, a stevedoring company, leased a ship under a bareboat charter; the plaintiff, a longshoreman, was injured while loading the vessel. Although the plaintiff was entitled to his compensation benefits, he brought an action against his employer as charterer alleging unseaworthiness of the vessel. The employer defended on the basis of the exclusive remedy provision in the Longshoremen's and Harbor Workers' Compensation Act. Without using the dual-capacity terminology, the court's holding was consistent with the reasoning behind the dual-capacity theory. The employer was liable to his employee as a bareboat charterer for injuries arising from the unseaworthiness of the chartered vessel. The defendant had the duty as the bareboat charterer to provide the employee a seaworthy vessel. That duty was "traditional, absolute and nondelegable" (id., at p.415 (10 L.Ed. 2d at p.452) and could not be avoided by the exclusive remedy provision of the Longshoremen's Act.

"In sum, Bell's complaint discloses *injuries arising from two concurrent causes: the employment relation* (for which Vangas is liable under workers compensation law) *coinciding with a defective product* (for *which Vangas is here sought to be held liable as the manufacturer).*

"The principle enunciated and approved by this court from Duprey, supra, 39 Cal.2d 781, to D'Angona, supra, 27 Cal.3d 661, compels the conclusion that *a coincidental employment relationship will not shield an employer from a common law liability where the concurrent cause of the injury is attributable to the employer's separate and distinct relationship to the employee and which invokes a different set of obligations than the employer's duties to its employees.*"

"Section 3600 of the (California) Labor Code provides that an employer is liable for injuries to its employees arising out of and in the course of employment, and section 3601 declares that where the conditions of workers compensation exist, the right to recover such compensation is the *exclusive remedy against an employer* for injury or death of an employee. *The issue to be decided (in this proceeding) is whether an employee is barred by these provisions from prosecuting an action at law against his employer for the intentional torts of fraud and conspiracy in knowingly ordering the employee to work in an unsafe environment, concealing the risk from him, and, after the employee had contracted an industrial disease, deliberately failing to notify the state, the employee, or doctors retained to treat him, of the disease and its connection with the employment, thereby aggravating the consequences of the disease.*

"We conclude that while the workers compensation law bars the employee's action at law for his *initial injury*, a cause of action may exist for *aggravation of the disease* because of the employer's *fraudulent concealment* of the condition and its cause.

The rationale for this opinion was explained as follows: "Where the employer is charged with intentional misconduct which goes beyond his failure to assure that the tools or substances used by the employee or the physical environment of a workplace are safe, some cases have held that the employer may be subject to common law liability (several applicable cases occurred from 1959 to 1978). For example, "it was held that an action for fraud could be maintained against an employer who made misrepresentations regarding the employee's right to medical care and conspired with a third party to conceal from the employee that his injuries, which occurred while he was working, were caused by the third party against whom he had recourse, and we allowed an action at law against an insurer for assault, battery, and intentional infliction of emotional distress, based upon its deceitful conduct in investigating a workers compensation claim." The court stated, "the reasons given in these cases for allowing a common law action for intentional misconduct of the employer vary.....the rationale was based, at least in part, on the ground that since an employee may sue a fellow employee at law for assault,...he should have the same right against his employer, and that an intentional assault by the employer has a questionable relationship to the general conditions of employment.

Finally, the court held that, "we conclude the *policy of exclusivity* of workers compensation as a remedy for injuries in the employment *would not be seriously undermined* by holding defendant liable for the aggravation of this plaintiff's injuries, since we cannot believe that many employers will aggravate the effects of an industrial injury by not only deliberately concealing its existence but also its connection with the employment. Nor can we believe that the Legislature in enacting the workers compensation law intended to insulate such flagrant conduct from tort liability. Finally, although plaintiff filed an application for workers compensation and may receive an award in that proceeding, double recovery may be avoided by allowing the employer a setoff in the event plaintiff is awarded compensation for the aggravation of his injury in that proceeding and in the present case as well."

Editor's Note — Information in Note 3 quoted from sections of Bell v. Industrial Vangas Inc., 30 Cal. 3d 268; California Law Reporter P.2d. and Johns-Manville Products Corp. v. Superior Court 27 Cal. 3d 465; California Law Reporter 858, 612 P.2d 948.

4. *As an example of recent Workers Compensation law reform, the California Assembly recently approved legislation (AB 64) which made three major changes:*
   * *It permits injured employees to sue an employer for failure to have proper point-of–operation guards on punch presses (including press brakes).*
   * *It appears to give punch press manufacturers full authority to mandate specific guards for each punch press.*
   * *It makes any employer liable who, "knowingly, removes, or does not provide" the recommended guards, liable for damages beyond workers compensation awards.*

The Labor Code Section 4558 of this new law reads as follows:

(a) As used in this section:

(1) "Employer" means a named identifiable person who is, prior to the time of the employee's injury or death, an owner or supervisor having managerial authority to direct and control the acts of employees.

(2) "Failure to install" means omitting to attach a point of operation guard, either provided or required by the manufacturer, when such attachment is required by the manufacturer and made known by him to the employer at the time of acquisition, installation, or manufacturer-required modification of the punch press.

(3) "Manufacturer" means the designer, fabricator, or assembler of a punch press.

(4) "Punch press" means any material-forming machine utilizing a die mechanism which is designed for use in the manufacture of other products.

(5) "Removal" means physical removal of a point of operation guard which is either installed by the manufacturer or installed by the employer pursuant to the requirements or instructions of the manufacturer.

(6) "Specifically authorized" means an affirmative instruction issued by the employer prior to the time of the employee's physical injury or death, but shall not mean any subsequent acquiescence in or ratification or removal of a point of operation safety guard.

(b) An employee, or his or her dependents in the event of the employee's death, may bring an action at law for damages against the employer where the employee injury or death is proximately caused by the employer's knowing removal of or knowing failure to install a point of operation safety guard on a punch press and such removal or failure to install is specifically authorized by the employer under conditions known by the employer to create a probability of serious injury or death.

(c) No liability shall arise under this section absent proof that the manufacturer designed, installed, required, or otherwise provided by specification for the attachment of such guards and conveyed knowledge of the same to the employer. Proof of conveyance of such information to the employer by the manufacturer may come from any source.

(d) No right of action for contribution or indemnity by any defendant shall exist against the employer, however, a defendant may seek contribution after the employee secures a judgment against the employer pursuant to the provisions of this section if the employer fails to discharge his comparative share of such judgment.

The Employer's Liability Beyond Workers Compensation

George A. Peters, J. D.

Here Dr. Peters provides additional case law information on the dual capacity doctrine, which is having an ever-stronger impact on safety and health programs of all organizations.

The Employer's Liability Beyond Workers Compensation

In their overall effect, workers compensation laws minimized, controlled, and made more predictably certain the seemingly inevitable accident costs for the employer. Most importantly for the employer, accident costs were minimized. The reality is that lower claims costs translated into less incentive for loss prevention efforts, such as more effective safety engineering. But, if the cost of accidents were to increase, the motivation for more appropriate or effective accident prevention measures would be increased almost in direct proportion to the threatened loss or cost of the accidents.

The sacred protective walls, epitomized by the exclusive remedy clauses of workers compensation statutes, now are being breached by both legislative and judicial actions. Awareness of this trend in the law should serve as justification for employers to undertake improved accident prevention and loss control measures. Prevention of injury is the surest means of preventing the personal inconveniences and financial hemorrhage of court awards that may attempt restitution or punishment under newer legal theories and current measures of damages. A quick review of employer's liability, beyond workers compensation, may illustrate the need for more comprehensive safety programs on the part of the industrial employer.

1. **CRIMINAL LIABILITY (What Work Supervisors Should Understand About Safety)**
   The superintendent of a city sewage treatment facility was convicted of involuntary manslaughter after two of his employees died. The workers died as a result of being overcome by hydrogen sulfide gas in a manhole. One man died trying to rescue the other, neither were furnished a gas mask nor a safety harness for use in confined workplaces. Previously, other workers had complained to their supervisors and to OSHA about the lack of safety equipment required by the City's own safety manuals. Although the criminal conviction was appealed, based on conflicts in various administrative directions relating to safety, the conviction was upheld. *People v Gaglione, 2 Crim. 41012, 2nd District Court of Appeals, California* (as reported in the Los Angeles Daily Journal, 14 December 1982, Section 2, page 1).
2. **DUAL CAPACITY — AGGRAVATION OF INJURIES**
   In some situations, the employer has been found to perform two roles or a "dual capacity"; first, as an employer and, secondly, in some other "capacity" or role (other than as an employer). For example, as an "employer," he could be found liable, under workers compensation laws, for the initial industrial injury. In his second role or dual capacity, he could be held liable for an aggravation of that injury. In *Duprey v Shane, 39 Cal.2d 781, 249 P.2d 8 (1952)*, it was held that a nurse could recover workers compensation benefits from her employer for injuries received in the course of her employment. But, she could also maintain an action at law against her employer for aggravation of those injuries if caused by the negligent medical treatment she received from her employer.

   In *Guy v Arthur H. Thomas C., 55 Ohio St. 2d 183, 9 Ohio Ops.3d 138, 378 N.E.2d 488 (1978)* a hospital was held to have occupied a dual capacity as an "employer" (liable for mercury poisoning) and as a "treating hospital" (liable for malpractice because of negligent treatment of her as a patient). Also see *Stevens v County of Nassau, 56 App. Div.2d 866, 392 N.Y.S.2d 332 (1977)* and *Volk v. City of New York, 284 N.Y. 279, 30 N.E.2d 596 (1940)*. A more recent case is *D'Angona v County of Los Angeles, 27 Cal.3d 661, 166 Cal. Rptr. 177, 613 P.2d 238 (1980)* involving a physical therapist who recovered workers compensation benefits for injuries resulting from contracting meningococcemia on the job and was permitted to bring an action at law for negligent medical treatment of her illness by her employer.

The hospital, as an employer, was under a duty to provide compensation for her injuries, but was not under an obligation to treat her disease. In assuming the doctor-patient role, the hospital became liable for any malpractice in that second capacity. Also see *McCormick v Caterpillar Tractor Co., 402 N.E.2d 412 (Ill. App. 1980).*

3. **DUAL CAPACITY — PRODUCT LIABILITY**

The same logic has been applied to industrial injuries. A company may be found to have been an "employer" and also a "manufacturer." In *Douglas v E. & J. Gallo Winery, 69 Cal. App.3d 103, 137 Cal. Rptr. 797 (1977)* two workers, injured using a scaffold (that collapsed) manufactured by their employer were able to sue for workers compensation benefits and also institute a product liability action against their employer. The key issue was whether the product (the scaffold) was intended for the sole use of the employer or was also sold to the general public. If the product is not sold to the general public, there is no dual capacity; see *Shook v Jacuzzi, 59 Cal. App.3d 978, 129 Cal. Rptr. 496 (1976), Williams v State Compensation Insurance Fund, 50 Cal. App.3d 116, 123 Cal. Rptr. 812 (1975), Goetz v Avildsen Tools & Machines, Inc., 403 N.E.2d 555 (Ill. App. 1980), and De Paolo v Spaulding Fiber Co., Inc., 397 A.2d 1048 (N.H. 1979).*

In *Moreno v Leslie's Pool Mart, 110 Cal. App.3d 179, 167 Cal. Rptr. 747 (1980)* a part time stock boy was disposing of leaking bottles of muriatic acid and chlorine. The chemicals mixed, creating fumes that caused serious injury, and he sued the employer under the dual capacity doctrine. The court held that "there is no reason to relieve a manufacturer who sells to the general public of liability as a manufacturer by the chance circumstance that the defendant manufacturer also happens to be an employer of the injured person." The "exclusive remedy" or "sole remedy" of workers compensation did not prevail; the employee was entitled to sue his employer, at law, under the dual capacity doctrine.

In *Bell v Industrial Vangas, Inc., 30 C.3d 268, 179 Cal. Rptr. 30, 637 P.2d 266 (1981)* the court held that there is nothing to "commend a rule of law that would encourage manufacturers to do less in the area of product safety if by chance the product is to be used by their own employees." It stated that "the inherent deterrent aspect of a manufacturer's strict liability is thwarted if the manufacturer has no responsibility to its employees (or the third party joint tortfeasors) beyond a workers compensation award."

There may be dual capacity as an "employer" and a "lessor" of a truck (with a defective emergency brake) as in *Smith v Metropolitan Sanitary Dist., etc., 396 N.E.2d 524 (Ill. 1979)*. In *Reed v The Yaka, 373 U.S. 410, 10 L. Ed.2d 448, 83 S. Ct. 1349 (1963)*, the employer was considered both an "employer" of a longshoreman and a "bareboat charterer." Also see *Hoffman v Rogers, 22 Cal. App.3d 655, 99 Cal. Rptr. 455 (1972); Dorado v Knudsen Corp., 103 Cal. App..3d 605, 163 Cal. Rptr. 477 (1980*. In essence, whenever an employer assumes an additional role, he may be assuming the greater liability of common law.

4. **INTERNATIONAL TORTS — ASSAULT, FRAUD, DECEIT**

Intentional torts may be cumulative or alternative to workers compensation benefits. In *Magliulo v Superior Court, 47 Cal App.3d 760, 121 Cal. Rptr. 621 (1975)*, it was held that physical assault on the employee, by the employer, justifies an action at law against the employer. Also see *Meyer v Graphic Arts International Union, 88 Cal. App.3d 176, 151 Cal. Rptr. 597 (1978)*.

Fraud, by the employer, overcomes the exclusive remedy provision of workers compensation statutes; see *Ramey v General Petroleum Corp., 173 Cal. App.2d 386, 343 P.2d 787 (1959)*. One of the most significant decisions occurred in *Johns-Manville Products Corp. v Superior Court, 27 Cal.3d 465, 165 Cal. Rptr. 858, 612 P.2d 948 (1980)*, known as the "Reba Rudkin Case," where an employee alleged misconduct beyond that of failing to assure safe working conditions, charging her employer with the intentional torts of fraud and conspiracy in knowingly ordering the employee to work in an unsafe environment, concealing the risk, and aggravating the consequences of the disease by failing to notify the employee, the state, or the treating physicians that the employee had contracted a disease (asbestos related diseases).

Intentional torts can be considered as a type of dual capacity. For example, in *Unruh v Truck Insurance Exchange, 7 C.3d 616, 102 Cal. Rptr. 815, 498 P.2d 1063 (1972)*, an insurer stepped "out of its proper role" (investigating claims) and allegedly committed an intentional tort against its employee (assault, battery, and intentional infliction of emotional distress based on deceitful conduct).

The dual capacity doctrine has been rejected in *Kohr v Raybestos-Manhattan, Inc. 522 F. Supp. 1070 (E.D. Pa., 1981)*. The employer's concealment of health hazards was not an intentional tort sufficient to overcome the exclusive remedy provisions of workers compensation, in *Tysenn v Johns-Manville Corp., 517 F. Supp. 1290 (E.D. Pa., 1981)* and *Kofron v Amoco Chemicals Corp., 441 A.2d 226 (Del. 1982)*.

5. **IMMEDIATE FAMILY**
In some cases, the spouse (wife) and minor children may recover in an action against the employer of an injured worker, despite an exclusivity clause in the state workers compensation law. The cause of action could be for loss of consortium (by the spouse), loss of companionship and society (by the children), and negligent infliction of mental suffering (shock at seeing the severe injuries). In other words, the exclusive remedy restriction may apply to the worker but not to his immediate family. This is a relatively rare form of lawsuit, but an example may be found in *Ferriter v Daniel O'Connell's Sons, Inc. 413 N.E.2d 690 (Mass., 1980)* which involved quadriplegic injuries suffered when a load of beams fell from a nylon sling. Also see, *King v Viscoloid Co., 219 mass. 420, 106 N.E. 988 (1914).*

6. **CORPORATE SUBSIDIARIES**
In *Gigax v Ralston Purina Co., 136 Cal. App.3d 591 (1982),* a laborer who lost his left arm while cleaning a conveyor belt that unexpectedly started, received a workers compensation award, then sued his employer on the basis of products liability, negligence, and wanton and reckless conduct. The trial court granted summary judgment on the exclusive remedy provisions of the workers compensation scheme (that is, the defendant was the statutory employer immune from a common law tort action). The appellate court ruled that "a host of cases hold an employee of a wholly owned subsidiary, who has obtained workers compensation benefits from the subsidiary, may maintain an action in tort against the parent corporation and this is so even though the parent and subsidiary are covered by the same workers compensation policy." What seems to be controlling is the degree of "separateness" of the entities; for example, are the parent and subsidiary sufficiently distinct in location, function, identity, and enterprise. The court held that it was not the name given to a business enterprise that determines its status as an employer, but rather the substance and hard realities as to whether the entities are separate and distinct.

In *Mercer v Uniroyal, Inc., 361 N.E.2d 492 (Ohio App. 1976)* a tire manufacturer's employee was able to sue his employer, under product liability law, after a truck tire blowout. The court reasoned that corporations have entered a variety of fields and so diversified that each merger could erase, cut off, or pre-empt the tort causes of action of many innocent employee victims. Each shift in corporate restructuring, acquisition, or divestiture could erase the legal rights of large numbers of employees. Also see *Boggs v Blue Diamond Coal Co., 590 F.2d 655 (6th Cir. 1979), Thomas v Hycon, Inc., 244 F. Supp. 151 (D.D.C. 1965),* and *Tucker v Union Oil Co., 603 P.2d 156 (Idaho 1976).*

7. **LEGAL MALPRACTICE**
The gross disparity, between a workers compensation award and a full recovery under the common law, is such as to create a viable cause of action against the lawyer who fails to recognize a third party action. In other words, it may be legal malpractice for the lawyer processing a workers compensation claim to fail to take timely action to have a possible concurrent common law action evaluated and filed. For example, in *Cassol v Kaplan, Los Angeles Superior Court, No. 114702, 1 June 1979,* a worker lost a finger in an unguarded punch press, and the workers compensation lawyer obtained an award of approximately $6,500 for the injured worker. However, the lawyer failed to institute a product liability action against the press manufacturer and supplier prior to the expiration of the applicable statute of limitations, so a legal malpractice action was instituted against the lawyer for negligently disregarding the product liability claim. A jury awarded the worker $400,000 in the action against the lawyer. In other words, an attorney is under a legal compulsion to initiate legal action to obtain *all* appropriate remedies for injured workers. Half a loaf is not enough for the injured worker, if he has a legal right to seek a full remedy. These rights should be construed, by those who might be sued, as an adverse warning or signal to emphasize a reasonable and professional approach to employee health and safety.

Insurer's Liability

John E. Russell, CSP, P.E.

Mr. Russell, 1980-81 Society President, is Vice President-Loss Control of Maryland Casualty Company in Baltimore. He is a veteran of 30 years experience in safety engineering and occupational health, most of it from an insurance perspective. In June, 1982, he received one of ASSE's highest honors — that of 1981-82 Safety Professional of the Year.

A. Controlling Liability from the Safety Function

Whenever there is serious personal injury or extensive property damage, those suffering the injury or damage often look for someone else to whom they can shift all or part of the loss. This, combined with the contingency fee system for plaintiffs' attorneys, sets the stage for the "sue everyone in sight" approach. Anyone, company or individual, who could possibly be considered at fault or a contributor to the injury or damage, may be named as a defendant. The approach is to let the courts select those who are responsible and who should accept all or part of the loss.

It is common practice in the insurance industry to combine fact-finding for underwriting purposes and policyholder safety services. Plaintiffs' attorneys are well aware of this almost omnipresent target for the third-party suits. Considering that the insurance representatives make thousands of policyholder visits each working day, and that there are hundreds of serious injuries, the number of suits against the representatives or their companies is relatively small. The number of successful suits is even less.

Even so, there have been some very sizable judgments. The cost of legal defense against these claims, whether valid or not, has become enormous. It is, therefore, *important that the safety representative and those in the insurance company who in any way provide, describe or market the safety services know that: Anytime a serious personal injury or extensive property damage loss has occurred, the safety representative and/or the insurance company may be a defendant in ensuing litigation, even though the safety services may have been either exemplary or non-existent.*

Therefore, the optimum defense against "negligent inspection" suits is the prevention of extensive harm in the first place. While that Utopian objective is not likely to ever be reached, it must always be the first consideration. It often eliminates the exposure to large judgments as well as high legal defense costs.

It must be accepted that there will be accidents or occurrences resulting in extensive loss which may expose the insurance company or its safety representative to negligence litigation. The occasional large awards are highly publicized, while the multitude of successfully defended cases are not. This one-sided exposure could cause one to conclude that defense is hopeless. Nothing could be more misleading. There is much that can be done.

Defense doesn't start in the courtroom. *It starts with understanding how the courts work,* what conduct by insurance company personnel is likely to lead to vulnerability, and taking action to avoid or lessen that vulnerability. To understand how the courts function, it is necessary to review some of the history of the activities and important cases.

There are, in general, two classes of suits for negligent inspection against insurance representatives. They are the first-party suits and third-party suits. The typical first-party suit is one where a policyholder claims that the insurance safety representative was relied upon to inspect property and that because of negligence, the inspection, or lack of it, resulted in damage to the policyholder's property. The policyholder then brings legal action against the insurance company for that part of the loss not covered by the insurance policy. Typical cases quoted are *Hartford Steam Boiler Inspection and Insurance Company vs. Pabst Brewing Company*[1] and *Pennsylvania Millers Mutual vs. Thomas Milling Company.*[2]

A typical third-party negligent inspection suit is one where someone other than a policyholder is injured and brings suit against the insurance company. The most common negligent inspection case is one where an employee of the policyholder is injured and claims that the injury could have been prevented or lessened, except for negligence of the insurance safety representative.

Negligent inspection suits often use as their basis historical cases (case law). A committee of the American Law Institute, consisting of law professors and practicing attorneys, periodically publishes its interpretations of current law. These interpretations are often adopted in the State Legislatures and the courts. The *Second Restatement of Torts, Section 324A,* published by this comittee, is often quoted in negligent inspection suits, and it is as follows:

324A — Liability to Third-Person for Negligent Performance of Undertaking.

One who undertakes, gratuitously or for consideration, to render services to another which he should recognize as necessary for the protection of a third person or his things, is subject to liability to the third person for physical harm resulting from his failure to exercise reasonable care to protect his undertaking, if

(a) his failure to exercise reasonable care increases the risk of such harm, or

(b) he has undertaken to perform a duty owed by the other to the third person, or

(c) the harm is suffered because of reliance of the other or the third person upon the undertaking.

A preponderance of negligent inspection suits arise out of workers compensation insurance. Where an employee is injured, the plaintiff's attorney will usually attempt to show that the insurance company assumed the policyholder's responsibility for employee safety. For this reason, most insurance carriers have worded their workers compensation policy to state that the *company has a right but not a duty* to inspect the policyholder's premises. Typical wording would be as follows:

"The Company shall be permitted, but not obligated, to inspect the workplace, operations, machinery and equipment covered by this policy. Neither the right to make the inspection, nor the making thereof, nor any report thereon shall constitute an undertaking on behalf of, or for, the benefit of the insured or others, to determine or warrant that such workplaces, operations, machinery or equipment are safe."

There is no way of knowing how many legal actions this precaution has eliminated, but there have been a few where it was obviously a factor. *(Kennard vs. Liberty Mutual Insurance Company.)*[3]

The court may reject the policy wording argument, and the insurance company may argue that even so, its actions do not justify the conclusion that it has assumed the policyholder's responsibility for safety. That argument has prevailed in some cases, such as the following: *Gerace vs. Liberty Mutual Insurance Company,*[4] *Zamecki vs. Hartford Accident and Indemnity Company,*[5] *Stacey vs. Aetna Casualty and Surety Company,*[6] *Tillman vs. Travelers Indemnity Company.*[7]

The court in the Tillman case reiterated the decision in the Stacey case. That is, that proof the insurer had conducted a negligent inspection, by itself, was not a sufficient basis for recovery. In other words, it was not proof that the insurer had assumed the policyholder's responsibility for safety.

The plaintiff's attack on such a defense usually is that the insurance company's actions speak louder than words and that their actions *implied* they have *assumed at least in part* the policyholder's responsibility for safety. In attempting such proof, the plaintiffs often very carefully scrutinize the advertisements of the insurance carrier. In the Nelson/Wire Rope case *(Nelson vs. Union Wire Rope Corporation),*[8] the plaintiff used the defendant insurance company's advertising to successfully argue that the insurance company had, in fact, undertaken safety on the part of the policyholder.

Insurance companies sometimes have successfully argued that the *scope* of their service did not include inspection of the hazard which resulted in the injury. For example, a crane boom fell, causing injury. *(Smithhart vs. AAA Contracting Company).*[9]

The insurance company successfully contended that inspection of the crane was outside the scope of their service. There was a similar case in which a pipe burst, allowing hot sulphur to spray in the face of a worker. The insurance carrier successfully argued that the inspection of the pipe in detail was beyond the scope of its service. *(Fuller vs. Aetna Casualty and Surety Company).*[10]

Part (c) of the *Second Restatement of Torts, Section 324A,* is concerned with "harm suffered because of the other's *reliance* upon the undertaking." The matter of reliance has been a key issue in several negligent inspection suits. Some courts hold that reliance is essential for recovery. Others have held just the opposite. In the Viducich case *(Viducich vs. Greater New York Mutual),*[11] the court ruled that "the insured did nothing which would have led either the insured or the plaintiff to *rely* upon the inspections it has made." The court in the Nelson/Wire Rope case specifically rejected this argument and ruled the opposite.

Just what the courts will find that constitutes *reliance* is not clear, but being careful not to do or say things which make it easy for the plaintiff to prove reliance is an important way of avoiding potential liability.

The question often arises as to just what duty the insurance safety representative has in seeing that recommendations are followed. The courts have been divided on this issue. In one case *(Hubbard vs. Aetna Insurance Company),*[12] an employee was killed when a piece of equipment exploded. Even though Aetna had told the insured the equipment was unsafe, they were made a defendant in a suit wherein the plaintiff argued that the Aetna should have been required to remove the hazard. The court disagreed. A similar case *(Clark vs. Employers Mutual of Wausau),*[13] was also decided in favor of the insurance company.

In another case of similar circumstances *(Andrews vs. Insurance Company of North America),*[14] the result was the opposite. Over a period of two years, INA had repeatedly made recommendations for correcting unsafe conditions of punch presses. After repeated requests, the policyholder had installed two hand trip safety buttons and had provided tongs for use when the two hand trips were not practical. One day, an employee, with the permission and assistance of her foreman, taped down the dual safety buttons and discontinued use of the safety tongs. As a result, she lost several fngers in the press. The court found, in this case, that the repeated inspections, recommendations and contacts with upper management was sufficient evidence to give rise to a duty on the part of INA to provide a safe place of employment for the insured's employees. INA was found liable.

Insurance representatives could become discouraged reading the foregoing case, as it appears that no matter what one does, some courts will find for the plaintiff. It should be kept in mind that this is only one case out of thousands. *The same case tried in another jurisdiction would most likely have had the opposite result.*

In the defense of negligent inspection suits, argument has often been presented that the safety activities of the thousands of insurance safety representatives serve to reduce accidents. Without protection from the negligent inspection suits, the service may be curtailed or even disappear, resulting in an economic loss to the whole community.

Responding to this, several states have provided immunity in their workers compensation statutes against the negligent inspection suit. Since statutory relief is an erosion of common law, the courts are very careful in interpretation. Relief will only be granted to the extent that it is specifically spelled out in the statute. These statutory immunities with the ever-changing legislation and court actions are in a constant state of flux. *Even so, every Safety Professional should be aware of the current status in the state where he/she provides safety service.*

B. Avoiding Legal Liability Arising Out Of The Insurance Company Safety Function

If no injury or damage occurs, there can be no common law negligence liability. Therefore, to avoid liability, the first and foremost consideration should be the avoidance of accidents which result in harm. Since in the forseeable future there will continue to be serious accidents, it is necessary to consider what steps can be taken to lessen the chances of negligent inspection suits against the insurance company or representative and the chances of an adverse award.

1. *Policy Wording.* The policy wording should state that the insurance company has the right, but not the duty, to inspect the policyholder's premises and that none of the company activities should be construed to imply that the insurance company is assuming any part of the policyholder's responsibility to provide a safe workplace.
2. *Advertisements.* The insurance company advertisements, whether prepared by the Advertising Department or a Loss Control Representative, may be just what is needed for the plaintiff to prove that the insurance company had assumed all or part of the policyholder's responsibility for safety. All advertising copy, all pamphlets and the policyholder safety promotional material should be reviewed by the Legal Department prior to final printing.

   Where field offices present local safety seminars or participate in marketing seminars, it is not unusual for the Safety Department to prepare their own special leaflet or brochure. *Such items should have the same careful review as the company advertisements.*
3. *Policyholder Communications.*

A. Visit Confirmation: Most safety representatives confirm the findings of a policyholder visit with a letter typed at the local company office or a handwritten list of recommendations written during the visit and left with the policyholder. In either case, the following suggestions will apply:

1) Be *specific* and report only what was done. Never make a blanket statement such as, "I inspected your Jones Street plant." Instead, be more specific such as, "I observed the operation of the three power presses and recommend that all be equipped with suitable barrier guards."
2) Be *prompt* in reporting serious hazards. Even though one may normally confirm the visit by letter, any serious hazard noted should be brought to the policyholder management's attention in *writing* before leaving the premises, even though all recommendations may have been reviewed orally with the management during the visit.
3) Avoid the use of *unnecessary specifications.* If a recommendation stated, "the guard should be bolted to the machine with a 3/8" bolt," and the bolt failed, causing injury, it would have been better to say, "the guard should be attached to the machine with a suitable bolt." Even better would have been, "the guard should be designed and attached as specified by your Engineering Department."
4) Some companies use a *Disclaimer* with each piece of policyholder correspondence. While it is of questionable value, at least one claim was abandoned when the disclaimer was pointed out. A typical disclaimer is as follows:

"This confirmation of service concerns only such conditions and practices as were observed and considered during the visit. It does not purport to list all hazards. Neither does it purport to indicate that other hazards do not exist, nor that you are in compliance with Federal and State safety and health laws."

5) Attempt to do only that for which you are *qualified.* For example, one shouldn't recommend medical items for First Aid, unless he or she has medical training. One should not attempt to do a floor loading analysis without proper training.
6) Do not *misrepresent* qualifications. In most states, it is illegal to use the title *Engineer* in relation to services performed or offered, unless the person is a Registered Professional Engineer in that particular state.
7) Avoid actions which can be interpreted by the courts to imply that you have *assumed* part of the policyholder's responsibility for safety. For example,

dealing directly with policyholder employees, other than management, may imply the assumption of a policyholder management function. The insurance safety representative should never discuss recommendations with employees, nor give instruction to them. Such discussions should be confined to the policyholder management. The insurance safety representative should never hold a safety meeting with policyholder employees. The meeting should be a policyholder function called and directed by the policyholder management. There should be nothing wrong with the insurance representative performing as a guest speaker or providing instructions as a guest speaker.

8) When recommending safety products, strive to give at least *three (3) sources* and allow the policyholder to make the choice.

Following the above suggestions and always striving to perform in a professional, businesslike, manner will reduce one's exposure to the negligent inspection suits.

References

1. *-201 F 617 (7 Cir (Wis) 1912)*
2. *-224 SE2d 55 (Ga App 1976)*
3. *-277 So2d 170 (La App 1973)*
4. *-264 FSupp 95 (DC 1966)*
5. *-95 A2d 302 (Md App 1953)*
6. *-484 F2d 289 (5 Cir (Miss) 1973)*
7. *-506 F2d 917 (5 Cir (Miss) 1975)*
8. *-199 NE2d 769 (Ill 1964)*
9. *-260 So2d 8 (La App 1972)*
10. *-369 FSupp 967 (SD Miss 1974)*
11. *-192 A2d 596 (NJ App 1963)*
12. *-347 NE2d 396 (Ill App 1976)*
13. *-297 FSupp 286 (Penn 1969)*
14. *-230 NW2d 371 (Mich App 1975); on remand, -231 NW2d 645 (Mich 1975)*

Health and Safety Law for American Companies Operating in Europe

Allan St. John Holt

Mr. Holt, a long-time International Member of ASSE, is managing director of E. St. John Holt and Associates Ltd., an accident prevention and industrial safety consulting firm in Southampton, England. He has long experience in both forensic and management consulting work in British business and industry. He is Vice President and a Fellow of the Institution of Occupational Safety and Health in the United Kingdom.

The systems of laws controlling health and safety at work in Europe differ widely, as do standards of protection required of employers. Although statutory rules and standards vary in their complexity and the extent of their technical demands, there is little doubt that employers who are prepared to meet the standard of worker care imposed by OSHA will have little more than fine tuning to do to achieve compliance in Europe. However, there are a number of areas where OSHA and ANSI standards are exceeded, and others where European provisions exist in the absence of American equivalents. This article will outline general requirements based upon the British system — the most comprehensive and demanding in Europe — and provide reference points for further information.

The introduction of the Health and Safety at Work etc. Act in 1975 in Britain extended existing statutes to all fields of employment, and extended coverage to some 8 million workers not covered by previous specific legislation. *This Act imposes general duties upon all employers and employees, in addition to applying controls on those who manufacture, import, design or supply anything to be used at work.* Breaches of these provisions, which are written as objectives rather than as lists of specific requirements, constitute *criminal offences.* A greater involvement of the workforce was also sought by allowing for the appointment of safety representatives, with rights of inspection and immunity from prosecution, by the labour unions, and for the creation of statutory safety committees.

Powers of the inspectors of the Health and Safety Executive, and of other enforcing authorities with delegated powers, are unlimited under the Act. They have unlimited right of entry to premises, can require management and employees to give statements about particular circumstances, and have power to stop any work with potential to cause serious personal injury. These and other powers are not used lightly, *since inspectors possess university master's degrees* and are experienced in their industries. If persuasion fails, prosecution may result. Individual indictment of members of management and workers alike is common. Inspectors have no power to propose penalties for violations — this is a matter for the criminal courts at various levels. The average fine per offence charged is £300 (about $480).

One of the provisions which affects all employers with more than five workers is that they must develop and publish a written statement of safety policy. This legally-required document provides a basis for regulatory assessment of the employer by the authorities, for assessing criminal responsibility of individuals, and allows the employer to set a standard of conduct for himself by which his reasonable actions may be judged in the event of civil claims. Failure to produce such a statement constitutes a criminal offence; some guidance is available from official sources on methods of writing suitable statements. (see references).

Compliance with the general duties section of the Act is not easy, as the standard to be achieved is that the employer must take all reasonably practicable steps to ensure the health, safety and welfare at work of his employees. Existing statutory specifics, such as the Factories Act and the Offices, Shops and Railway Premises Act remain in force meanwhile, and provide examples of standards which are both acceptable and reasonable. But the decision as to which are reasonably practicable and which are not is left to the employer, on whom the burden of proof rests if the matter should be taken to court. Voluntary standards such as those promoted by trade associations and especially those of the British Standards Institution (a non-governmental body) are usually acceptable to the enforcing authorities looking for compliance with the general duties clauses.

It is important to realise that payment of the compulsory National Insurance premium *does not bar the employer from suits by his injured employees.* Although the employer's duty derives from the contract of employment, *almost all civil cases are brought under the tort of negligence.* Claims may be presented under breach of either statutory duty or common law duty of care, and usually both, so as to add to the compensation paid under the state benefit scheme. Under the Employers Liability (Defective Equipment) Act 1969, *the employer is held strictly liable for injuries caused by defective equipment, while he is able to pursue a subsequent counter-claim against the manufacturer, producer or importer of the goods.* Although the manufacturer is still open to claims from injured parties, and to criminal prosecution under the Health and Safety at Work etc. Act (Section 6), the 1969 Act offers an easy route for compensation claims and the "product liability case" initiated by the injured worker against a manufacturer is not often encountered.

Machine guarding standards are set by the Factories Act 1961 (Section 14), and the most comprehensive guide to achieving safety in this area is contained in British Standard 5304; 1975. *Modern authorities consider that guarding is an integral part of machine design.* Guards will be fitted on imported machines by specialist guarding manufacturers working in conjunction with the importer and the purchaser. Strict application of statutory controls has produced dramatic results: injuries from all kinds of power presses in Great Britain dropped from 441 in 1965 to 48 in 1979, largely as a result of the regular press and guard examinations required by the Power Presses Regulations introduced in 1965, and amended in 1972, so as to require the person making the periodical examinations and tests to report serious defects to the Factory Inspectorate of the Health and Safety Executive.

Although Britain does not have a Freedom of Information statute, Section 6 of the Health and Safety at Work etc. Act 1974 requires all manufacturers, importers, designers and suppliers to provide necessary information about the proper use of their products so as to prevent possible injury. This means that the employers, employees and representatives of labour unions will ask for full details of all testing procedures and perfomance specifications of any product of foreign origin. Failure to provide this data could lead to an importation ban.

British health and safety law and standards are regarded as being the most comprehensive and detailed in Europe. Other countries have different legal systems and enforcement practices. The Common Market, or EEC, may issue legal instruments known as Directives, which are binding upon member states of the EEC but leave the members to decide about the way in which they will be put into operation. Health and safety directives have been aimed at harmonising standards so that unfair competition is removed by ensuring that employers in one country do not have to meet higher safety standards than those in another. The trend to date has been to move towards the British requirements as a base line. Directives issued so far have included one on VCM, and one on safety signs at work, and drafts are in progress on major hazards, such as lead and asbestos. Details of regulatory requirements can be obtained from the listed regulatory bodies, and information on standards from the major standards organisations. Corporate managers and visiting safety professionals may find it useful to attend an orientation briefing given by a consultant familiar with both European and American procedures.

(see next page for references)

References

COUNTRY	STANDARDS BODY	REGULATORY BODY
AUSTRIA	Austrian Standards Institute 1010 Wien 1 Borsegasse 18	Verlag der Osterreichischen Staatsdruckerei, Vienna
BELGIUM	Translations available from VDMA Corneliusstrasse 4 6000 Frankfurt/Main, W. Germany Acts and decrees available from publishers:- SACED Samson, 7, rue Phillippe de la champagne, B1010, Brussels	Administration de la securite du travail
BULGARIA	Comite de la Qualite 21 rue 6 Septembre Sofia	Industrial Safety Central Council Bulgarian Trades Administration Sofia
DENMARK	Dansk Standardiseringsraad Aurehøjwej 12 2900 Hellerup	Direktoratet for arbejdstilsynet Rosenvaengets Allé 16-18 2100 Copenhagen
EIRE	Institute for Industrial Research Ballymum Road Dublin 9	Industrial Inspectorate Department of Labour Mespil Road Dublin 4
FINLAND	Finnish Standards Association PO Box 205 SF - 00121 Helsinki 12	Yrkes Inspektionen Ministry of Social Affairs Helsinki
FRANCE	AFNOR Tour Europe, Cedex 7 92080 Paris La Defénse	Regulatory codes acts, decrees etc. available from publishers:- L'Imprimerie Nationale 27,rue de la Convention, Paris
WEST GERMANY	DIN Beuth-Vertrieb GmbH Berlin 12	(Regulations and index from:-) Carl Heymanns Verlag, 5000 Koln, Gereonstrasse 18.
GREECE	Ministry of National Economy General Directorate of Industry 20, Canning Street, Athens 141	Trade Inspectorate Directorate E/2 Ministry of Labour Piraeus Street 14, Athens.
ICELAND	Nordisk Maskinkomite Baungegardsvij 73 S-2900 Hellerup Sweden	Oruggiseftirlit rikisins Braedraborgarstig 9 Regkjavik
ITALY	UNI Piazza Armando Diaz 20123 Milano	ENPI Via Alessandria 220-E 00198 Roma
NETHERLANDS	NNI Polakweg 5 Rijswijk ZH-2106	Labour Inspectorate Ministerie van Sociale Zaken Balen van Andelplein 2 Postbus 69 Voorburg
NORWAY	NSF Haakon VII's gt 2 Oslo 1	Statens arbeidstilsynet Direktor Fr. Nansens vei 14 Oslo
PORTUGAL	IGPAI Avenida de Berna 1 Lisbon 1	Ministerio da Economia Instituto Nacional Rue Garcia de Orto 68 Lisbon 2
SPAIN	INRN Serrano 150 Madrid 6	Ministerio de Industrial Serrano 35 Madrid 1
SWEDEN	(See Iceland) *Schandinavian countries co-operate in the formulation of standards	Trades Safety Inspectorate KAS Wennersbergsgatan 10 S-10026 Stockholm 34
SWITZERLAND	SUVA, Abteilung Unfallverhütung Postfach, 6002 Lucerne	SUVA, Abeteilung Unfallverhütung Postfach, 6002 Lucerne
USSR	Gosudarstvennyi Komitet Standartov Soveta Ministrov USSR Leninsky Prospekt 96 Moscow M 49	State Committee for Labour Safety UL. Kuibisheva 4 Moscow

UK	British Standards Institution 2, Park Street, London W1A 2BS	Health and Safety Executive. Baynards House, 1-13 Chepstow Place, London W2 4TY

REFERENCES

Statutes

Health and Safety at Work etc. Act 1974
Factories Act 1961
Offices, Shops and Railway Premises Act 1963
Power Presses Regulations 1966
- all available from Her Majesty's Stationery Office

49, High Holborn
London WC1V 6HB

Official Guidance (all obtainable from HMSO)

HSE Publications Catalogue - a complete guide to all health and safety governmental publications

A guide to the Health and Safety at Work Act	- HS(R) 6	
Packaging and Labelling of Dangerous Substances	- HS(R) 1	
A Guide to Agriculture Legislation	- HS(R) 2	
A Guide to the 1963 OSRP Act	- HS(R) 4	
A Guide to the Safety Signs Regulations 1980	- HS(R) 7	
First Aid at Work (guide to 1981 Regulations)	- HS(R)11	£2.50
Effective Policies for Health and Safety (ISBN 0 11 883254 9)		£1.00
Managing Safety	- OP3	£2.25

Books

N. SELWYN-	Law of Health and Safety at Work, (a general guide)	published by Butterworth (ISBN 0 406 66750 0)	£7.50
	British Standards Yearbook (complete list and descriptions of all current standards)	published by British Standards Institution	£15.50

(See Appendix B, p. 123)

Criminal Prosecution Under OSHA

James T. Patterson, CSP

***Mr. Patterson, a Professional Member of the Society, is a loss control consultant for the Talbert Corporation, a Surety Bonds and Insurance firm in Denver. He has extensive experience in and has devoted considerable time to study of legal aspects of occupational safety and health. This article originally appeared in the March 1979 issue of Professional Safety* Magazine and is reprinted here, with permission of the author.**

Editor's Note — The author is not an attorney and this review of OSHA's criminal prosecution powers cannot substitute in any way for legal counsel. However, it should assist the reader in locating the case history on this matter and emphasize the need to develop corporate strategy for dealing with death in the workplace.

This article reviews the individual and corporate risk of criminal prosecution under the Occupational Safety and Health Act of 1970. Even though OSHA has instituted criminal proceedings in only a few cases since the Act became effective, the risk is still significant to the individual, particularly since "Miranda" warnings against self-incrimination may not be required during the initial phases of an OSHA inspection. Enforcement policies will vary; a lack of criminal prosecution one year may not be the next year. Employers and those individuals within the corporation who possess the power to prevent or correct corporate violations of the Act may wish to have an attorney present during questioning by an OSHA compliance officer, when a fatality has occurred.

One often sees corporate safety policies which announce that:

The safety department has full and complete authority to: (1) stop the work, if hazardous conditions exist; and (2) approve corrective action taken by local management.

This is an exceptionally broad statement, which may carry serious risk of both civil damages[1] and criminal prosecution by OSHA.[2] Since the "power to stop the work" has been interpreted as the "duty to stop the work"[3] when hazardous conditions exist, one has to question the wisdom of including such statements in corporate policy.

As safety becomes increasingly professionalized, one of the inescapable risks is the safety professional's increased vulnerability to civil damage suits. Although criminal OSHA prosecutions are infrequent, these actions are also threatening to the safety professional.

This paper will review the criminal prosecution that OSHA could institute. The few criminal cases filed by OSHA and one criminal case prosecuted in California will be examined to determine, if possible, what factors were common to these proceedings. Finally, the question of the indiviudal's right to counsel and protection against self-incrimination will be reviewed.

Criminal sanctions in OSHA

Section 17(e) of OSHA provides that:

"Any employer who willfully violates any standard ... or .. regulations prescribed pursuant to this Act, and that violation caused death to any employee, shall, upon conviction, be punished by a fine of not more than $10,000 or by imprisonment for not more than six months, or by both."

The origin of this criminal sanction can be traced to a bill introduced in 1965 by Congresswoman Sullivan.[5] The bill was designed to protect workers exposed to hazardous materials and relied almost exclusively upon criminal penalties for enforcement. The bill was re-introduced in every Congress after 1965, including the 91st, which passed OSHA.

The bills introduced at the beginning of the 91st Congress drew upon the 1965 bill by Congresswoman Sullivan for much of their criminal penalty provisions.

The Conference Committee version retained what was basically an all-civil penalty provision for all substantive violations, with the criminal penalty at 17(e) and other criminal penalties[6] for giving advance notice of an inspection (Section 17(f)), making false reports (Section 17(g)), and killing an OSHA inspector (Section 17(h)).

Cases involving section 17(e)

OSHA has attempted only a few criminal prosecutions since the Act became effective in April, 1971. In most cases an attempt was made to hold both the corporation and one or more individuals liable.

In *U.S. v. Turcon Co.*[7], action was brought against the corporation and the president as an individual. Three weeks prior to the fatality, the corporation had received a citation for violation of a trenching standard and the president was "active in conducting and supervising construction activities at the time of the violations." Although the president was acquitted, the corporation was fined $5,000.

In *U.S. v. Dye Construction Co.*[8], the trial court dismissed all counts against the president, holding that the corporation was the "employer," despite testimony that the president was involved in daily operations and "might have been out on the (fatal) site that day." Despite the fact that state safety inspectors had issued "imminent danger" notices six times in the nine months preceding the fatality, two of the three charges against the corporation were dismissed, leaving a corporate fine of $3,500.

In *U.S. v. Pinkston-Hollar, Inc.*[9], Pinkston, a vice-president, was supervising placement of roof insulation in a high wind. One employee fell through a roof opening, but managed to catch himself and avoided falling to the concrete floor thirty-five feet below. The employee then warned Pinkston that protection against falls was necessary. Despite Pinkston's awareness of applicable OSHA regulations — two previous citations had been issued for failure to provide fall protection — work proceeded. Shortly thereafter, another employee fell through a roof opening to his death. Despite this, the jury acquitted on both individual and corporate charges.

In *U.S. v. Crosby and Overton*[10], two officers and the corporation were charged with four counts of willfully failing to provide equipment and procedures necessary to enter closed tanks that contained toxic atmospheres. The District Court refused to impose either jail sentences or fines, allowing the plea of *nolocontendere*, and handing down a sentence of four years parole and implementation of a safety program. This case also has simultaneous civil action, that resulted in penalties of $14,250 and an abatement order more severe than that issued under criminal action.

It can easily be seen that OSHA has been neither effective nor active in criminal prosecution. *Other jurisdictions, notably California, have been very active in using criminal sanctions.* During one period of approximately 15 months, there were, in California, over 100 investigations of criminal violations, with 31 convictions out of 34 criminal proceedings.[11]

Although tried earlier than the cases mentioned above, the case of *California v. Lockheed Shipbuilding and Construction Company*[12] is interesting, in that it is a case in which the project safety director was charged with criminal action. Although the convictions were reversed because of trial court error, the tunnel project manager and project safety engineer were sentenced to terms of 20 years and 18 months, respectively, and the corporation was fined $120,000. The case was brought after 17 men lost their lives in a methane gas explosion and fire in a water diversion tunnel near Los Angeles.

Careful reading of these cases reveals the following factors common to each:

1. **Each involved a construction company.**[13]
2. **In each case, either "near misses" or citation for violation of identical standards had taken place shortly prior to the fatality.**
3. **The individuals charged with criminal violations knew, or should have known, of the circumstances surrounding the fatal accident.**
4. **Each of the individuals charged had either the "power to stop the work" or the responsibility of planning such procedures as would control the risk of serious danger.**

In theory, many, if not all, corporate safety professionals will face the factors listed above. If called upon to face OSHA personnel investigating a fatality, what rights does the individual have?

Defenses available

The foundation of our individual rights in criminal proceedings is the Fifth Amendment, under which we cannot be forced or coerced into self-incriminating statements. However, the application of this right during interrogation by OSHA (and other government regulatory agencies) is not a simple matter.

The first question that arises is, "Are 'Miranda'-type warnings[14] required?" This question was ruled upon in *U.S. v. Pinkston-Hollar, Inc.*[9], in which defendent Pinkston immediately reported the fatality to the nearest OSHA office. The investigation began the following day and lasted one week, with the investigator talking to fellow employees of the deceased and with Pinkston.

When criminal charges were filed against both the corporation and Pinkston, both attempted to raise the question of self-incrimination, as they had attempted to cooperate with the OSHA compliance officer, and had not been issued a "Miranda" warning.

The court held that a corporation has no Fifth Amendment rights against self-incrimination[15] and that three disclosures made by Pinkston were made prior to the initiation of any criminal proceedings, stating that the "(Miranda) procedure, however, is required *ipso facto* only when the suspect has been taken into the Government's custody or is otherwise deprived of his freedom by the Government."[16]

Two other cases dealing with the question of legal counsel and/or self-incrimination have been decided by the OSHA Revised Commission. In the case of *Secretary of Labor v. Capital Dock and Dredge*[17], the vice-president of Capital, upon legal advice, refused to make a deposition unless the OSHA attorney would offer assurance that both Capital and its vice-president were "immune from any criminal sanction that is provided for in the (Act)." The Review Commission found a procedural error in the case, remanded it to the Administrative Law Judge (ALJ), with the case ultimately being settled out of court, with the willful citation and penalty reduced.[18]

In the case of *Secretary of Labor v. Phillip J. Estere, dba The Upstairs*[19], the finding was that in "(civil) proceedings .. there is no requirement that an employer must be in the presence of an attorney when he is being interviewed."

Conclusion

Federal courts, including the Review Commission, will probably follow the precedents established in *Pinkston* and *Estere, dba The Upstairs*. This means, in the author's opinion, that employers and "responsible employees" should give strong consideration to consulting with an attorney before undergoing any questioning by OSHA when a fatality has occurred. This is of particular relevance in jurisdictions, such as California, where pursuit of criminal cases is active.

References

1. *Damages for negligence, as in "wrongful death" suit brought against a third-party defendant, other than the employer (who is usually granted immunity by the workers compensation law). At least one corporate safety director has been held liable for damages in a fellow-employee suit. Graven v. Oggero,* 213 NW 2[d] 678 (Iowa S. Ct, Dec. 19, 1973).
2. In this paper the term "OSHA" will be used to refer to both the Occupational Safety and Health Act of 1970 and the Occupational Safety and Health Administration. The context of the use will clearly indicate which meaning is intended.
3. See the following for discussion of architect-engineer liability for injury and/or death:
   Davidson, D. M., "The Legal Implications of Quality Control," *Civil Engineering*, 37:72–73, Nov., 1967.
   Goldbloom, J., "Safety in Construction: Whose Responsibility?," *Civil Engineering*, 39:42–46, Nov., 1969.
   Malone, E. F., "The Power to 'Stop the Work': A Serious Source of Potential Liability," *Consulting Engineer*, 36:24, 26, June, 1971.
   Millman, P. and D. A. Ostrower, "Engineering Liability: Where Does the Buck Stop?" *Consulting Engineer*, 51:42, 44, 46, 48, Nov., 1978.
4. Individuals cited as references are attorneys. Other references are: (1) summaries of cases published by the Bureau of National Affairs (cited as BNA); material found in Subcommittee on Labor, Senate Committee on Labor and Public Welfare, *Legislative History of the Occupational Safety and Health Act of 1970, 92*[d] Congress, 1st Session, 1971 (cited as *Leg Hist*); and citations of decisions in the various court reporters.
5. H. R. 1179, 89th Congress, 1st Session. Text of the bill may be found in 13 *House of Representatives Bills*, 89th Congress (1965-66). See also *Leg. Hist, op cit*, pp. 1080–84.
6. None of the latter sanctions has ever been invoked as far as I know.
7. No. 72-D-239 (D. Neb., Feb. 21, 1974).
8. BNA, 2 OSHC 1510 and 510 F. *2*[d] 78 (10th Circuit Court of Appeals, Jan. 29, 1975).
9. BNA, 4 OSHC 1697 (No. 76-33-CR-6, D. Kan, Oct. 12, 1976).
10. No. CR-74-1832-F (S.D., Calif., Feb. 24, 1975).
11. Fisher, R. N., "Criminal Trials on Safety Issues," *Proceedings of the ABA National Institute on Occupational Safety and Health Law* (Chicago: American Bar Assoc., 1976). p. 178.
12. BNA, 1 OSHC 1450.
13. If one agrees that the tank cleaning work of Crosby and Overton constitutes construction work.
14. *Miranda v. Arizona*, 384 U.S. 436 (1966).
15. *Campbell Painting Co. v. Reid*, 392 U.S. 286 (1968).
16. This ruling is consistent with the Supreme Court decision in the case of *Beckwith v. U.S.*, 425 U.S. 341 (1976), in which Internal Revenue Service agents interrogated without warnings complying with Miranda requirements. The Court ruled that warnings against self-incrimination are required only when there has been a detention and "focus" on the one being interrogated about possible tax fraud. Fisher, *op cit* p. 182, warns that "... federal courts will presumably follow the Beckwith rule in OSHA cases."
17. BNA, 1 OSHC 1066.
18. Personal communication with ALJ Sidney J. Goldstein, Dec. 26, 1978.
19. BNA, 2 OSHC 3011.

The Fellow-Employee Suit — Civil Liability of Safety Professionals

James T. Patterson, CSP

***The risk of civil litigation is an increasing threat to the practicing safety professional. Despite the "exclusive remedy" provisions of workers compensation, there are several states in which an injured employee or his estate may sue a fellow-employee. Here Mr. Patterson discusses what the safety practitioner may need as to specific protection for this possibility. This article originally appeared in the September 1980 issue of Professional Safety* Magazine and is reprinted here with permission of the author.**

During the past decade, the established professions — architecture, engineering, law and medicine — faced a substantial increase in claims against individual members for professional malpractice. Some indication of the magnitude of this problem can be found by reviewing the increases in professional liability insurance between 1962-72 (Table 1).[1]

There are several reasons why these professions faced a substantial increase in claims (and insurance premiums). Among them are: Changing concepts of the duty owed by a professional; weakening or elimination of legal barriers, such as privity of contract; and the increasing prevalence of the attitude that when one suffers economic loss, regardless of negligence, someone else has to compensate him for that loss.

Safety is becoming increasingly professionalized.[2] As this process continues and safety becomes recognized by society as an established profession, the risk of lawsuits will become of increasing concern to all of us, regardless of our employment situation or our certification/ registration.

This article will review only one aspect of the safety professional's liability — that of action brought by a fellow-employee alleging that the safety professional discharged his duties in a negligent manner. Included in this article are the following: A brief review of Workers Compensation Law, as it pertains to the subject; a review of the insurance coverage problems peculiar to this matter; and suggestions for personal conduct in discharging one's responsibilities as a safety professional.

Consideration of the insurer's liability for negligent safety inspections is excluded, as this has been discussed thoroughly.[3] Also excluded is any consideration of the liability problems of the independent safety consultant.[4]

The reader is cautioned to seek legal counsel as it is impossible in an article of this nature to discuss the laws of any state. The law changes too rapidly in response to legislation and case law for one to attempt this. Furthermore, one may wish to consult with an insurance agent concerning his personal insurance coverages and consult with his corporate insurance manager concerning corporate insurance protection.

"Exclusive Remedy" Provisions

Workers compensation acts differ from state to state. However, the concept underlying all this legislation is relatively uniform:

1. The employer surrenders his common-law defenses of fellow-servant rule, assumption of risk, contributory negligence and acts of God.
2. The employee surrenders his right to sue his employer, in return for a guaranteed recovery.
3. When the party causing the injury is someone other than the employer, the injured employee has a right of common-law action against this "third party."

Most states have, either through legislation or court decisions, limited the right of an employee to sue a fellow-employee, usually on the grounds that the fellow-employee normally has no insurance protection and thus, the award of damages would be "... as debilitating to his economic welfare as the original loss was to the injured worker's ...."[5]

In order to protect fellow-employees from the risk of litigation and subsequent award of damages, legislatures have sought to make workers compensation the "exclusive remedy." A typical legislative statute on this matter might read as follows:

"The right to compensation or benefits under this chapter shall be the exclusive remedy to an employee, or in the case of death his dependents, when such employee is injured or killed by the negligence or wrong of another in the same employ."[6]

However, the safety professional who researches the law in his state and finds a similar "exclusive remedy" provision in the Compensation Act has no assurance that a court decision might not overturn such protection. This happened recently (1978) in Alabama when the Supreme Court held that the provision of the Alabama constitution which preserves common-law rights and remedies overrode the legislature's power to grant co-employees immunity from suit for injuries covered by the Workers Compensation Act.[7]

Obviously, no one can predict when similar decisions might occur in his own state.

Insurance coverage problems

As the intent of this article is to bring this exposure to the attention of the safety professional and cause him to consider seeking competent legal and insurance counsel, the insurance coverages involved will be limited to the personal homeowners policy of the safety professional and the employer's comprehensive general liability policy. Considerations mentioned herein will also probably apply to automobile liability policies.

With respect to the employer's liability policy, one will find that the insuring agreement provides protection only for the company and its "executive officers, directors, and stockholders while acting in their capacities as such." Furthermore, the policy may exclude coverage for industrial injuries. The language of such exclusion typically reads as follows:

"This insurance does not apply ... to any obligation for which the insured or any carrier as his insuror may be held liable under any workers compensation ... law ... or ... to bodily injury to any employee of the insured arising out of and in the course of his employment by the insured ..."

If the fellow-employee (safety professional?) named in a suit does not fall within the policy definition of a named insured, he will normally be informed by the employer's liability carrier that he should notify the carrier which provides personal liability insurance coverage for him, normally his homeowner's policy carrier.

However, the individual who informs his homeowner's carrier (or personal liability carrier) that he has been named in a lawsuit for damages, may well receive the chilling news that his personal policy excludes coverage for this type of occurrence. The language of such an exclusion typically reads as follows:

"This policy does not apply ... to bodily injury or property damage arising out of the rendering or of failing to render professional services ... or ... to bodily injury or property damage arising out of business pursuits *(emphasis added) of any insured ..."*

It is possible for the employer to provide coverage against the risk of fellow-employee suits.[8] In consideration of an additional premium the employer, acting through his insurance agent, can negotiate with the liability carrier to endorse the liability policy so that the exclusion relating to fellow-employees is modified to provide coverage in any case where an employee is allowed to bring suit against a fellow-employee. This endorsement should be added to both the comprehensive general liability policy and the automobile liability policy.

The insurance carrier may be reluctant to extend this coverage, because of fear that, should this extension become known throughout the organization, injured employees will attempt to bring common-law action against fellow-employees, hoping to receive awards of much higher value than those possible under the workers compensation statute.

The individual, of course, can also attempt to have this exclusion removed from his personal liability policies. This course of action, obviously, is less desirable than having the protection afforded through the employer's coverages.

There is another course of action available to all of us, of course, and that is to try to influence legislation in one's state to preclude fellow-employee suits.

Personal conduct

Again, for definitive advice in this area, one should consult with legal counsel.

Another action that the safety professional can take is to review the decisions of appellate courts that have rendered judgment on cases involving action by an injured employee against one or more fellow-employees, including the corporate safety manager. Appendix A contains several citations to recent decisions of this nature. If these legal references are not available through one's corporate counsel, one should be able to gain access to them through his personal attorney, or possibly through the law library at his county courthouse.

With respect to one's personal conduct, lawyers have provided guidance to architect/engineers along the following lines:

1. Keep a personal daily diary in enough detail to allow you to reconstruct months or even years later any conversations, discussions, or inspections.
2. Confirm in writing decisions reached in the course of conversations, conferences, and inspections.
3. Confine your actions to those areas in which you have expertise.
4. Keep all your written memoranda in good order, until such time as any possible suit is barred by statute of limitations.
5. Review your corporate job description with legal counsel to determine if it leaves you vulnerable and responsible for the acts or omissions of others over whom you have no control.[9]

Conclusion

The Society studied the problem of legal liability during the early 1970's and was able to offer insurance protection to the membership. Due to lack of participation by safety professionals, the carrier dropped the program after a short time.*

With increasing emphasis on professionalization of safety and given the increasing trend toward litigation by those who feel victimized, there is an apparent need for this protection. This should be given serious consideration by the Society staff and elected officers.

***A new liability insurance program for Society members was launched in 1982.**

References

1. *Shear, B. W., "Professional Liability Problems*

Among Architects, Engineers, Lawyers, and Accountants: A Comparison With the Medical Profession," Appendix to the Report of the Secretary's Commission on Medical Malpractice. Health, Education and Welfare Publication No. (OS) 73-89, Washington, D.C., 1973, pp 637–643.

2. Patterson, J. T., "Safety — an Aspiring Profession," *Professional Safety*, Vol 23. No. 4, April, 1978, pp 20–26.
3. a. -----. "Liability of insurer for Safety Inspections," *Defense Law Journal*, Vol 20, 1971, pp 284–293.
   b. Rosen, Paul A., "Nelson Decision and the Safety Engineer," *The Liability of the Safety Professional*, Monograph No 2. (Park Ridge, Ill: American Society of Safety Engineers, 1972) pp 5–7.
4. I have been unable to locate any published material or court decisions on the liability problems of the independent safety consultant. Does this mean they have successfully avoided this risk, thus far?
5. -----. "The Third Party Action — Expanding the Circle of Immunity: Co-Employees," *Mississippi Law Journal*, Vol 48, #1, Jan. 1977, p 108.
6. New York Workmen's Compensation Law, Art 29 (6), 1975.
7. Grantham v. Denke, *Southern Reporter*, 2d Series, Vol 359, p 785. For an excellent discussion of this decision, see "Workmen's Compensation —Coemployee Liability," *Cumberland Law Review*, Vol 9, #3, Winter 1979, pp 921–935.
8. Special endorsements to hospital liability policies that declare all employees to be "named insureds" have been available for approximately 25% of the regular malpractice premium for the institution. No definitive information was available on the number of hospitals that used this endorsement Shear, "The Malpractice Problem for non-Physician Health-Care Professions as Reflected in Professional Liability Rates," *Appendix to the Report ... op cit.*, p 652.
9. For a discussion of a fellow-employee suit in which a written job description was an important part of the defense, see Kerrigan v. Erett, *North Western Reporter*, 2d Series, Vol 394, p 394 (Supreme Court of Iowa, 7-29-77).

Selected Court Decisions Involving Fellow-Employee Suits, with descriptions:

1. Adams v. Fidelity & Casualty of NY, (Vol) 107 *Southern Reporter, 2d* Series, (page) 496 (Louisiana First Circuit Court of Appeals, 11-21-58).
   Widow of decreased employed had right of action in wrongful death suit against corporate officers, including safety director, all of whom should have seen the hazard that resulted in death.
2. Cacibanda v. Gajenni, Jr. *etal*, 350 Southern, *2d*, 572 (Louisiana Fourth Circuit Court of Appeals, 12-13-74).
   Company supervisor of administrative services, who was responsible for safety of employees, was personally liable in a suit brought by widow of deceased employee.
3. Craven v. Oggero, 213 *North Western, 2d*, 678 (Iowa Supreme Court, 12-19-73).
   Construction company's safety director and job superintendent were held to be proper defendants in suit by estate of deceased employee.
4. Hysell v. Iowa Public Service Co. *etal*, 534 *Federal 2d*, 775, (United States Eighth Circuit Court of Appeals, 4-12-76).
   Co-employee of injured employee was defendent in damage suit because he failed to maintain lookout for clearance between boom truck and overhead electric line.
5. Kerrigan v. Errett, 256 *North Western 2d*, 394 (Iowa Supreme Court, 7-29-77).
   In order to impose liability on co-employee, the court ruled that "the following criteria must be met: (1) the ... employer must owe a duty of care to the injured person, breach of which caused the damage for which recovery is sought; (2) the duty must have been delegated by the ... employer to the co-employee; (3) the defendant ... co-employee must have breached its duty through personal as contrasted with technical or vicarious fault; and (4) with regard to the personal fault, personal liability cannot be imposed simply because of the co-employee's general administrative responsibilities ..."
6. Pipkin v. Southern Electrical and Pipefitting Co., Inc., *etal 358 Southern, 2d*, 1015 (Alabama Supreme Court, 5-5-78).
   Trial court's dismissal of suit against co-employee (safety director) on grounds that the Workers Compensation Act provided immunity was reversed by Supreme Court.

employee (safety director) on grounds that the Workers Compensation Act provided immunity was reversed by Supreme Court.

Table 1
Malpractice Insurance Rates for Lawyers, Architects Engineers: Physicians, Surgeons, and Dentists Shown as Percentages of 1962 Rates For Each Profession

	Lawyers	Architects/ Engineers	Physicians	Surgeons	Dentists
1962	100 %	100 %	100 %	100 %	100 %
1964	99.0%	109.4%	115.8%	135.5%	100.3%
1966	106.9	109.4	134.0	157.1	115.9
1968	109.8	181.4	217.6	204.2	121.0
1970	170.7	300.3	540.0	673.9	164.4
1972	*	493.3	667.7	826.7	177.8

Source Shear page 643, Note 1

Regulatory Law — An Overview

David Swankin, Esq.

Editor's Note — Mr. Swankin is a long-time Washington-based attorney and former U.S. Dept. of Labor official with wide experience in government-related occupational safety and health matters. Much of the information he shares here is from a course in occupational health and safety law he teaches at the Washington campus of the University of Southern California. He is a partner in the Washington law firm of Swankin and Turner.

A. Introduction

For the non-lawyer to understand safety law as it has developed in the United States is no easy task. Other sections of this book have treated, at length, the developments in product liability law. Whether one agrees with the way product liability law has been developing or not, it cannot be denied that the "private" law has had a profound impact on safety. *One cannot be involved in the design, manufacture, distribution, installation, maintenance or repair of both consumer and industrial products without having a good working knowledge of the law of negligence, contracts, and strict liability.*

But that is only one part of the equation. Since the beginning of the 20th century, a blanket of safety regulation has emerged from the federal government (and, to a lesser extent, from state and local governments). This body of law can be loosely described as regulatory law.

It most certainly is a patchwork blanket. Congress has not seen fit to write a comprehensive National Safety Law. Instead, it has from time to time reacted to public pressure of one sort or another and enacted a variety of special safety laws, as well as an alphabet of agencies to administer these special laws. Most often the administration of these laws has resulted in the promulgation of thousands (collectively) of rules and regulations to implement the legislation.

The purpose of this section on regulation is to give the safety professional a "basic handbook" on the federal regulatory network. Moreover, it is also the purpose of this section to help the safety professional (1) in knowing how to stay on top of new developments in the field, and (2) in knowing how to ferret out more detailed information on any particular subject.

Perhaps the best way for the layman to understand the relationship between regulatory law and the so-called "common law" is to describe what it is *not*. It is not a neat, interlocking system, where one picks up where the other lets off. Far from it. Rather, we have in the United States a dual, overlapping system, where *the regulatory system of law has been superimposed on the tort system*. For example, a company that manufactures an unsafe product is subject to a private law suit by a person who has been injured by that product. That company may also be subject to the enforcement arm of a Federal regulatory agency. The two are not dependent on each other. The private law suit can go forward, without regard to the action (or inaction) by the federal regulatory agency.

That is not to say that there is no relationship between law suits by individuals and actions by federal regulatory agencies.

Some laws are silent on the relationship, and others deal with it head on. For example, section 25(a) of the Consumer Product Safety Act reads as follows:

> "Sec. 25. (a) Compliance with consumer product safety rules or other rules or orders under this Act shall not relieve any person from liability at common law or under State statutory law to any other person."

This means that a private law suit can be brought by an injured person even though the product that caused the injury met an applicable Federal mandatory safety standard. Of course, the manufacturer of the product would try to have himself relieved from liability on the grounds that his product was indeed safe, because it complied with a mandated standard. However, under the law, meeting the standard cannot be used to *presume* that the manufacturer would win such a case.

B. Administrative Law[1]

Administrative law is the legal requirements and restrictions on how government agencies make decisions which affect members of the public. It controls what agencies must do and what agencies cannot do. *Its concern is the process by which those decisions are made, as opposed to the substance of the decisions themselves.* The final part of the definition — the limitation to decisions affecting members of the public — indicates that administrative law, at least as will be described here, is not concerned with the internal management of the government, but rather is concerned with the relationship of government agencies to the so-called "private sector."

[1]This section borrows heavily from Philip Harter's "Regulatory Use of Standards", published by the U.S. Department of Commerce in 1979.

There are basically four sources of administrative law.

• *Administrative Procedure Act*. The first is the Administrative Procedure Act (APA). The procedures that agencies should follow when making decisions affecting the public matured during the growth of the federal government in the thirties, and the APA largely codified these precepts. Although the Freedom of Information Act, the Privacy Act and the Sunshine Act have been added to the APA recently, its general principles remain unchanged. The Act provides the basic procedures that agencies must follow when issuing rules and in adjudicatory proceedings. It also provides the criteria courts use to review the decisions of an agency.

• *Substantive Statutes*. The second major source of administrative procedure is the particular statute that gives it the power to issue the rule in the first place. Most of the statutes creating regulatory authority that have been passed within the past decade set forth the procedures the agency must follow in implementing the statute. Generally, the procedures supplement those of the Administrative Procedure Act. Thus, for example, the Occupational Safety and Health Act, unlike the Administrative Procedure Act, requires OSHA to conduct an oral hearing if anyone requests it before issuing a regulation. The Act also provides a different criteria for judicial review, so that one could argue that OSHA is obligated to develop more specific factual information to support one of its rules than would be an agency operating under the Administrative Procedure Act alone. To take another example, the Consumer Product Safety Act (CPSA) contemplates an entirely different sort of rulemaking process than that envisaged by the APA. Under the CPSA, as originally enacted, whenever the Consumer Product Safety Commission desires to issue a product safety standard, it could solicit offers to develop the standard from groups in the private sector, instead of developing it inside the agency as is normal.

• *Due Process Clause of the Constitution*. The third source of requirements imposed on agencies is the Due Process Clause of the Fifth Amendment to the Constitution of the United States. It provides, "No person. . . shall be deprived of life, liberty, or property, without due process of law". This clause means that if the government does something that takes or destroys the property of an individual or firm, then it can only do so by adhering to at least minimally acceptable procedures. Usually, the due process clause is applied in non-commercial situations involving private individuals. But it does serve to constrain arbitrary conduct on the part of a government agency even when the issue is commercial.

• *Courts*. The final source of the requirements on agencies is the federal courts. For the past decade, the courts have continually expanded the procedures agencies must follow. In part, these requirements have been based on the due process clause, although the courts have not explicitly relied on it, and on an expanded reading of the APA. Very recently, however, the Supreme Court chastised the lower courts for imposing these additional requirements, saying that so long as the agencies follow the procedures established by Congress, the courts are not free to require additional steps. The implications of this decision are not yet clear.

During its formative years, most administrative law was adjudicated because that was how the government conducted its business. Thus, most of the early writing and judicial decisions concerned the refinements of the trail type hearings that were modeled after court proceedings and used in agency adjudication.

But, in the late sixties, administrative agencies entered the era of rulemaking with the creation of many new regulatory programs that were designed to issue highly complex technical rules. With the change in how the government conducts its business came an increased concentration of administrative law on rulemaking that has specifically focused on the information agencies develop to support their technical rules and the methodology they used to promulgate final versions of those rules.

C. Enforcement

(1) Introduction

Each regulatory law has a particular scheme of enforcement, whereby the enforcement agency is given one or more powers to exercise in order to achieve the purposes for which the law was enacted. No two laws have exactly the same enforcement scheme. Moreover, because most enforcement decisions are discretionary, even understanding what the agency *can* do is not a guarantee that in fact the agency *does* exercise all of its enforcement powers.

At the end of this section on regulatory law, there are brief synopses of the powers and functions of the federal health and safety agencies. At the end of each, there is a section marked "Enforcement." A glance through these summaries will give the user of this reference book an appreciation for the wide range of enforcement tools that exist. They include:

• *Mandatory Standard Setting*: This is an enforcement power given to most safety and health agencies. However, the scope of the power varies greatly. For example, OSHA was authorized to (and did) adopt thousands of voluntary national consensus standards as mandatory standards. FDA (Food and Drug Administration), on the other hand, has an elaborate system for developing mandatory medical decree standards, but in six years has never mandated a single one. It cannot adopt, by reference, voluntary consensus standards the way OSHA can.

• *Premarket clearance*: This allows an agency to approve a product *before* it can be sold. FDA, for example, has this power for prescription drugs, but not for foods.

• *Hazard reporting*: Most agencies are allowed to require regulated industries to file accident, injury, and/or hazardous product reports. The CPSC, for example, must be informed of every product that a producer has reason to believe *could* be a substantial hazard, even if further examination proves that no real substantial hazard exists.

• *Certification requirements*: The Federal Aviation Administration, for example, requires airlines to have in their possession certificates of air worthiness for the planes they fly. Others involve certification by independent laboratories, or other accredited laboratories, as to whether or not a product meets a mandated standard.

• *Continuous Inspection*: The U.S. Department of Agriculture has this power, whereby its meat inspectors are permanently located in the manufacturing plants they regulate. This can be contrasted with the inspection authority of other agencies, such as OSHA, who never get to inspect all of the firms over which they have jurisdiction.

• *Good Manufacturing Practices*: This enforcement power allows the regulatory agency to regulate not only end products, but also the manufacturing *process* (i.e., inventory control, general cleanliness, etc.). FDA has this authority, for example.

• *Product Bans*: This is a power that enables an agency to prohibit the sale of a regulated product it finds dangerous.

• *Product Recalls*: The Department of Transportation, for example, uses this power to recall automobiles that need various types of safety "fixes." It is also commonly used to recall tainted foods.

• *Blacklisting*: This is a power generally limited to the government. Under the Walsh-Healey Public Contracts Act, for example, the Labor Department could prohibit a manufacturer from receiving government contracts if it did not meet various standards, including safety standards.

• *Red-tagging*: This power is somewhat akin to a ban, only it applies more to a manufacturing process instead of a product. OSHA, for example, can shut down (red-tag) a piece of equipment that is imminently dangerous.

• *Fines*: Many agencies have authority to levy civil fines, and some are empowered to bring criminal enforcement actions, leading to fines and even imprisonment. Use of criminal enforcement tools is rare, even when it exists.

• *Injunctions and Cease and Desist Orders*: This is a common enforcement power, and allows an agency not only to correct a problem, but to take steps to assure that the unsafe process will be eliminated. Sometimes cease and desist orders can be issued by the agency itself, but more often the agency must go to court to seek such an order.

There now follows brief summaries of the workings of 10 major federal safety and health agencies:

CONSUMER PRODUCT SAFETY COMMISSION

PURPOSE– The U.S. Consumer Product Safety Commission (CPSC) was established in 1973, as an independent regulatory agency charged with reducing unreasonable risks of injury associated with consumer products.

COVERAGE– Because the Commission is responsible for implementing the Consumer Product Safety Act, the Federal Hazardous Substances Act, the Poison Prevention Packaging Act, the Flammable Fabrics Act and the Refrigerator Safety Act, its jurisdiction includes consumer products, fabrics and related materials, substances, mixtures of substances and medicines (limited to child-resistant packaging) injurious to young children.

FUNCTIONS– CPSC's functions can best be described by examining its responsibilities under the five acts which it administers:

(1) *The Consumer Product Safety Act* (CPSA) enacted in 1972 and recently amended, applies to consumer products used in or around homes, schools, in recreation and otherwise. Exemptions from this act include products not customarily produced for consumers, tobacco, firearms, motor vehicles, pesticides, aircraft, boats, drugs, devices, cosmetics and food.

One of the main responsibilities of the Commission is the promulgation of consumer product safety standards and rules. Where necessary these standards are mandatory in nature and manufacturers of products which are subject to these standards must certify that their products conform with the standard. However, CPSC also participates in and monitors voluntary standards proceedings and encourages, where appropriate, industry compliance with such voluntary standards.

Under section 8 of the CPSA, CPSC has the authority to ban a consumer product where it presents an unreasonable risk of injury and where no feasible safety standard could protect the public from that unreasonable risk of injury.

Under section 15 of the CPSA the Commission also has authority to determine whether a product presents a substantial product hazard and, if it does, to order the manufacturer, distributor or retailer to notify the public, repair or replace the item, or refund the purchase price.

Section 12 of the CPSA authorizes the Commission to file suit in a federal district court against imminently hazardous consumer products.

In order to better protect consumers, the Commission maintains an Injury Information Clearing House to collect, investigate, analyze and disseminate injury data and information, as it relates to the use of consumer products. In addition to conducting investigations, CPSC has the authority to test products and safety devices and to provide training in product safety investigations and test methods.

The CPSA also provides requirements for imports and exports. Consumer product imports which fail to meet mandatory standards or violate other CPSC rules are refused admission into this country. CPSC's export regulations exempt products from CPSC regulation in certain export circumstances.

(2) *Federal Hazardous Substances Act*– Under this Act substances which are toxic, corrosive, irritants, strong sensitizers, flammable or combustible or which generate pressure through decomposition, heat or other means, are deemed hazardous substances (if, through reasonably foreseeable use, they may cause serious illness or injury). Additionally, certain naturally occurring radioactive substances and toys which present electrical, mechanical or thermal hazards may also be included as hazardous substances. There are eight prohibited acts under the FHSA, including: introducing into interstate commerce a misbranded or banned hazardous substance and the failure to permit inspection of records of interstate shipping of hazardous substances. The Act also allows the Commission to ban hazardous substances, impose labeling requirements, and exempt substances from the requirements of the FHSA. Penalties, injunctions and seizures are additionally authorized by the Act.

(3) *Flammable Fabrics Act*– The purpose of this Act is to prohibit the introduction or movement in interstate commerce of articles or fabrics, related material or products which are so flammable that they present an unreasonable risk of fire. The statute provides CPSC the authority to promulgate flammability standards and regulations in order to provide necessary protection. Failure to conform to these standards and regulations is deemed a prohibited transaction and constitutes a misdemeanor, thereby invoking criminal penalties. The Act further allows CPSC to: impose injunctions, seize goods violative of the FFA, conduct investigations and research, develop flammability test methods and testing devices and offer training in the use of these test methods and devices. The Act does not apply to any fabric or material to be exported from the United States.

(4) *Poison Prevention Packaging Act*– The law applies to substances used by individuals in or around the household that are either: a hazardous substance; a poison; a food, drug or cosmetic; or a fuel *and* which pose hazards to children in the availability of such substances. The Act's basic function is to provide standards or regulations for the special (child-resistant) packaging of these substances.

When the household substance subject to requirements under this Act is one that is used by elderly or handicapped persons who are unable to use the substance when packaged in compliance with the Act, a manufacturer may package the substance in a single size which does *not* comply with the standard. However, in order to do so the manufacturer must also supply the substance in packages which do comply with the standard and on the packages that do not meet the standard there must be a label stating: "This package for households without young children." Prescription drugs may also be dispensed in noncomplying packages when directed by the prescriber or when requested by the purchaser.

The PPP Act (as do the other statutes administered by the Commission relative to the issuance of substantive rules) contains provisions which allow any person who will be adversely affected by a packaging standard to file a petition with the U.S. Court of Appeals for judicial review of the standard.

(5) *Refrigerator Safety Act*– This Act makes it unlawful for anyone to introduce into interstate commerce a household refrigerator that is not equipped with a device enabling the door to be opened from the inside. Any person who violates this Act is guilty of a misdemeanor and is upon conviction subject to one year imprisonment, or a fine of not more than $1,000, or both.

ENFORCEMENT– Section 15 of the Consumer Product Safety Act requires firms to report products that could create substantial product hazards. In addition the Commission staff investigates numerous incidents involving unreported products. It is the responsibility of the manufacturers, distributors, and retailers of a product found to be substantially hazardous to repair or replace the product or refund the purchase price. They also may be required to notify the public of the hazard. In carrying out the CPSA, the officers and employees of the Commission have the authority to inspect factories, warehouses or other establishments to investigate compliance with CPSC regulations.

The Commission's enforcement authorities under the five acts it administers also include:

- injunctions to prevent violations of safety-related laws and regulations
- seizures of products that are in violation of regulations
- cease and desist orders
- mandatory and voluntary recalls of hazardous products, and
- civil and criminal penalties.

OTHER SIGNIFICANT ASPECTS– In order to better identify hazards, CPSC established the National Electronic Injury Surveillance System (NEISS), a computer-based network of statistically selected hospital emergency rooms throughout the country which collect injury data. These data allow the Commission to estimate the number of product-related injuries treated in all hospital emergency rooms in the U.S.

Another source of information for CPSC is the Medical Examiners and Coroners Alert Project (MECAP). Under this project, the 50 states, Washington, D.C., Puerto Rico, and the Virgin Islands supply CPSC with certificates for product-related deaths on a monthly basis. Data on potentially hazardous products and product-related injuries are also obtained through poison control centers, field office reports, news clippings, hotline calls, and consumer letters. In-depth investigations in a selected sample of all injury reports are conducted to determine the role of the product in the injury incidents.

CPSC also operates an Information and Education Program to help consumers choose products and alert them as to safety problems. Materials and projects produced as a result of this program include: news releases, consumer alert bulletins, product safety fact sheets, notices of recalled and banned products, educational programs, work shops, films, and public service announcements.

ACTS ADMINISTERED– Consumer Product Safety Act
Federal Hazardous Substances Act
Poison Prevention Packaging Act
Flammable Fabrics Act
Refrigerator Safety Act

CROSS REFERENCE– See also sections on Environmental Protection Agency, and the National Highway Traffic Safety Administration.

FOR MORE INFORMATION– Contact the Consumer Product Safety Commission, Washington, D.C., 20207; hotline: 800-638-8326; in Maryland: 800-492-8363; in Alaska, Hawaii, Puerto Rico, and the Virgin Islands: 800-638-8333.

ENVIRONMENTAL PROTECTION AGENCY

PURPOSE– The United States Environmental Protection Agency (EPA) was created in 1970 to consolidate a number of federal environmental activities into a single agency. An independent agency, EPA is responsible for executing federal laws aimed at protecting the environment.

COVERAGE– In consolidating all federal environmental activities into a single agency, EPA gained authority over air pollution control, solid waste management, radiation, drinking water, water pollution control, pesticides, environmental radiation protection standards.

FUNCTIONS– EPA's functions can best be understood by examining briefly the federal acts which it administers.

Clean Water Act — This Act is the basic authority for water pollution control programs and aims to make national waters fishable and swimmable. Included in this Act are requirements for water quality standards, effluent limitations defining the amount and kinds of material that can be discharged, planning to choose the best waste treatment methods for particular areas, administration of federal grants for construction or modification of sewage treatment plants, wastewater discharge permits which conform to overall effluent limitations and dredge and fill permits to regulate dredging, filling of wetlands, or dumping of dredged material affecting navigable waters of the U.S.

Marine Protection, Research and Sanctuaries Act of 1972 — Under this Act EPA is required to protect the oceans from indiscriminate dumping of wastes by designating areas where dumping is permitted, issuing permits for dumping, and assessing penalties for unauthorized dumping.

Safe Drinking Water Act of 1974 — This Act gives EPA the authority to regulate public drinking water supplies and requires EPA to administer and enforce the Drinking Water Regulations and protect underground water supplies against contamination by underground ingestion of wastes and other materials.

Resource Conservation and Recovery Act — Enacted in 1976, this Act gives EPA the authority to establish regulations and programs to ensure safe waste disposal. Major provisions include: hazardous waste management through the issuance of standards and regulations covering the generation, storage, transport, treatment and disposal of hazardous wastes; solid waste disposal planning; research and development to find new methods of waste disposal; resource and energy recovery and innovative technology. The Act also places responsibilities on the states to develop waste disposal plans and to work with EPA in projects to recover and reuse valuable materials from waste, such as glass, plastic, silver and aluminum.

Federal Insecticide, Fungicide and Rodenticide Act — This Act authorizes EPA to regulate the manufacture and distribution of pesticides, and to conduct research into their health and environmental effects. EPA Pesticide Control Program has three major components — registration of pesticides, training of pesticide applicators, and monitoring and research.

Food, Drug and Cosmetic Act — EPA has authority under this Act (the majority of which is administered by the Food and Drug Administration) to establish tolerance levels for pesticide levels in food and animal feed.

Toxic Substances Control Act of 1976 — This Act authorizes regulation of the development, distribution and marketing of chemical substances. Included in the Act are provisions for: regulation of chemical substances; testing by manufacturers if a chemical substance presents an unreasonable risk to health or the environment; identification and priority listing of up to 50 chemicals an interagency committee determines should be tested for health and environmental effects; pre-market notification to EPA by manufacturers of new chemicals or existing chemicals where there is a planned significant change in the use or purpose of the chemicals, research and monitoring into the effects of toxic chemicals. This Act also contains what is essentially a ban of all further manufacture of PCBs and places restrictions on disposal of equipment containing PCBs.

Clean Air Act — This law provides the basic legal authority for air pollution control. Among its provisions are the following: national ambient air quality standards for specific air pollutants to protect public health and welfare; EPA review of state plans to achieve satisfactory air quality; new source performance standards for new, or modified, stationary sources of air pollution; hazardous air pollutants national standards which limit emissions of certain substances; prevention of significant deterioration of air quality in areas having pristine or good to moderate air quality; and automobile emission controls limiting the emissions of carbon monoxide, hydrocarbons and nitrogen oxide. This Act also provides for active involvement by the states in attaining control of air pollution.

Noise Control Act of 1972 — EPA under this Act is responsible for noise abatement and control. The Act gives EPA the authority to: establish noise emission standards for products identified by EPA as major sources of noise; propose aircraft and airport noise standards to the Federal Aviation Administration; set labeling regulations for consumer products which produce noise capable of affecting public health and welfare and for those products sold on the basis of their effectiveness in reducing noise; establish noise emission standards for railroads, trucks and buses; perform research into the psychological and physiological effects of noise on people; and administer state and local grants to help reduce community noise.

ENFORCEMENT– In order to achieve compliance with the Acts and regulations under its jurisdiction EPA utilizes a variety of enforcement measures. These include:

- encourage voluntary compliance
- encourage state and local governments to perform direct enforcement activities
- conduct inspection and testing: for example, unleaded gasoline regulations, monitoring of air and water quality
- bans: for example, under the Toxic Substance Control Act EPA had the authority to ban PCBs
- litigation
- environmental trust fund concept
- recalls: for example, EPA can recall automobiles that fail air pollution control standards
- enforcement task force: for example, to clean up existing hazardous waste sites.

OTHER SIGNIFICANT ASPECTS– Authority for protecting the public from dangerous radiation is established in EPA through an Executive Order and several pieces of federal legislation. The agency's major repsonsibilities in this area are to set radiation guidelines including standards to protect the general environment from radiation, to assess new technology and to monitor radiation in the environment, such as that resulting from above-ground nuclear weapons testing.

EPA's Office of Research and Development is responsible for major research efforts in a variety of areas. These projects have more recently included determining the health effects of various pollutants on human beings, examining technology for controlling pollutants, increasing domestic energy sources without sacrificing environmental quality, identifying hazardous wastes and selecting safer disposal sites.

ACTS ADMINISTERED

Clean Water Act of 1972 (also known as the Federal Water Pollution Control Act)

Safe Drinking Water Act of 1974

Resource Conservation and Recovery Act of 1976

Federal Insecticide Fungicide and Rodenticide Act (1972, 1975, 1978)

Toxic Substances Control Act of 1976

Clean Air Act (1970, 1977)

Noise Control Act of 1972

Marine Protection, Research and Sanctuaries Act of 1972

Food, Drug & Cosmetic Act (regulation of pesticides in food and animal feed)

CROSS REFERENCE– See also sections on Nuclear Regulatory Commission and Consumer Product Safety Commission.

FOR MORE INFORMATION– Contact the Office of Public Awareness, (A-107) Environmental Protection Agency, Washington, D.C. 20460; (202) 755-0707.

FEDERAL AVIATION ADMINISTRATION

PURPOSE– The Federal Aviation Administration (FAA) traces its beginnings back to the Air Commerce Act of 1926. Through a series of organizational changes and as a result of the Federal Aviation Act of 1958, which was passed to regulate civil aviation and provide for the safe and efficient utilization of the nation's airspace, the Federal Aviation Administration was incorporated into the Department of Transportation in April 1967. Thus, the FAA is the primary federal agency charged with aviation regulation.

COVERAGE– The FAA's authority includes all commercial aircraft, air navigation facilities, pilots, air traffic controllers, and other air personnel.

FUNCTIONS– One of FAA's principal responsibilities is the operation and maintenance of the air traffic control and air navigation systems. There are currently 25 air traffic control centers, over 400 airport control towers and more than 300 flight service stations. Air traffic control centers handle enroute aircraft operating under instrument flight rules between airport terminal areas. Airport traffic control towers direct the movement of aircraft on and in the vicinity of an airport. Flight service stations provide weather data, airport conditions and other flight planning data. General aviation flights (non-airline), not utilizing the enroute air traffic control system, are subject to FAA regulation through visual flight rules. The FAA is currently in the process of implementing a computer-based semi-automated system which tracks control-led flights automatically. Installation at the enroute centers has been completed and automated radar systems at terminal locations are being installed so as to tie together the enroute centers and terminal locations into a nationwide system for the exchange of data.

A second function of the FAA is to establish and enforce standards relevant to the training and testing of airmen and the manufacture and airworthiness of aircraft. Every civil aircraft in the U.S. must receive FAA's certification. This certification occurs in three stages. The airplane must receive a Type Certificate to show that it meets FAA standards of construction and performance; a Production Certificate is issued to the manufacturer when its capability to duplicate the type design has been established; finally, each airplane must receive an Airworthiness Certificate stating that it conforms to the Type Certificate and is safe to fly.

The FAA must also approve of airline maintenance programs. Repair stations that perform the required maintenance checks as well as repairs and alterations on general aviation aircraft are also licensed by the FAA. In addition to the aircraft and repair facilities, FAA also certifies personnel affecting the safety of airflight; included are pilots, flight engineers, navigators, aviation mechanics, air traffic controllers, aircraft dispatchers and parachute riggers. Pilot and mechanic schools and their instructors must also receive FAA certification.

Another major function of the FAA is airport aid and certification. Under the Airport Development Aid Program, FAA is authorized to allocate funds for airport improvement and construction projects. Funds are allocated on a cost-sharing basis for such projects as acquisition of land, construction of runways, taxiways and aprons, purchase of fire/crash/rescue equipment, and installation of lighting and navigation and landing aids. Grants for two types of planning projects — master plans at individual airports and statewide or regional airport system plans are also available.

In addition to authorizing the FAA to give aid to airports, the Airport and Airway Development Act of 1970 also authorized FAA to certify airports to assure their safe operation. As a basis for certification, FAA promulgated regulations setting safety standards in 18 areas, including the availability of firefighting and rescue equipment, reduction of bird hazards, marking and lighting of runways and taxiways, and handling and storage of dangerous materials. Advisory circulars, standards which address safety and efficiency, are also developed by the FAA. These circulars are mandatory for FAA grant recipients and have received broad acceptance by others.

In an effort to maintain air quality and limit noise, FAA has initiated regulations designed to quiet older jets and has adopted standards limiting engine noise for new aircraft including supersonic transports. FAA serves in an advisory capacity to the EPA in the latter's actions to set standards governing the emissions of noise, carbon monoxide, hydrocarbons and nitrogen oxides.

The FAA Civil Aviation Security Program, strengthened further by the Anti-hijacking Act of 1974, is aimed at preventing or deterring such criminal acts as air piracy, sabotage, extortion and other crimes which could adversely affect aviation safety. Requirements of the program include screening of all enplaning airline passengers and their carry-on baggage and a security system in each airport aimed at keeping unauthorized persons from gaining access to air operations areas.

ENFORCEMENT– In carrying out its responsibilities, the FAA has the authority to use the following enforcement procedures:

- investigations, hearings, subpoenas, production of documents, records and property
- consent orders
- cease and desist orders
- injunctions
- civil penalties
- criminal penalties
- seizure of aircraft
- suspension or revocation of Certificates of Aircraft Registration.

OTHER SIGNIFICANT ASPECTS– An engineering and development program is conducted by FAA at its Technical Center, the Transportation Systems Center and at the Civil Aeromedical Institute. Included in these engineering and development projects are efforts to upgrade the present air traffic control radar beacon surveillance system, development of collision avoidance systems that will operate independently of the air traffic control system but will be compatible with it, the development of automated weather observation systems for airports without control towers and the development of a Microwave Landing System to replace the present Instrument Landing System.

FAA's aeromedical research includes studies to examine crash impact and survival, toxic hazards of burning cabin materials following a crash, and the effect of aging and stress on airmen's performance. FAA also conducts a comprehensive health program for air traffic controllers, providing annual physical examinations and laboratory procedures to determine controllers' ability to perform their duties.

FAA is involved with international aviation matters including: sending Civil Aviation Assistance Groups abroad to provide technical aid to other nations; training foreign nationals at the FAA Aeronautical Center; working with the International Civil Aviation Organization in establishing worldwide safety and security standards; providing technical advice on the export and import of aviation products; and handling certification of foreign-made aircraft engines and parts under the terms of bilateral airworthiness agreements.

The FAA investigates most non-fatal and many fatal general aviation accidents on behalf of the National Transportation Safety Board (NTSB). FAA also participates with NTSB in the investigation of major aircraft accidents to determine if any immediate action is needed to correct deficiencies and prevent recurrences. The FAA also operates 3 airports: Washington National Airport, Dulles International Airport and an airport at the FAA Technical Center.

Under the Hazardous Materials Transportation Act, the FAA also has jurisdiction over the transportation of shipment of hazardous materials by air. This Act prohibits the shipment of certain hazardous materials and allows for stringent regulation of the shipping of other types of hazardous materials. FAA additionally operates the training program required by the Hazardous Materials Act which is directed at personnel who handle the transport of hazardous materials.

ACTS ADMINISTERED– Federal Aviation Act of 1958

Airport and Airway Development Act of 1970

Anti-hijacking Act of 1974

Clean Air Act of 1970 (EPA's responsibility; however, FAA serves in advisory capacity)

Hazardous Materials Transportation Act (as related to transportation by air)

CROSS REFERENCE– See also sections on Environmental Protection Agency (portion of Clean Air Act); and the National Transportation Safety Board.

FOR MORE INFORMATION– Contact Public Inquiry Center, APA-430, Federal Aviation Administration, Washington, D.C. 20591; (202) 426-8058.

MINE SAFETY AND HEALTH ADMINISTRATION

PURPOSE– The Mine Safety and Health Administration (MSHA) was established in 1978 to administer federal laws that protect the health and safety of miners. The Federal Mine Safety and Health Act of 1977 created MSHA and thus transferred the responsibility for administering and enforcing mine safety and health from the Department of Interior to the Department of Labor. The Act also had the effect of repealing the Federal Metal and Nonmetallic Mine Safety Act, amending the Federal Coal Mine Health and Safety Act of 1969 and, for the first time, placing all of mine safety and health responsibilities under a single federal law.

COVERAGE– The requirements of the Federal Mine Safety and Health Act of 1977 apply to all underground and surface mining operations, including noncoal as well as coal mines.

FUNCTIONS– Under the Federal Mine Safety and Health Act of 1977, MSHA is required to develop, promulgate, and revise, where appropriate, improved mandatory health and safety standards for the protection of life and the prevention of injuries and illnesses in mines. The Act specifically mandates the issuance of certain standards and regulations; for example, the Act requires regulations providing that mine rescue teams be available to each undeground mine for rescue and recovery work in the event of emergency. Petitions for modification or variances are granted in specific cases where investigation shows that an equal or greater measure of safety can be achieved by an alternative method, or that application of the standard would reduce the miners' safety.

Inspection of mines is another primary function of MSHA. Under the Act, MSHA must conduct four complete annual inspections of all underground mines, coal and noncoal alike. The law also requires two complete annual inspections for all surface mines. Should an inspector find a violation that poses an immediate threat to miners, the affected area of the mine is ordered closed until the condition is corrected. Mine operators shall also be assessed penalties for violations. (See section on Enforcement).

The Act also provides that a miner or representative of miners be allowed to accompany an MSHA inspector during a mine inspection and attend any conference at full pay for time spent in such activities. Miners may also request inspections and file discrimination complaints.

MSHA also maintains a system of mandatory reporting and record keeping for injuries in the mining industry. Injuries are classified as fatal, nonfatal occurrences with work days lost or restricted work activity, and nonfatal occurrences that require medical treatment but do not result in lost workdays. First aid cases are not reportable.

Administratively, MSHA divides the regulations of mines into two areas: Coal Mine Safety and Health; and Metal/Nonmetal Safety and Health. In addition to meeting their respective duties under the Act and its subsequent regulations, these divisions also conduct special programs related to mine safety. Under a Congressional action of December, 1981, MSHA lost its jurisdiction over surface stone operations, clay, colloidal phosphate and sand and gravel operations.

Coal Mine Safety and Health has instituted a Resident Inspection Program for coal mines which are especially hazardous or large. Under this program, one mine inspector is assigned to a mine fulltime and is responsible for conducting all the regular inspections and also any spot inspections which may be required.

The Metal and Nonmetal Safety and Health Division's program in accident reduction is aimed at mines with high injury rates and potentially serious safety problems. Each year the mines selected for this program are evaluated ad recommendations to prevent accidents and injuries are made to mine management and labor. MSHA offers assistance in carrying out these recommendations and evaluations are made throughout the year.

A second program in this division is the Compliance Assistance Visit (CAV) program. Under this, when a noncoal operation is started, re-commenced after a shut-down, or when a new piece of equipment is introduced to the mine site, the operator may request a CAV inspection. The inspector will note all violations, but no penalty will be assessed. On his next inspection, the inspector will check each citation to see that the violation was corrected. If not, he will issue another citation and this one *will* have an assessment penalty.

ENFORCEMENT– Under the Federal Mine Safety and Health Act of 1977, MSHA is able to impose civil penalties for violations of mandatory standards or the Act's provisions. Penalties may be assessed against operators and against miners who willfully violate standards against smoking or carrying smoking materials or who falsify records. Corporate operators, their directors, officers or agents who knowingly authorize, order or carry out a violation are subject, individually, to civil penalties.

In assessing the size (dollar amount) of the penalty MSHA considers six criteria established by the Act: history of previous violations; size of the operator's business and company to which the mine belongs; negligence, if any, on the part of the operator; effect of an assessment upon the operator's ability to continue in business; gravity of the violation; and demonstrated good faith by the operator in attempting to achieve rapid compliance after notification of a violation. Following this assessment by MSHA officials, an operator can request a conference where additional facts or arguments can be made prior to final determination of the penalty. Under a proposed reorganization, the conference would be conducted by the District Manager.

Assesssments may be contested before the Federal Mine Safety and Health Review Commission whose administrative law judges conduct formal adjudications (similar to those of the Occupational Safety and Health Review Commission). Where a final order of the commission remains unpaid, the Act authorizes a separate collection action to reduce the assessment order to a judgment.

The Department of Labor's Office of the Solicitor, Division of Mine Safety and Health is also involved in MSHA enforcement efforts. Injunctions may be sought to prevent mine operators from denying the entry of MSHA inspectors into the mines, from otherwise impeding mine inspections, or from operating mines in the face of MSHA withdrawal orders. Contempt actions may also be brought against operators who refuse to obey court injunctions. MSHA also assists the Department of Justice in preparing criminal litigation against companies and individuals alleged to have "willfully" violated the Act.

OTHER SIGNIFICANT ASPECTS– Technical Support is a division within MSHA which provides technical services to MSHA's enforcement activities, assists in solving technological problems encountered in enforcing the Act, and coordinates interagency research activities. Technical Support also provides criteria and technical information for development and modification of federal mine safety and health standards. In addition it collects, analyzes and publishes data on mining injuries and illnesses; approves and certifies equipment and materials as safe for mining use; assists in transfer of newly developed technology to industry; maintains special mine rescue and recovery capabilities; helps prepare technical course materials; and offers consultative services to federal, state and local agencies on request.

MSHA's Education and Training division is responsible for assisting industry in complying with regulations which require appropriate training for new and experienced workers in mines and mineral mills, and require that each mining operation submit a training plan for MSHA's approval. The Education and Training division provides training courses to prepare instructors who provide the mandatory training for industry and also must approve all training plans under the regulations. Other activities in MSHA Education and Training include: qualifying and certifyng miners through training or examination, developing special courses in response to accident trends and changes in regulations, and sponsoring the National Coal Mine Rescue and First Aid Contest. Under the proposed reorganization, much of this Education and Training work will also become the responsibility of the District Manager.

MSHA also operates the National Mine Health and Safety Academy located in Beckley, West Virginia. The Academy's mission includes reducing accidents and improving health conditions in the nation's mines and mineral industries through education and training. The Academy has primary responsibility for training MSHA inspectors and technical support personnel. It also offers programs and services for industry, labor, other government agencies and the academic community.

ACTS ADMINISTERED– Federal Mine Safety and Health Amendments Act of 1977 (incorporating the Coal Mine Health and Safety Act of 1969).

CROSS REFERENCE– See also sections on Occupational Safety and Health Administration; National Institute for Occupational Safety and Health, Occupational Safety and Health Review Commission and the Environmental Protection Agency.

FOR MORE INFORMATION– Contact Mine Safety and Health Administration, Office of Information, 4015 Wilson Boulevard, Arlington, VA 22203, (703) 235-1452.

NATIONAL HIGHWAY TRAFFIC SAFETY ADMINISTRATION

PURPOSE– The National Highway Traffic Safety Administration (NHTSA) is the agency within the Department of Transportation responsible for reducing the number of accidents on the nation's highways and the deaths and injuries which result.

COVERAGE– NHTSA is responsible for regulation of the safety characteristics of motor driven vehicles, including automobiles, trucks and buses, the ease and safe movement of traffic, and the skill and awareness of drivers.

FUNCTIONS– The functions of NHTSA relate to two subject categories: motor vehicle safety and highway safety.

With respect to motor vehicle safety NHTSA issues motor vehicle safety standards based on a level of performance required under specific test conditions. These standards apply to all vehicles, domestic and foreign, manufactured for sale in the United States. They concern those parts of the vehicle which affect its safe operation and protect drivers and riders from death or serious injury in the event of a crash. The Agency also investigates possible defects related to the safety of vehicles and motorists. NHTSA receives information on defects from consumer complaints, manufacturer's bulletins, police reports, and automobile fleet operators. NHTSA motor vehicle research efforts, aimed at establishing new and better ways of improving the safety of cars, drivers and occupants, have included:

- modifications to production vehicles so that

the passenger compartment will be safe in the event of a crash
- specially constructed research vehicles designed with safety, fuel economy, lack of pollution and consumer cost in mind
- scientific accident investigation to determine accident causes and resulting deaths and injuries so that remedies can be designed
- safer brakes and tires, vehicle handling qualities, and expanded area of vision for the driver to help prevent crashes
- crash testing new cars to determine existing levels of occupant protection.

NHTSA's second major area of activity is highway safety. There are currently 18 uniform national standards covering such subjects as driver education, traffic records, emergency services, highway design, alcohol use, school buses, motorcycle and pedestrian safety. Other highway safety activities include managing a grant program for the states and communities to accelerate their highway safety programs; and assisting the states in training highway safety personnel in a variety of specialties. Research on highway safety has included focus on issues such as:

- studies of the influence of alcohol and drugs on driving abilty
- driver education and traffic safety awareness for all ages
- improvement of emergency medical services
- better court records, court procedures, driver licensing and vehicle registration.

There are currently six priority programs for federal funding under the State and Community Highway Safety Grant Program, including: alcohol countermeasures; police traffic services; occupant protection; traffic records; emergency medical services; and safety construction and improvements to existing roads.

ENFORCEMENT– In order to assure compliance with its standards, NHTSA utilizes the following enforcement measures:

- testing programs to measure compliance
- manufacturers recall campaigns
- surveys of imported cars
- imposition of civil penalties (fines)
- litigation.

OTHER SIGNIFICANT ASPECTS– NHTSA has three advisory committees which make recommendations to the Agency on a variety of motor vehicle and highway safety issues. The National Highway Safety Advisory Committee advises the Secretary of Transportation on highway safety standards, projects, programs, and ways in which travel on roads and highways can be made safer. The Biomechanics Advisory Committee reviews procedures and projects which require the use of live and deceased human subjects for research. This committee also makes recommendations regarding the need for the use of human test subjects, minimizing the risks to volunteers, and protecting the rights and dignity of subjects. The National Accident Sampling System Advisory Committee reviews documents and provides advice on NHTSA's National Accident Sampling System program which collects and analyzes accident data.

NHTSA has also been given the responsibility for issuing fuel economy standards for future model passenger cars, light trucks and vans, and for enforcing those standards.

Authority to issue bumper standards to reduce damage in low-speed accidents has also been given to NHTSA, along with the monitoring of compliance with federal odometer regulations which prohibit tampering with vehicle mileage readings.

ACTS ADMINISTERED– National Traffic and Motor Vehicle Safety Act of 1966; and Highway Safety Act of 1966.

CROSS REFERENCE– See also sections on the National Transportation Safety Board and the Environmental Protection Agency.

FOR MORE INFORMATION– Contact the National Highway Traffic Safety Administration, Office of Public Affairs, 400 7th St., SW, Washington, D.C. 20590; (800) 424-9393; or (202) 426-9550.

NATIONAL INSTITUTE FOR OCCUPATIONAL SAFETY AND HEALTH

PURPOSE– The National Institute for Occupational Safety and Health (NIOSH) was established by the Occupational Safety and Health Act of 1970. The Institute is a part of the Department of Health and Human Services' Public Health Service, Centers for Disease Control. NIOSH is the primary federal agency engaged in research directed at eliminating on-the-job hazards.

COVERAGE– Because NIOSH was initiated as an integral part of the OSH Act, its authority over employers includes, where applicable, any "person engaged in a business affecting commerce who has employees." (See separate section on OSHA for further discussion).

FUNCTIONS– Under sections 20, 21, 22 of the OSH Act, NIOSH has the authority to:

- develop criteria for the establishment of national occupational safety and health standards
- collect and analyze records and statistics on occupational safety and health necessary for promulgation of new or improved mandatory occupational safety and health standards
- conduct research or demonstrations relevant to occupational safety and health, including studies of behavioral and motivational factors
- develop criteria for dealing with toxic materials and harmful physical agents, indicating safe exposure levels for workers for various periods of time, in consultation with the Department of Labor
- publish an annual listing of all known toxic substances and the concentrations at which such toxicity is known to occur
- conduct education and training programs aimed at providing an adequate supply of qualified personnel to carry out the purposes of the OSH Act, and informational programs on the importance of and proper use of adequate safety and health equipment

- conduct and publish industrywide studies of the effect of chronic or low-level exposure to industrial materials, processes and stresses on the potential for illness, disease, or loss of functional capacity in aging adults.

OTHER SIGNIFICANT ASPECTS– NIOSH also administers the Proficiency Analytical Testing Program which is a quality assurance service provided to industrial hygiene laboratories. This program helps participating laboratories that use conventional industrial hygiene analytical procedures to determine their analytical competence and improve their analytical performance.

The Health Hazard Evaluation Program of NIOSH allows employers or authorized representatives of employees to make a written request to NIOSH for a determination of whether a substance normally found in their place of employment has potentially toxic effects in such concentrations as used or found in their workplace. Where NIOSH finds that an investigation is warranted, inspection of the workplace, collection of samples and performance of tests, including medical examination of employees are authorized. Investigations which reveal the presence of an imminent danger call for NIOSH to report such danger to the employer, the employees, and the Department of Labor or, if applicable, the state agency administering occupational safety regulations.

NIOSH also maintains its own laboratories in order to conduct research on a variety of topics, including: the effect of exposure to certain hazardous substances, occupationally related respiratory diseases, and testing and certification of personal protective equipment. In order to foster long term training to upgrade the knowledge and skills of occupational health and safety professionals, NIOSH also provides support for Education Resource Centers at major U.S. colleges and universities.

Under the 1977 Mine Safety and Health Act, a number of responsibilities related to miners' health were given to NIOSH. As a result, NIOSH works closely with the Mine Safety and Health Administration in conducting research into miners' health problems; for example, an effort was initiated to identify and establish criteria for toxic mine substances leading to development of standards to further protect miners.

ACTS ADMINISTERED– Occupational Safety and Health Act of 1970 (sections 20-22 pertain to NIOSH). Mine Safety and Health Act of 1977

CROSS REFERENCE– See also sections on Occupational Safety and Health Administration, the Occupational Safety and Health Review Commission, and the Mine Safety and Health Administration.

FOR MORE INFORMATION– Contact the National Institute for Occupational Safety and Health, Room 844, Parklawn Building, Rockville, MD 20857; (202) 443-2140.

NATIONAL TRANSPORTATION SAFETY BOARD

PURPOSE The National Transportation Safety Board (NTSB) is an independent federal accident investigation agency. The Board's mission is to determine the "probable cause" of transportation accidents and to formulate safety recommendations to improve transportation safety. Established by the Independent Safety Board Act of 1974, NTSB's functions were formerly performed by the Department of Transportation and prior to that by the Bureau of Safety of the Civil Aeronautics Board.

COVERAGE– The Safety Board is mandated to investigate the probable cause of:

- civil aviation accidents
- highway accidents selected in cooperation with the states
- all passenger train accidents, any fatal railroad accident, any railroad accident involving substantial damage
- major marine accidents, any marine accident involving a public and non-public vessel
- pipeline accidents involving a fatality or substantial property damage.

FUNCTIONS– In investigating those accidents described above NTSB follows several steps. Upon receiving notification of a major accident, an NTSB Go-Team travels to the accident site. A Go-Team is a group of Board personnel who possess a wide range of accident investigation skills; for example, a team might include one of the five members of the Safety Board, an expert trained in witness interrogation, a meteorologist, a metallurgist and a hazardous materials expert. Individual investigators are regularly dispatched to the scene of less spectacular accidents from one of the Board's ten field offices. Following the investigation at the accident site, more work is often required. This may include engineering studies and laboratory tests. NTSB operates its own technical laboratory to support these investigations. The Board may also decide to hold a public hearing to collect additional information. The final stage of the accident investigation is the analysis of the factual findings. The Final Report, which includes "the probable cause of the accident," is presented to the full five-member Board for discussion and approval at a public meeting. Also resulting from the accident investigation is the Safety Recommendation. Since timeliness is important, the Safety Recommendation is issued as soon as a problem is identified, without necessarily waiting until an investigation is complete. Each recommendation issued by the Board designates the person, or party, expected to take action, describes the action the Board expects, and states the safety need to be satisfied.

The Independent Safety Board Act also requires NTSB to conduct special studies on safety problems. In the past such topics as weather, crashworthiness, in-flight collisions, commuter airlines, and railroad track maintenance have been the subject of NTSB special studies.

The Safety Board is also required to evaluate the effectiveness of government agencies involved in transportation safety; evaluate the safeguards used in the transportation of hazardous materials; and review appeals from airmen and merchant seamen whose certificates have been revoked or suspended (in this capacity NTSB acts as an appellate authority for actions taken by the Federal Aviation Administration or the U.S. Coast Guard).

ENFORCEMENT– In order to carry out its investigatory responsibilites, the Safety Board has the power to:

- conduct hearings for which it may subpoena witnesses and the production of evidence
- enter any property where an accident has occurred to inspect records, files, papers, processes, controls and facilities relevant to the investigation of the accident
- obtain copies of autopsy reports prepared by state and local officials on any person who dies as a result of a transportation accident. If necessary, the Board may order the autopsy
- in the case of refusal to obey a subpoena, order or inspection notice, the U.S. District Court, at the request of NTSB, has jurisdiction to issue an order to comply. Failure to obey such an order is punishable as a contempt of court.

ACTS ADMINISTERED– Independent Safety Board Act of 1974.

CROSS REFERENCE– See also sections on the National Highway Traffic Safety Administration and the Federal Aviation Administration.

FOR MORE INFORMATION– Contact the National Transportation Safety Board, Office of Government and Public Affairs, Washington, D.C. 20594; (202) 382-6600.

NUCLEAR REGULATORY COMMISSION

PURPOSE– In 1974, the Energy Reorganization Act created two new agenices, the Nuclear Regulatory Commission (NRC) and the Energy Research and Development Administration, now part of Department of Energy, and abolished the Atomic Energy Commission. NRC is the independent regulatory agency charged with assuring adequate protection of public health and safety with respect to commercial nuclear energy facilities and materials.

COVERAGE– NRC has authority over all nuclear power plants, during both their construction and operating phases. NRC is also responsible for licensing the export of nuclear reactors and the export and import of uranium and plutonium and other radioactive materials. Licenses for fuel-cycle facilities, the packaging and handling of nuclear materials and the use of radioisotopes are also issued by NRC.

FUNCTIONS– The Nuclear Regulatory Commission has three basic functions:

(1) Licensing — NRC reviews and issues licenses for the construction and operation of nuclear power plants and other uses of nuclear materials, including medical, industrial, educational and research activities. Regulatory authority for some nuclear materials licensing has been transferred to the states under NRC's Agreement States Program. Under NRC's Reactor Licensing Program, a utility must first obtain a permit to construct a power reactor. Later when the facility is constructed the utility must then obtain a license to operate it. Prior to approval of a construction permit several stages of review must be conducted; these include:

- *Environmental Review* — An environmental impact statement is developed by NRC staff. This evaluation considers the effects of construction and operation of the plant on the local environment and weighs the benefits to be gained against the possible risk to the environment. This statement may require changes to the plant design or operational mode.
- *Safety Review* — An in-depth safety review of the proposed design of the plant is conducted by NRC staff. Where design features do not meet NRC standards changes by the applicant are required. A Safety Evaluation Report is then prepared by the staff and made public.
- *Advisory Committee on Reactor Safeguards* — This committee conducts an independent review of the application and submits its own recommendations to the Commission. (See Other Significant Aspects.)
- *Public Participation* — A public hearing conducted by the Atomic Safety and Licensing Board must be held before a decision to grant or deny a permit to build a nuclear power plant can be made. At these hearings, the applicant, the NRC staff and other interested parties make presentations in support of their positions.
- *Antitrust Review* — NRC also conducts a pre-licensing antitrust review of each application for a major nuclear facility in order to assure the proposed facility is in compliance with antitrust laws.

Following these reviews the Licensing Board makes its decision on the construction permit. This decision is subject to review by the Commission and by the Atomic Safety and Licensing Appeal Board. During construction, nuclear power plants are inspected by NRC representatives and before construction is completed the utility submits an application for an operating license. Another safety review is prepared by the staff and the Advisory Committee on Reactor Safeguards makes its independent review and report. At this stage any person may petition the Commission for a public hearing.

(2) Inspection — The NRC conducts periodic inspections of nuclear plants and other licensees to determine compliance with NRC requirements for health and safety, security of nuclear materials and facilities and environmental protection. Independent measurements of radioactivity in nuclear facility effluents are taken to determine whether the licensee's measurements are accurate

and that discharges are maintained at levels required by NRC regulations. NRC also inspects the quality assurance programs of reactor manufacturers, architect-engineering firms and suppliers of major nuclear components for nuclear power plants. Additionally, the regulatory compliance of other licensees, including hospital nuclear medicine programs, industrial applications, academic and research activities and nuclear material processing, are checked by NRC. The Commission also investigates accidents and incidents at licensed facilities as well as complaints or allegations from licensee employers or members of the public concerning activities of NRC licensees.

A program of resident inspectors for operating nuclear power plants is administered by NRC. Technical specialists in NRC's regional offices assist resident inspectors in inspecting areas such as environmental monitoring, emergency planning, radiation protection, security and inservice inspection of nuclear components.

(3) Regulatory Research — NRC's research program focuses on areas of safety, safeguards and environmental assessment. Recent research efforts have included programs in water reactor safety, probabilities risk assessment, the behavior of nuclear fuel, computer codes to predict the nature and consequences of severe accident damage to reactor fuel and containment systems, advance safety technology relating to high temperature, gas-cooled reactors and liquid metal fast breeder reactors, and fuel cycle, environmental and waste management.

The NRC also establishes regulations, standards and guidelines governing the various licensed uses of radioactive materials. These regulations and standards address, among other things, the siting, design, construction, operation, decommissioning and safeguarding of nuclear reactors and other nuclear facilities, as well as the storage, processing, transporting, safeguarding and use of nuclear materials.

ENFORCEMENT– When appropriate, NRC utilizes the following enforcement actions:

- notice of violations requiring corrective action
- imposition of fines and modification
- suspension or revocation of licenses.

OTHER SIGNIFICANT ASPECTS– The Nuclear Regulatory Commission is comprised of five members appointed by the President and confirmed by the Senate for five-year terms. In carrying out its licensing duties, NRC is assisted by three independent licensing units. The Advisory Committee on Reactor Safeguards is composed of fifteen scientists and engineers who review and make recommendations to the Commission on all applications for construction and operation of nuclear power reactors and related nuclear safety matters. The Atomic Safety and Licensing Board Panel, a board of lawyers and others with expertise in various technical and environmental fields, appoints three of its members to conduct each public hearing on nuclear power plant applications. Likewise the Atomic Safety and Licensing Appeal Panel appoints three-member appeal boards to review decisions of the licensing board.

ACTS ADMINISTERED– Atomic Energy Act and the Energy Reorganization Act.

CROSS REFERENCE– See also section on Environmental Protection Agency which has authority for protecting the public from certain types of radiation hazards.

FOR MORE INFORMATION– Contact U.S. Nuclear Regulatory Commission, Office of Public Affairs, Washington, D.C. 20555; (301) 492-7715.

OCCUPATIONAL SAFETY AND HEALTH REVIEW COMMISSION

PURPOSE– The Occupational Safety and Health Review Commission (OSHRC) was created by the Occupational Safety and Health Act of 1970. OSHRC is an independent administrative court and is not connected with the Department of Labor or the Occupational Safety and Health Administration (OSHA). The Commission's main goal is settling disputes which arise out of violations of the Occupational Safety and Health Act.

COVERAGE– All cases heard by OSHRC are the result of citations or proposed penalties by OSHA. Actions may be brought by either employers or employees as described below.

FUNCTIONS– As a result of the issuance of a citation and/or proposed penalty by an OSHA inspector, an *employer* may bring an action to contest all or part of the citation or proposed penalty. The initial case is heard by one of OSHRC's 27 Administrative Law Judges who presides at the hearing and renders a decision. The parties can object to the Judge's decision and seek a Discretionary Review by the Commission, which is comprised of three members appointed by the President and who serve six-year terms. In order that a case be heard by the Commission, one or more of the Commissioners must direct that the decision be reviewed by the full Commission. There are four bases for review of a Judge's decision within the OSHRC framework; these are:

1) that the Judge made findings of material facts which are not supported by the evidence
2) that the Judge's decision is contrary to law
3) that a substantial question of law, policy or abuse of discretion is involved, or
4) that a prejudicial error was committed.

An employer may also Petition for Modification of Abatement, or, in other words, request that the period of time stated in the citation for the correction of the alleged violation be extended. The major difference procedurally between the two actions — contesting a citation/penalty and petitioning for modification of abatement — is that the burden of proving the case rests on different parties. In a contest of a citation/penalty, the burden of proof rests with the Secretary of Labor because it is OSHA, an agency of the Department of Labor, that is alleging the wrongdoing. Whereas in a proceeding where the abatement period is being challenged, the party which must prove the necessity for such modification is the employer.

An *employee* may also use the procedures of OSHRC to contest the reasonableness of the period of time given to the employer for correcting a hazardous condition. In such cases the procedures are similar to those used for contests by the employer. The Secretary of Labor has the burden of proof and must establish that the period allowed the employer to correct the condition is not unreasonable. An employee may also petition for permission to intervene in any proceeding where the hearing has commenced. Thus, where an employer may be contesting the short duration of the period of abatement, the employee must request permission to intervene as an interested party in the interest of supporting the short abatement period because of health hazards being addressed by the citation.

OSHRC cases are similar to lawsuits in the civil court system. In cases before the OSHRC Administrative Law Judges, the Federal Rules of Civil Procedure and the Federal Rules of Evidence are followed, in addition to OSHRC's own Rules of Procedure. At the hearing, both sides call and cross-examine witnesses, introduce evidence, and present written and oral arguments. In hearing appeals, the Commission may issue a stay, request briefs from the parties and request oral arguments of the issues by the parties. The Commission also has the authority to hear appeals of interlocutory orders of the Administrative Law Judge, or those decisions made before or during the course of the case.

Appeal of Commission decisions may be heard by the 12 federal courts of appeal.

OTHER SIGNIFICANT ASPECTS– Under OSHRC procedures, petitions for modification of abatement periods and employee contests of abatement periods are placed on a special docket and are treated as expedited proceedings. Also, upon application of any party of intervenor or upon his motion, any Commission may order an expedited proceeding. Under such a format, shortened time limits are imposed and the judge has authority to take other measures which minimize time and maintain fairness.

Simplified proceedings are also available upon the request of any party. However these proceedings are not allowed for all OSHRC cases. Certain complicated cases, such as occupational noise exposure and toxic substances, are excluded. Simplified proceedings differ from conventional OSHRC proceedings in that there are no pleadings, discovery is greatly restricted, the Federal Rules of Evidence do not apply and interlocutory appeals are not permitted. Additionally, the parties are required to attempt to reach a settlement and must discuss narrowing of the issues, an agreed statement of issues and facts, defenses, witnesses and exhibits, motions and any other pertinent matter. In simplified proceedings, the judge presides over both the conference, at which he/she attempts to have the parties reach further agreement, and at the hearing if subsequently needed.

ACTS ADMINISTERED– Occupational Health and Safety Act of 1970 (section 12 pertains to OSHRC).

CROSS REFERENCE– See also sections on the Occupational Safety and Health Administration and the National Institute for Occupational Safety and Health.

FOR MORE INFORMATION– Contact the Information Office, Occupational Safety and Health Review Commission, 1825 K St., NW, Washington, D.C. 20006; (202) 634-7943.

OCCUPATIONAL SAFETY AND HEALTH ADMINISTRATION

PURPOSE– The Occupational Safety and Health Administration (OSHA) was created within the Department of Labor as a result of the Occupational Safety and Health Act of 1970. It is the responsibility of OHSA to administer this Act, the purpose of which is "to assure so far as possible every working man and woman in the Nation safe and healthful working conditions and to preserve our human resources."

COVERAGE– In administering the OSH Act, OSHA has jurisdiction over all employers and their employees in the 50 states, the District of Columbia, Puerto Rico, the Canal Zone and all other territories under Federal Government jurisdiction. While an employer is defined as any "person engaged in a business affecting commerce who has employees," those *not* covered by the Act include self-employed persons, farms which employ 10 or fewer persons and do not maintain temporary labor camps, workplaces already protected by other federal agencies under other federal statutes, and state and local governments in their role as employers.

FUNCTIONS– One of OSHA's primary responsibilities is the promulgation of occupational safety or health standards. Currently, these standards fall into four major categories — General Industry, Maritime, Construction and Agriculture. OSHA can begin standards-setting procedures on its own initiative, or on petition from other parties including the National Institute for Occupational Safety and Health, state and local governments, standards organizations or any interested person. OSHA publishes notice of plans to propose, amend or delete a standard, invites public comment and in some instances it holds public hearings on the proposal. Where workers are in grave danger due to exposure to toxic substances or new hazards, OSHA is authorized to set emergency temporary standards. OSHA may also issue variances where the employer can prove their facilities or methods of operation provide employer protection at least as effective as that required by OSHA. Any person who may be adversely affected by a final standard may file a petition for judicial review of the standard.

In order to help define high hazard industries, to inform employees of the status of their employer's record and to compile statistical information regarding occupational safety, employers of eleven or more employees must maintain records of occupational injuries and illnesses as they occur. All occupational illnesses must be recorded regardless of severity. All occupational injuries must be recorded if they result in: death, one or more lost work days, restriction of work or motion, loss of consciousness, transfer to another job, or medical treatment other than first aid. Record-keeping forms must be maintained for each calendar year, be kept for five years, and be available for inspection. Employers are also required to post for employees, statistics regarding the totals of work-related illnesses and injuries (to be posted during each February); copies of OSHA citations for violations of standards; summaries of petitions for variances from standards of recordkeeping procedures; and a list of employees' rights and responsibilities under the OSH Act.

ENFORCEMENT– To enforce its standards, OSHA is authorized to conduct workplace inspections of every establishment covered by the Act. Given the enormity of such a task, inspection priorities have been developed and are currently comprised of: imminent danger situations, catastrophes and fatal accidents, employer complaints and programmed high-hazard inspections. OSHA is also currently in the process of implementing a variety of experimental programs whereby some establishments which meet certain conditions would be exempt from routine OSHA safety checks, though not from the agency's standards or other types of inspections.

OSHA is also authorized to issue citations and penalties. Citations inform the employer and employees of the regulations and standards alleged to have been violated, and of the proposed time for their abatement. Penalties up to $10,000 per violation may be proposed. Employers and employees can contest citations and proposed penalties in actions before the Occupational Safety and Health Review Commission's administrative court system (see separate section on OSHRC).

OTHER SIGNIFICANT ASPECTS– As part of the OSH Act, states have the option of developing their own safety and health programs. To receive OSHA approval a state must demonstrate that it will within three years provide adequate legislation, standards-setting, enforcement and appeals procedures, public employee protection and a sufficient number of competent enforcement personnel. After such a plan has been in operation for three years OSHA may then certify that the legal, administrative and enforcement means are adequate to operate effectively. Final approval of the state plan is then possible one year later following certification. Once a state plan has been initially approved, OSHA funds fifty percent of the program's operating costs. Monitoring and evaluation of the state programs continue following its approval. Employees in those states which do not adopt their own program are subject to the OSH Act as previously described.

As a means of identifying hazardous conditions and determining corrective measures, OSHA administers a free on-site consultation service for employers in every state. These visits are done at the request of the employer and are conducted by consultants from the state government or private contractors. The consultant may not issue citations or invoke penalties for violations found on his/her visit and the consultant's files cannot be used to trigger an OSHA inspection. However, the employer must agree, in accepting a consultation visit, to eliminate any serious hazards identified. Failure of the employer to do so then requires the consultation project manager to notify OSHA.

ACTS ADMINISTERED– Occupational Safety and Health Act of 1970.

CROSS REFERENCE– See also sections on Occupational Safety and Health Review Commission and National Institute for Occupational Safety and Health.

FOR MORE INFORMATION– Contact the OSHA Information Office, Room N3637, Occupational Safety and Health Administration, Department of Labor, Washington, D.C. 20210; (202) 523-8151.

Access to Medical Records—An Update

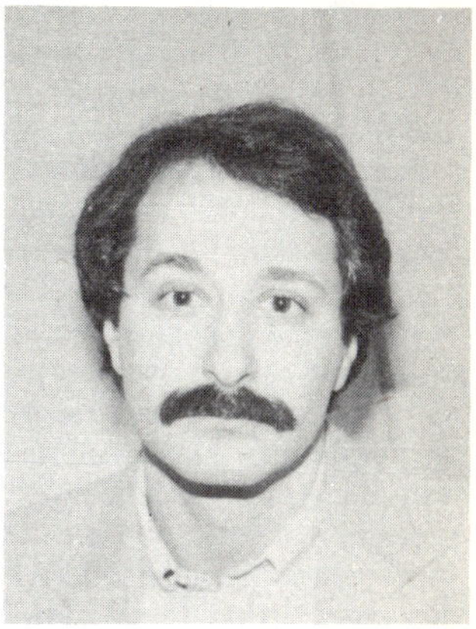

Gary Nothstein, Esq.

Editor's Note — This description and commentary on the access to employee medical and exposure records issue was published originally in the ASSE Society Update member newsletter in the Fall of 1980.* It is updated here, with permission, to again remind safety professionals of the important requirements in this potentially controversial area. Mr. Nothstein is a Washington D.C.-based attorney specializing in occupational safety and health matters.

BACKGROUND

On May 21, 1980, OSHA issued a final standard requiring the preservation of and access to "employer maintained exposure and medical records" relevant to employees exposed to toxic substances and harmful physical agents, 29 CFR 1910.20. Access is also provided to "analyses" using exposure and medical records.

The standard applies to each general industry, maritime and construction employers of employees exposed (both past and present) to toxic substances or harmful physical agents. There is no exemption for small businesses or employers with multiple or transient work sites or transient work forces.

Subject to access are employee medical records, employee exposure records and analyses using exposure or medical records.

Upon request, access to employee exposure records and analyses must be provided to employees, designated representatives of employees and OSHA. OSHA access is not conditioned upon employee consent, but requires a written order approved by the Assistant Secretary of Labor for OSHA.

RECENT CHALLENGES, INTERPRETATIONS AND MODIFICATIONS TO THE STANDARD

In August, 1981 OSHA published an *interpretation* of the records access standard addressing four issues of concern raised by interested parties: (1) the standard requires that access be provided in a reasonable time, place and manner, but not later than 15 days after the access request is made. OSHA stated, however, that as long as an employer makes diligent, good faith efforts to provide the records as soon as possible and keeps the employee (representative) informed, OSHA will not cite for violations. (2) although the standard requires access to exposure records of other employees with similar or related working conditions, the employer need conduct only a good faith, diligent search but the search need not be "heroic"; (3) records created solely in anticipation of litigation which are otherwise privileged from discovery, need not be produced; (4) finally, OSHA stated that disciplinary actions against employees for breach of confidentiality agreements are solely a matter of labor-management relations, about which OSHA is neutral.

Finally OSHA proposed to *modify* the trade secrets provision of the standard 1910.20(f) to permit employers to include liquidated damage clauses in confidentiality agreements which employee (representatives) may be required to sign prior to disclosing toxic substance information which is a trade secret.

Soon after its promulgation, the "standard" was challenged in the U.S. Court of Appeals for the D.C. Circuit and the U.S. District Court in Louisiana. The D.C. Circuit case has been put on a deferral basis; but in late 1981, the Fifth Circuit reviewing the District Court decision stated that the access "rule" could be reviewed in the District Court since OSHA exceeded its statutory authority by mislabeling a Section 8 "regulation" (reviewable in a district court) as a Section 6 "standard" (reviewable only in a court of appeals.) When Congress authorized in Section 6 a special class of rules reviewable only in the appeals court, it did not provide for any such accelerated procedure for review of recordkeeping and other rules promulgated as "regulations" under Section 8. To allow OSHA to confer the benefit of accelerated review on the records access regulation merely by characterizing it as a "standard" would frustrate Congress's intent. A standard must purport to correct a particular identified risk, while the records access rule is an enforcement or detection procedure designed to further the goals of the Act generally by possible detection, over a long period, of significant risks not covered by standards.

Partially in response to the 5th Circuit's decision, OSHA in July, 1982 proposed to modify the "Access Rule." Under the proposal, only employees whose work involves *direct* exposure to toxic substances or harmful physical agents would

---
*see *Appendix E, p. 135.*

be covered by the rules governing access to employee exposure and medical records. Eliminated from coverage would be most "white collar" workers and employees in service or other industries where exposure does not typically occur. However, records for employees not otherwise covered would have to be maintained if accidental exposure required medical treatment. The definition of employee exposure record is also being narrowed to include only those records traditionally regarded as occupational exposure records (environmental and biological monitoring results, material safety data sheets). The definition of employee medical records is also to be narrowed to remove those records not typically related to occupational disease. Further modifications are proposed for the construction industry.

Also proposed is a redefinition of "toxic substance" to include only those chemicals on the NIOSH Registry of Toxic Effects of Chemical Substances (RTECS) which meet specified criteria for toxicity. (The NIOSH RTECS currently lists over 39,000 chemicals; the OSHA proposal would limit the number by applying toxicological criteria used by the American National Standards Institute, reducing the number of regulated chemicals to about 3,500); limiting medical record retention to employment plus five years or a total of 30 years, whichever is longer; and permitting employers to withhold the identities of trade secret chemicals which are not highly toxic and to make confidentiality agreements more meaningful as protection.

In addition to the limit on long-term retention of medical records, OSHA is considering eliminating the employer retention requirements for construction workers and employees who work less than one year. OSHA also proposes to eliminate requirements for keeping purchase orders and inventory-type records of chemical identities, as well as records of first aid and emergency treatment, and allowing employees to micro-film X-rays under the supervision of qualified experts. The status of records created under contract is also being relaxed, to remove the "strict liability" for compliance by persons not under an employer's control. Finally the proposal modifies the "immediate" access requirement for records, and lessens the burden on employers to supply requested records to OSHA and unions. Once comments are received and evaluated, OSHA will once again publish in final form the revised "Access Rule."

On November 5, 1982 the federal district court in the case of *Louisiana Chemical Ass'n. v. Bingham*, C.A.No. 801178 (W.D.La.), placed OSHA in the awkward position of having successfully defended the rule it is in the process of revising. The court upheld OSHA's rule requiring employee access to medical and exposure records. Although OSHA has completed hearings on proposed revisions to the rule, it is expected that the court's decision could make it legally and politically more difficult for OSHA to follow through on the revisions. Industry attorneys have not yet decided whether to appeal this ruling.

NOTE: In November 1982, the federal district court in Louisiana upheld the "access rule" in its entirety, saying its content was "quite directly related" to the purpose of the OSH Act. However, the employer group challenging the rule in January, 1983 appealed the decision to the United States Court of Appeals for the Fifth Circuit. OSHA is still considering comments and testimony on its proposed administrative changes to the rule.

(See Appendix E, p. 135)

The Employer's Rights on Inspections Under OSHA Law

by Robert E. Rader Jr.

Mr. Rader is a member of the law firm of McCarty, Wilson, Rader and Mash in Ennis, Texas. He specializes in representing employers in litigation against government regulatory agencies, with an emphasis on OSHA. He was the first attorney to obtain a judicial holding that OSHA must obtain a search warrant in order to compel on OSHA inspection.

This material is adapted by permission from a booklet of the same title by the author originally published in 1980.

HOW OSHA WORKS

The Occupational Safety and Health Act of 1970 covers all employers engaged in a business affecting commerce.[1] Practically speaking, that includes virtually every employer in the country.

The Act requires employers to

(1) Furnish employees a place of employment that is free from recognized hazards, and

(2) Comply with safety and health standards promulgated by the Secretary of Labor (OSHA).[2]

The Act is enforced by means of workplace inspections and record keeping requirements. Section 8 of the Act[3] grants OSHA Compliance Officers the unlimited right to inspect any place where work is performed by an employee of an employer, and requires employers to maintain accident and illness records and to make such records available to OSHA upon request.

When the Secretary finds a violation, he is authorized to issue a citation and assess civil monetary penalties of up to $10,000. There are also criminal penalties of up to $20,000 and imprisonment for a willful violation that results in an employee death.[4]

An employer has 15 working days from receipt of a citation and notice of proposed penalties in which to contest the citation, proposed penalties and abatement date by filing a Notice of Contest. Otherwise, the citation and penalty become final and unappealable.[5]

If an employer files a Notice of Contest, the matter is referred to the Solicitor of Labor who files a complaint before the Occupational Safety and Health Review Commission, which appoints an Administrative Law Judge to hear the case. After the hearing, or trial, the Administrative Law Judge makes his findings as to whether the employer has violated the Act or any safety standards promulgated thereunder.

After the Administrative Law Judge has rendered his decision, both the employer and the Solicitor have the right to appeal to the Review Commission by filing a Petition for Discretionary Review within 30 days. Such petition must state with particularity the issues upon which review is sought, since review will be limited to the issues specified in the petition. A member of the Review Commission may also direct a case for review upon his own motion any time within 30 days after the Administrative Law Judge's decision. If no member of the Review Commission grants a party's Petition for Discretionary Review or otherwise directs review of the Administrative Law Judge's decision within 30 days, the Judge's decision becomes the final order of the Commission.[6]

If review is granted, both parties will be afforded opportunity to file briefs with the Commission, but oral argument is not normally allowed.

It is important to note that the granting of review by the Commission operates as an automatic stay of the Administrative Law Judge's decision during the pendency of the review period.

Any person adversely affected by a final order of the Occupational Safety and Health Review Commission[7] has 60 days to appeal to the United States Court of Appeals.[8] Such appeal does not operate as an automatic stay of the Commission's final order, however, and the courts will allow such an appeal only as to issues previously raised in a Petition for Discretionary Review to the Review Commission.[9]

DECISIONS AN EMPLOYER MUST MAKE

When an employer is confronted with an OSHA inspection, he must decide initially whether to insist on a valid search warrant as a prerequisite to allowing such an inspection. Should OSHA obtain a warrant, the employer must then decide whether to honor the warrant. If and when OSHA does inspect, the employer must decide on what protective measures he will take during the course of the inspection. Finally, if after an inspection OSHA issues citations against the employer, he must decide whether to contest the citations. The purpose of this article is to discuss the employer's right to a warrant and the procedures for contesting an invalid warrant.

SHOULD THE EMPLOYER INSIST ON A SEARCH WARRANT?

The United States Supreme Court has held that an employer has a constitutional right to insist on a search warrant, based on probable cause, as a prerequisite to an OSHA inspection.[10] There are several advantages in requesting a warrant. First, it requires OSHA to convince a neutral judicial officer that there is "probable cause" to conduct the desired inspection, and thus prevents discriminatory and harassing inspections.[11] Second, a warrant may serve to limit the scope of OSHA's inspection.[12] Third, a warrant protects against inspections triggered by disgruntled employees, ex-employees, competitors and contentious labor organizations.[13] And fourth, by insisting on a warrant, the employer establishes a judicial record of the number of times he has been inspected, thus preventing unduly repetitious and numerous inspections.

When confronted with an OSHA inspection, an employer needs to know certain critical facts in order to decide whether to request a warrant.

WHAT TYPE OF OSHA INSPECTION IS IT?

First, the employer should determine the *type* of inspection OSHA is requesting. There are four basic types of OSHA inspections.[14] In order of priority these are:

1. Imminent danger inspections
2. Fatality-catastrophe investigations
3. Complaint inspections
4. General schedule (random) inspections

In addition, OSHA conducts follow-up inspections to insure that previously cited violations have been abated.

If the desired inspection is an imminent danger or fatality situation, the employer may not want to insist on a warrant since there is obviously probable cause to conduct the inspection.[15]

However, if the desired inspection is based on a complaint, it is important to determine whether the complaining party is a current employee, or a labor organization, or a non-employee. In a complaint situation, the OSHA Compliance Officer is required by law to furnish the employer with a written copy of the complaint.[16] If the complaint is not in writing and has not been made by a current employee, and does not specify with some particularity the location and nature of the alleged violations, it is advisable to request a warrant, since no other type complaint is authorized by the Act.[17]

Finally, if the desired inspection is a general schedule inspection, the employer should ascertain why his particular establishment was chosen for inspection. Unless the employer is satisfied that OSHA has inspected every other establishment in his area with a higher accident-illness rate, he should again insist on a warrant.[18]

WHAT WILL THE SCOPE OF THE INSPECTION BE?

After determining the type of inspection OSHA desires to conduct, the employer should determine the proposed *scope* of the inspection. This is particularly important where the inspection is pursuant to a complaint, since Section 8(f)(1) of the Act itself limits inspections to the complained of items.[19]

Likewise, follow-up inspections should be limited to an examination of the previously cited items. And in most instances, fatality and imminent hazard investigations should be limited in scope to the actual accident site. The only wall-to-wall search contemplated by the Act is a general schedule inspection, and even that must be limited as to the documents and persons examined.[20]

Therefore, if the inspection requested by OSHA is based on a complaint, or is a follow-up inspection, but the OSHA Compliance Officer expresses his intent to inspect the entire premises—then demand a warrant. Even if the Compliance Officer agrees to limit his inspection, you may still want to insist on a warrant, since actual experience indicates that if the Compliance Officer spots any violation, he will cite it, even if it is outside the scope of his agreed inspection. The *only* way to *insure* that an OSHA inspection will be limited to complained of violations or follow-up items is to insist on a warrant, suitably limited in scope.

In making the decision whether to request a search warrant, the employer should not be dissuaded by the fear that OSHA will treat him more severely for requesting a warrant. OSHA Compliance Officers are sworn to cite every violation they observe—and will do so whether or not the inspection is pursuant to a warrant. Further, OSHA's own case-law precedent holds that an employer may not be penalized for exercising his constitutional right to a warrant.[21]

Finally, if the employer does request that OSHA obtain a warrant, he should also request adequate notice and opportunity for hearing on the warrant application. OSHA's own regulations previously required such notice and hearing.[22] Effective November 3, 1980, OSHA amended its regulations to provide for *ex parte* warrant applications. However, the courts are not *required* to grant OSHA warrants *ex parte*, and have the discretion to grant hearing on the warrant application.[23] It is therefore appropriate to ask OSHA for notice and hearing on any warrant application. It is also appropriate—particularly where the employer suspects harassment—to contact the court or magistrate directly to request a hearing in the event OSHA applies for a warrant. Such a hearing will afford the employer an opportunity to examine OSHA's probable cause to inspect, and to present his own arguments as to why the warrant should not be issued, or restrictions that should be placed upon the scope of the search.

SHOULD THE EMPLOYER HONOR AN OSHA SEARCH WARRANT?

If OSHA obtains a warrant *ex parte* and appears at the employer's establishment to inspect, the employer should not automatically honor the warrant and allow the inspection. If the warrant is legally deficient, the employer may waive his constitutional right to a valid warrant by allowing the inspection.[24] In addition, once the warrant is executed, OSHA will insist the employer litigate any questions as to the constitutionality of the warrant before the Occupational Safety and Health Review Commission, rather than before the court that issued such warrant.[25] Therefore, if the employer allows entry pursuant to the warrant, he may lose his right to have the constitutionality of that warrant ruled on by a district court in the first instance.

In short, the employer must decide *before* allowing the inspection whether the warrant is constitutional and should be honored. If the employer believes with some certainty that OSHA's warrant is legally defective, he should not waive his rights by allowing an inspection pursuant to that warrant. Instead, the employer should either file a motion with the issuing court to quash the warrant, or, alternatively, simply refuse to honor the warrant and defend against any civil contempt action OSHA may bring.[26]

On the other hand, an employer should be very careful about disregarding an OSHA warrant, since he may be subjected to civil contempt penalties if the warrant proves valid. This is presently a very sensitive area in the law, and no decision should be made to disregard a warrant without the advice of informed OSHA counsel.

In making the decision whether to disregard an OSHA warrant, the employer and his attorney should know that there are two general constitutional defenses to such a warrant. The first defense is that there is no probable cause to support the warrant. The second defense is that the warrant is unconstitutionally overbroad in scope.

IS THE WARRANT BASED ON PROBABLE CAUSE?

It should first be noted that the warrant application and supporting affidavit will not normally be served along with the warrant. It may therefore be necessary to obtain those supporting documents either from OSHA or from the magistrate's file before allowing the inspection. The documents furnished to the magistrate must in and of themselves demonstrate probable cause to support the warrant issued.

If the requested inspection is a general schedule inspection, the warrant application and supporting affidavit should demonstrate that OSHA is inspecting on a "worst-first" basis, that OSHA has already inspected every other establishment in the area with a higher accident-illness rate, and that there are no higher priority inspections pending.[27]

Alternatively, an application for an OSHA warrant based on a complaint must identify the complainant as a current employee who has made a written, signed complaint to OSHA,[28] specify the nature of the alleged violations in some detail,[29] and describe the size and general layout of the establishment to be inspected and the department or location wherein the violations are alleged to exist.[30] The application should also advise as to the length of time between the date on which the violations are alleged to have existed and the date that information is presented to the issuing judicial officer,[31] as well as the number and date of prior OSHA inspections of the establishment in question.[32] Additionally, the application should advise the issuing judicial officer whether any higher priority inspections are pending,[33] the time and date that OSHA proposes to inspect,[34] and the scope of the search.[35] If OSHA desires to examine any documents, they must be described with particularity.[36]

If the warrant application and supporting affidavit fail to meet the above criteria, the constitutionality of the warrant may be contested in good faith.

IS THE WARRANT OVERBROAD IN SCOPE?

As explained above, the question of scope arises primarily in the context of warrants based on complaints, or issued to conduct a follow-up inspection. In either event, once probable cause is established to issue a warrant, the warrant itself must carefully limit the scope of the search to the alleged violations or previously cited items.[37]

Once the type of inspection—i.e. complaint, follow-up, general schedule—is determined, it is usually possible to tell from the face of the warrant whether it is unconstitutionally overbroad in scope and should be disregarded and defended on that basis.

CONCLUSION

Employers know that safety pays, and most employers make a real effort to avoid job-related accidents and injuries.

Experience teaches that, unfortunately, OSHA is more interested in finding so-called violations and issuing citations than in whether an employer is conducting a safe operation. It is quite common for employers with excellent safety records, who have complied with every safety instruction their insurance carrier can think of, to be cited and fined heavily by OSHA.

Employers should realize that OSHA's right to inspect is not unlimited. And in the event of an inspection, employers should realize that they are not necessarily in violation of the law just because OSHA issues a citation. They should also realize that while acquiescing in an OSHA citation and paying a small penalty may be smart short-term economics, it may present significant long-term problems, from the standpoint of abatement costs and exposure to repeat violations and civil litigation.

It is therefore critical that employers know and understand their rights, and that they not waive any rights when dealing with OSHA.

References

[1] *29 USC (United States Code) §651* ***et seq.***

[2] *29 USC §654. The Secretary has adopted or promulgated thousands of such standards, which are divided into the following general categories:*
General Industry – 29 CFR 1910
Construction Standards – 29 CFR 1926
Maritime Standards – 29 CFR 1915, 1919
Mining Standards – 30 CFR 55, 56, 57, 70, 71, 75, 77

Other Miscellaneous Standards – 29 CFR 570, 41 CFR 50.

[3]*29 USC §657.*

[4]*29 USC §666.*

[5]*29 USC §659.*

[6]*29 CFR 2200* ***et seq.***

[7]*Whether the order becomes final by the Commission's failure to grant review, or whether the Commission, upon review, affirms or reverses the Administrative Law Judge.*

[8]*29 USC §660.*

[9]***Keystone Roofing Co. v. Dunlop,*** *539 F 2d 960 (3rd Cir. 1976).*

[10]***Marshall v. Barlow's, Inc.,*** *436 US 307 (1978).*

[11]*Compare* ***Weyerhaeuser v. Marshall,*** *425 F Supp 1375 (ED Wis. 1978).*

[12]***West Point Pepperell Inc. v. Marshall,*** *496 F Supp 1178 (ND Ga. 1980),* ***Marshall v. North American Car Co.,*** *626 F 2d 320 (3rd Cir. 1980).*

[13]*See, e.g.,* ***In re Cargill, Inc.,*** *CCH OSHD ¶ 24,298 (ND Tex. 1980),* ***Marshall v. Horn Seed Company, Inc.*** *647 F 2d 96 (10th Cir. 1981).*

[14]*See Chapter IV of OSHA* ***Field Operations Manual.***

[15]*However, in a fatality investigation, the employer should insist on having his attorney present during the course of OSHA's investigation, since finding of violation by OSHA can be used as evidence of negligence against the employer in a future civil lawsuit.* ***Bachner v. Rich,*** *CCH OSHD ¶ 20,970 (Sup Ct Alaska, 1976);* ***Koll v. Manett's Transportation Co.,*** *CCH OSHD ¶ 21,763 (Sup Ct Iowa, 1977);* ***Bayne v. Todd Shipyards,*** *CCH OSHD ¶ 22,213 (Sup Ct Wash. 1977);* ***Disabatino Brothers, Inc. v. Baio,*** *CCH OSHD ¶ 21,229 (Sup Ct Dela. 1976);* ***Arthur v. Flota Mercante Gran Centro Americana S.A.,*** *CCH OSHD ¶ 16,979 (5th Cir. 1976);* ***Schroeder v. C. F. Braun & Co.,*** *CCH OSHD ¶ 19,064 (7th Cir. 1974);* ***Dunn v. Judge Brimer, Jr.,*** *CCH OSHD ¶ 20,834 (Sup Ct Ark. 1976);* ***Knight v. Burns Kirkley & Williams Construction Co., Inc.*** *CCH OSHD ¶ 20,876 (Sup Ct Ala. 1976).*

[16]*29 USC §657(f)(1). Complaints are normally recorded on an OSHA-7 Form and a copy of that form is handed to the employer at the time an inspection is requested.*

[17]*29 USC §657(f)(1). See also, Legislative History of the Occupational Safety and Health Act, Committee Print, Senate Subcommittee on Labor, p. 399.*

[18]*To obtain a warrant to conduct a general schedule inspection, OSHA must show they are inspecting all establishments on a "worst-first" basis, that they have inspected every other establishment in the area with a higher accident-illness rate, and that there are no higher priority inspections pending at the time. See,* ***Marshall v. Weyerhaeuser,*** *456 F Supp 474 (D NJ 1978);* ***Reynolds Metals Co. v. Secretary of Labor,*** *442 F Supp 195 (WD Va. 1977).*

[19]*29 USC §657(f)(1).* ***Marshall v. North American Car Co., F 2d, (3rd Cir. 1980); Marshall v. Trinity Industries, Inc.,*** *7 BNA OSHC 1851 (WD Okla. 1979).*

[20]***Blocksom v. Marshall,*** *582 F 2d 1122 (7th Cir. 1978);* ***Marshall v. Pool Offshore Co.,*** *467 F Supp 978 (WD La. 1979).*

[21]***Walter H. Kessler Co., Inc.,*** *CCH OSHD ¶ 23,415 (1979).*

[22]*29 CFR 1903.4. See,* ***Cerro Metal Products v. Marshall,*** *620 F 2d 964 (3rd Cir. 1980).*

[23]*In the Matter of Establishment Inspection of CF&I Steel Corp., 489 F Supp 1302 (D Colo. 1980).*

[24]*See e.g.,* ***Southern Indiana Gas & Electric Company,*** *CCH OSHD ¶ 15,238 (1972).*

[25]***Babcock & Wilcox v. Marshall,*** *610 F 2d 1128 (3rd Cir. 1979);* ***Baldwin Metals Co. Inc., v. Donovan,*** *642 F 2d 768 (5th Cir. 1981);* ***Chromalloy American Corporation,*** *7 BNA OSHC 1547 (Rev Comm 1979). But see contra,* ***Weyerhaeuser v. Marshall,*** *592 F 2d 373 (7th Cir. 1979); "OSHA Warrants and The Exhaustion Doctrine," 84 Dickinson Law Rev. No. 4.*

[26]*Civil contempt may be defended on the ground that the underlying OSHA warrant was erroneously issued.* ***Blocksom v. Marshall,*** *582 F 2d 1122 (7th Cir. 1978);* ***Marshall v. Huffhines Steel Company,*** *488 F Supp 995 (ND Tex. 1979).*

[27]*For an example of an acceptable warrant application, see* ***Reynolds Metals Co. v. Secretary of Labor,*** *442 F Supp 195 (WD Va. 1977). Compare,* ***Marshall v. Weyerhaeuser,*** *456 F Supp 474 (D NJ 1978);* ***In The Matter of Establishment Inspection of Urick Property,*** *472 F Supp 1193 (WD Va. 1979);* ***Hall Foundries & Mfg., Inc. v. Marshall,*** *CCH OSHD ¶ 23,995 (ND Tex. 1979). See also, "OSHA Warrants and Administrative Probable Cause," 33 Baylor Law Review, 97 (1981).*

[28]***Marshall v. Horn Seed Company,*** *647 F 2d 96 (10th Cir. 1981).*

[29]***Weyerhaeuser v. Marshall,*** *592 F 2d 373 (7th Cir. 1979).*

[30]***Marshall v. North American Car Company,*** *476 F Supp 698 (MD Pa. 1979); aff'd 626 F 2d 320 (3rd Cir. 1980);* ***In the Matter of Inspection of: Central Mine Equipment Company,*** *7 BNA OSHC 1185 (ED Mo. 1979), Rev on other grounds, 608 F 2d 719 (8th Cir. 1980).*

[31]***Id.***

[32]***Michigan v. Tyler,*** *436 US 499, 507 (1978).*

[33]*Such as a fatality or imminent danger investigation. See,* ***Field Operations Manual,*** *Ch. IV;* ***Marshall v. Weyerhaeuser,*** *456 F Supp 474 (D NJ 1978).*

[34]***Michigan v. Tyler,*** *436 US 499, 507 (1978).*

[35]***Id.***

[36]***Marshall v. Barlow's, Inc.,*** *436 US 307, 327, n.22,* ***Blocksom v. Marshall,*** *582 F 2d 1122, 1125 (7th Cir. 1978);* ***Marshall v. Pool Offshore Company,*** *467 F Supp 978, 982 (WD La. 1979).*

[37]***In the Matter of Establishment Inspection of Urick Property,*** *472 F Supp 1193 (WD Pa. 1979);* ***Marshall v. Trinity Industries, Inc.,*** *F Supp, 7 BNA OSHC 1851 (WD Okla. 1979);* ***Marshall v. North American Car Company,*** *476 F Supp 698 (MD Pa. 1979), aff'd 626 F 2d 320, (3rd Cir. 1980);* ***Marshall v. Wollaston Alloys, Inc.,*** *F Supp---, 7 BNA OSHC 1944 (D Mass. 1979);* ***In the Matter of Establishment Inspection of Northwest Airlines, Inc.*** *437 F*

Supp 533 (ED Wis. 1977), aff'd 587 F 2d 12 (7th Cir. 1978); **Whittaker Corp. v. OSHA,** 6 BNA OSHC 1492 (MD Pa. 1978), appeal dismissed 1979, **In the Matter of Establishment Inspection of Central Mine Equipment Co.,**---F Supp---, 7 BNA OSHC 1185 (ED Mo. 1979), Rev on other grounds but affirmed on this issue, 608 F 2d 719, n.1 (8th Cir. 1980); **Marshall v. Barlow's, Inc.** 436 US 307 (1978); **Marshall v. Pool Offshore Company,** 467 F Supp 978 (WD La. 1979). See also, **Michigan v. Tyler,** 436 US 499, 507 (1978); **Stanford v. Texas,** 379 US 476 (1965); **Marcus v. Search Warrant of Property at 104 East Tenth Street, Kansas City, Missouri, et al.** 367 US 717 (1961); and **Marron v. United States,** 257 US 192 (1927) on the scope of civil inspections.

Negligent OSHA Inspections— A Commentary

R. Ben Hogan III, Esq.

This article on various state laws regarding OSHA inspections was written in 1982 by R. Ben Hogan III, associated with the Birmingham, Alabama law firm of Hogan, Smith and Alspaugh. He is vice chairman of the Environmental Law Section of the Association of Trial Lawyers of America and co-author of OSHA, published by Matthew Bender in 1977. The article originally appeared in the October 1982 issue of Trial Magazine, published by ATLA, and is reprinted here with permission.

The Occupational Safety and Health Act[1] (OSHA) requires that the Occupational Safety and Health Administration (OSH Administration), an agency of the federal government, conduct safety inspections of the workplace.[2] Congress did not intend that OSHA serve as the basis for any new right of action in tort. Accordingly, the act provides at § 653(b)(4):

"Nothing in this Act shall be construed to supersede or in any manner affect any workmen's compensation law or to enlarge or diminish or affect in any manner the common law or statutory rights, duties, or liabilities of employers and employees under any law with respect to injuries, diseases, or death of employees arising out of, or in the course of, employment."

State and federal courts have been unanimous in holding that § 653(b)(4) prevents plaintiffs from using OSHA or any of its regulations as the basis for an independent cause of action.[3] It is equally well established, however, that OSHA regulations are admissible evidence on the issue of the standard of care in those tort cases where the plaintiff has a remedy by statute or common law.[4] *Now a new line of cases stands for the proposition that the Federal Tort Claims Act[5] (FTCA) may serve as the basis for personal injury suit against the federal government for injury proximately caused by negligent OSHA inspections.*

OSHA INSPECTIONS

Under the authority of OSHA, the Department of Labor developed regulations for inspections, citations, and proposed penalties, which are published at 29 C.F.R. § 1903, and a Field Operations Manual and Industrial Hygiene Manual for use by compliance safety and health officers (CSHOs). The manuals, which provide basic policy, operational and administrative instructions, are revised regularly by the Labor Department to reflect current policies.[6]

A CSHO entering a workplace may be there — initially at least — for a variety of reasons. The CSHO may be investigating a work-related fatality or an employee complaint, responding to a specific administrative search warrant, or inspecting a small part of the plant or its entire premises. The employer may or may not choose to accompany the CSHO on the "walk-around." Even if the CSHO spots a potential hazard, the remedies available to require abatement of the hazard are numerous. For the most part, however, the procedures described in the written manuals guide the CSHO during the entire inspection procedure. These are public record and easily obtainable.[7]

It is, of course, the employer and not the CSHO who has the primary responsibility for enforcement of safety violations under OSHA.[8] In view of § 653(4), as one court has observed, "...[I]t is clear to us that the United States has not, through OSHA, undertaken to perform any duties of the employer, but rather has undertaken to make inspections that are supplemental to, but independent of, inspections required of employers by their common law duties to their employees."[9]

Can any duties flow to an injured plaintiff from the undertaking by CSHOs to inspect a workplace? Consider the *Restatement (Second) of Torts §§* 323 and 324A.

Section 323 provides:

"*Negligent Performance of Undertaking to Render Services.* One who undertakes gratuitously or for consideration, to render services to another which he should recognize as necessary for the protection of the other's person or things, is subject to liability to the other for physical harm resulting from failure to exercise reasonable care to perform his undertaking.

"(a) his failure to exercise such care increases the risk of such harm, or

"(b) the harm is suffered because of the other's reliance upon the undertaking."

Section 324A provides:

"*Liability to Third Person for Negligent Performance of Undertaking.* One who undertakes, gratuitously or for consideration, to render services to another which he should recognize as necessary for the protection of a third person or his things, is subject to liability to the third person for physical harm resulting from his failure to exercise reasonable care to protect his undertaking, if

"(a) his failure to exercise reasonable care increases the risk of such harm, or

"(b) he has undertaken to perform a duty owed by the other to the third person, or

"(c) the harm is suffered because of reliance of the other or the third person upon the undertaking."

Under the Restatement *version of what is sometimes misnamed "Good Samaritan Liability," there is breach of duty and subsequent liability where an inspection makes matters worse either through increased risk of harm or induced reliance. Many states, of course, recognize that liability may flow from negligently performed safety inspections of the workplace.*[10] There is authority for the proposition that the *Restatement* requires some showing that the safety inspector undertook to perform a duty owed by the employer or other third party defendant to the plaintiff,[11] *but under the better rule the safety inspector would be liable for a negligent undertaking regardless of the liability of the employer.*[12]

THE FTCA

The FTCA makes the United States liable for tortious acts of omissions committed by its agents "under circumstances where the United States, if a private person, would be liable to the claimant in accordance with the law of a place where the act or omission occurs."[13] The validity of a claim against the government for negligent OSHA inspection must, therefore, depend upon the law of the state where the inspection occurred.[14] Enacted as a waiver of the federal government's immunity for torts, the FTCA is broadly construed.[15] Although giving its general consent to suit in tort, the government prescribed as a condition the exhaustion of administrative remedies[16] and carved out a series of exceptions to its waiver of sovereign immunity.[17]

One such exception is that of "discretionary function," which, as set forth in 28 U.S.C. § 2680(a), provides:

"The provisions of this chapter and § 1346(b) of this title shall not apply to

"(a) any claim based upon an act or omission of an employee of the government exercising due care, in the execution of a statute or regulation, whether or not such a statute or regulation be valid, or based upon the exercise or performance of the failure to exercise or perform a discretionary function or duty on the part of a federal agency or an employee of the government whether or not the discretion involved the abused."

The determination of whether a governmental function is discretionary necessarily involves comparison of the facts with the lodestar case of *Dalehite v. United States.*[18] In it a personal injury action was brought under FTCA to recover damages for death resulting from an explosion of ammonium nitrate fertilizer produced for export at the insistence of and according to the specifications of the government. At trial, the government was found negligent in various phases of drafting the fertilizer plan as a whole, manufacturing, and shipboard loading.

The Supreme Court reversed this, in an opinion holding the action was barred by the discretionary function exception at § 2680(a). Refusing to define the boundaries of this exception, the Supreme Court clearly excluded "all responsibility made at a planning rather than operational level"[19] and involving "room for policy judgment and decision."[20]

In *Griffin v. United States,*[21] the Third Circuit was confronted with an FTCA claim brought for tragic injuries allegedly sustained when a defective polio vaccine, which the then Department of Health, Education, and Welfare had a duty to inspect, was ingested by the plaintiff. The court held that the government's duty to inspect was not a discretionary function within the meaning of § 2680(a), and that the mere fact of the regulatory nature of the inspection was insufficient to insulate the government's negligence.

In *Hendry v. United States,*[22] the Second Circuit discussed the method of distinguishing protected policy judgments from unprotected decisions:

"[S]tate tort standards cannot adequately control those governmental decisions in which, to be effective, the decision-maker must look to considerations of public policy and not merely to established professional standards or to standards of general reasonableness.

"The fact that judgments of government officials occur in areas requiring professional expert evaluation does not necessarily remove those judgments from the examination of courts by classifying them as discretionary function under the Act."[23]

Thus the government has been held liable for its agents' negligence in cases involving medical malpractice,[24] failure to equip a bulldozer with a canopy guard,[25] decisions to release psychiatric patients,[26] and air traffic control operations.[27] As the Fifth Circuit observed:

"The cases following *Dalehite* made clear that an absolutist interpretation of the discretionary function is improper. It is not sufficient for the government to demonstrate that some choice was made in the decision-making process. That showing could be made in almost every case. The nature of the judgment must also call for the balancing of policy considerations."[28]

Under the authority of Griffin *and similar holdings, every district court which has considered the question to date has ruled that the discretionary function exception does not exempt the United States from liability for its negligent OSHA inspections.*[29]

Several courts have expressly recognized that the so-called "Good Samaritan Liability" rule[30] is applicable to the United States in suits brought under the FTCA when the relevant state's tort law recognizes it.[31] Thus any state that follows *Restatement (Second) of Torts* §§ 323 and 324A, or which has case law with similar impact, should be an appropriate forum for an FTCA claim brought against the government for injuries or damages arising out of negligent safety inspections such as those performed by the OSH Administration. Several cases have considered such claims at the pleadings stage, with results depending upon the applicable law of the forum.[32]

What must be considered the lead case to date on this topic is *Blessing v. United States*,[33] which contains a brilliant discussion of all aspects of this question and has been cited with approval by at least one other court.[34] In *Blessing*, the U.S. District Court for the Eastern District of Pennsylvania actually considered in one opinion two similar complaints brought against the government under the FTCA alleging negligent OSHA inspections prior to the injuries to the plaintiffs. The court discussed the allegations in each complaint, finding them deficient in many respects, but allowing amendment rather than ordering dismissal under Rule 12(b)(6) Fed. R. Civ. P.

The 39-page decision found that the discretionary function exemption was not applicable, that Pennsylvania followed the "Good Samaritan Liability" rule, and that, therefore, the FTCA claims stated — although inartfully — good causes of action against the government.

The court discussed in detail the requirements of §§ 323 and 324A, which are applicable in Pennsylvania, and noted:

"That the Occupational Safety & Health Act precludes a finding of federal liability under § 324A(b) as a matter of law does not mean that the statute has the same effect on subsection (a) or (c) of § 324A. The latter subsections address the consequences of what a Good Samaritan undertook to do; they focus on what he did that either made matters worse than they were before his involvement (increased the risk of harm) or induced reliance. Subsection (b), on the other hand, is much more addressed to a definition of the undertaking itself; it focuses on whether, independently of any increased risk or induced reliance, the Good Samaritan undertook to perform a duty owed by another to a third person. Although the statute tells us what the United States, through OSHA, has undertaken to do so, it does not tell us what results flowed from the United States' undertaking."[35]

The court determined that, in Pennsylvania at least, it would be necessary to allege either reliance on the OSHA inspection (by employer or employee) or increased risk of harm, and cited several cases supporting that conclusion.[36] *With such allegations being present, however, the court in* Blessing *determined that a cause of action was stated. The court noted:*

"To the extent that the government's argument is that plaintiffs may not bring suit based on a putative private right of action found in the Occupational Safety and Health Act..., we have earlier noted the correctness of this argument, but have also noted its irrelevance to these cases.

"Insofar as the government's contention is that plaintiffs may not base their claims on alleged breaches of a duty arising solely out of federal law when there is no corresponding duty under state tort law... the government is once again correct. [Citations omitted.] Plaintiffs' claims, however, are based on alleged breaches of duty arising out of Pennsylvania, not federal, law. The government's argument on this point therefore misses the mark. Because we are concerned here with Pennsylvania law, irrelevant too is the government's discussion of *Davis, supra*, which is only authority for the proposition that under the particular facts and claims asserted in that case, Nebraska law recognized no viable action in tort. The relevant question here is whether Pennsylvania would recognize this action if the United States were a private person."[37]

CONCLUSION

In those states that recognize so-called "Good Samaritan Liability" for negligent safety inspections, the FTCA gives the right of action against the government for personal injuries caused by negligent OSHA inspections. In those states strictly adhering to the Restatement *requirements of "Good Samaritan Liability" stated in §§ 323 and 324A, proof requirements must include either increased risk or induced riots flowing from the OSHA inspection. It is not necessary, however, that the injured plaintiff prove that the OSH Administration assumed any duty owed to the plaintiff by the plaintiff's employer. The discretionary function exception in the FTCA is not a valid defense to such suits.*

(See Appendix C, p. 131)

How to Prepare an OSHA Case— the Employer's Viewpoint

Ludwig B. Gartner Jr., Esq.

Mr. Gartner, an attorney for Faegre and Benson in Minneapolis, has experience in occupational safety and health litigation related to OSHA. A graduate of the University of Notre Dame and Harvard Law School, he has been a lecturer at the American Bar Association's National Institute of Occupational Safety and Health Law.

This article is reprinted with permission from the March 1979 issue of Professional Safety Magazine.

This article addresses preparation for a hearing on the merits of a citation for a substantial violation. Technical, legal or procedural considerations, not involving the merits of the case, i.e., irregularities of inspection, inadequacy of pleadings, validity or construction of regulations, etc., which are primarily the responsibility of the attorney, will not be discussed.

Although the article approaches the problem from the employer's point-of-view, the same principles are applicable to preparation of the government's case.

The safety professional is often the key to the successful *preparation* and *presentation* of an OSHA case. As OSHA evolves, more and more important cases are reduced to a question of feasibility: engineering, administrative, economic. The question becomes not whether the workplace should be made safer; but rather, how it should be made safer, how much safer it should be made, at what cost and by what time table. The feasibility question is primarily one of fact. The party with the most thorough *command* of the relevant facts and the best-reasoned expert testimony based upon those facts has the best chance of success before the administrative law judge. The safety professional has the training and experience to identify the relevant facts, quantify them in the particular workplace, and evaluate the available choices. A lawyer who attempts to present an OSHA case without a qualified safety professional for expert guidance and testimony can only hope that the other side will be equally handicapped.

The in-house safety professional plays a central role in the preparation of the case. *First,* the in-house safety professional is familiar with the history of the workplace and has a detailed understanding of how it works, mechanically as well as administratively. He is familiar with local labor contracts, prior inspections, and company safety records. The in-house professional is also knowledgeable about safety trends in the particular industry and has access to industrywide information and statistics. Since OSHA tends to focus on selected industries for inspection, the in-house professional often has knowledge of prior citations at other facilities for similar or related problems. The in-house professional is familiar with the "state-of-the-art" for industry facilities and processes. He has access to the most recently designed installations in order to determine whether technology implemented in such installations is feasible or would be effective in the cited workplace. Such specific state-of-the-art evidence can do much to rebut broad generalizations about techniques available to abate a problem.

Second, the in-house safety professional can help the attorney to obtain access to personnel and premises involved in the citation and discuss available choices with management. One of the biggest obstacles to successful preparation of an OSHA case is the client's lack of cooperation. In-house safety professionals with daily responsibility for the nonlitigation aspects of OSHA can develop a "sour grapes" mindset. The are convinced that the law is lousy, that they have been singled out by a hostile bureaucracy, and they they cannot possibly win. Such a mindset gets in the way of the kind of effort and imagination that is required to successfully prepare and present an OSHA case. "Sour grapes" is no substitute for professionalism. Moreover, management is often reluctant to devote the money and manpower required to properly prepare the case for hearing. The effort and enthusiasm of the in-house professional in acquiring the essential factual data upon which the case will ultimately stand or fall and in persuading management of the importance of the case can increase the likelihood of success.

The decision whether or not to retain an outside "independent" safety consultant in addition to in-house personnel should be made immediately. It can be difficult for an attorney to discuss this question with the client's in-house safety professional. It should not be. The question does not imply a lack of faith in the in-house professional's ability. *As an attorney I prefer to retain an outside consultant to work with in-house experts in preparation of the case.* The outside consultant often has a wider range of experience, is able to relate the problem of a specific industry or workplace to others, and might offer approaches or solutions that have been successful elsewhere. He can facilitate communication between in-house personnel and the lawyer in technical areas. Finally, the outside consultant usually has more experience in preparing exhibits and actually testifying at hearings. Moreover, his objectivity may carry weight with both the judge and the government lawyer, especially if the government has used the expert in other cases and considers him credible.

If you decide to retain an outside expert, look for both educational qualifications and practical experience. Discuss the expert's personal philosophy of his field of expertise. If the expert has testified in the past, obtain transcripts of prior testimony or copies of prior reports. Reach an agreement in advance with the outside expert about his compensation. In my experience, outside consultants and in-house personnel complement each other in the preparation of the case. Together they produce a superior work product.

As early as possible the attorney, consultant and in-house professional should thoroughly discuss all aspects of the cited condition. Each should clearly understand his responsibilities in the preparation of the case. A general timetable should be established for completion of various phases of the preparation.

The first step is to gather necessary *factual data*, including statements from affected employees, photographs of premises, monitoring tests to determine ambient conditions, etc. Start as soon as possible after the inspection. If you have a problem, notify your attorney immediately. There may be evidence that should be preserved, photos taken, etc., before changes occur. Don't wait for the official citation to arrive in the mail. The consultant usually has the equipment to conduct necessary testing. The in-house professional has access to employees for obtaining statements. The attorney can request the government to produce its inspection information. Once the facts at the cited workplace have been ascertained, a second conference should be held to discuss possible lines of defense based upon the facts. Accurate, thorough knowledge and documentation of the facts are the foundations upon which all opinions must be based. The employer has the advantage in this respect, as the party with the best information usually has the best answer in the feasibility flight and the employer controls the workplace. (The government has recognized this fact, is retaining more consultants and requesting that they have additional access to premises for the purpose of conducting a feasibility evaluation.)

The second step is to *formulate opinions* on the basis of the facts and any additional outside investigation. Again, the responsibility of each person should be clearly defined and a timetable established for completion of the investigation. OSHA hearings are usually scheduled promptly. Don't get caught unprepared. The in-house professional can obtain necessary statistical and industry-wide data. The consultant can visit other facilities for analysis and comparison. The lawyer can obtain reports of the government's expert for evaluation. This process should result in the formulation of expert opinions for use at the hearing. One caveat: Throughout the investigation, remain as open and flexible as possible. Often the investigation will produce unexpected avenues of opportunity that can be missed in the rigid pursuit of a preconceived conclusion. Often the investigation will suggest solutions that may be acceptable to all parties. Never foreclose the possibility of settlement.

When opinions have been finalized, prepare the evidence for presentation at the hearing. Unfortunately, at this point a letdown often occurs. However, this step is no less important than the first two, for *the object of the preparation is persuasion of the judge.* A final meeting should be held to discuss the presentation of the facts and opinions. Simple demonstrative evidence sets the stage and makes difficult technical data easier to understand. Visual aids are important: Professional photographs of work areas and equipment; drawings and illustrations; graphs; flip charts; motion pictures; video tapes—be creative. Many companies have their own graphics and advertising departments. Use them. Professionalism is the key. Make is easy for the judge to understand the facts and he is more likely to be persuaded by your opinions.

Finally, *establish your credibility* at the outset; never lose it. Be honest with your attorney. Advise him of information within your knowledge that you think may be damaging to your case. Apparently damaging facts sometimes can be turned around or at least blunted if disclosed in a timely fashion; don't let your attorney be surprised during the hearing. Always deliver what you promise. Don't overstate your case or advocate weak positions out of a misguided sense of duty. Always remember that when the clock strikes thirteen it leaves the other twelve strikes in doubt.

In conclusion, an OSHA case should be prepared as thoroughly and professionally as any other piece of major litigation. The seductive informality of the administrative forum, the absence of formal discovery procedures, and the short calendar place an added burden upon attorney and expert to organize and complete preparation of the case in a timely fashion. Management must cooperate by giving priority to the case, including access to management personnel, and by allocating sufficient resources to do the job right. Unless an employer is willing to underwrite the effort to establish the facts, provide the expertise to interpret the facts, and present the case with imagination and candor, it is better to abate the cited condition and pay the penalty. *A poorly prepared OSHA case is not only a bad investment for the cited employer, it can make bad law for an entire industry.*

Organizing the Corporate Team for Product Safety

Honorable Warren W. Eginton

Judge Eginton is U.S. District Judge in Bridgeport, Conn. He is a past member of the Product Liability Committee of the American Bar Association and has authored many papers on this subject. He is a veteran of many years of litigation on product safety/liability, both as a trial attorney and judge. This article is adapted, with permission, from an article in the May/June 1978 issue of Hazard Prevention Magazine, a publication of the System Safety Society.

Until World War I, a manufacturing concern in the United States, in any product area, could safely believe that its contractual relationships provided a reasonably accurate frame of reference for its responsibilities and obligations. A rule of law based upon so-called privity of contract seemed clearly established. Essentially, privity of contract held that the purchase of a manufactured product was a private contract between buyer and seller and was not subject to any other separate legal action or claim.

I—The Exposure of a Manufacturer to Liability Based on Product Defect Has Increased Geometrically Since 1960 for Several Reasons.

A. Privity of contractual relationship has been abolished in almost every type of product claim.

In March of 1916, the solid earth trembled in New York and a fissure opened which seemed minor at the time. Justice Cardozo, then an Associate Justice of the New York Court of Appeals, listened with his fellow judges to the arguments, in a matter entitled *Donald C. MacPherson* v. *Buick Motor Company*.[1] MacPherson was the owner and operator of a Buick on which one of the wooden spoke wheels collapsed, causing an accident which injured MacPherson. His case against the automobile manufacturer was tried to a jury of the New York Supreme Court and he received a plaintiff's verdict. Buick appealed the case to the Apellate Division of the New York Supreme Court which affirmed the plaintiff's verdict. Buick had purchased its automobile wheels from a component manufacturer, and the Appellate Division based its affirmance squarely on the duty of Buick to provide inspection of every wheel entering its plant and being assembled on its motor cars.

However, the arguments of counsel before the Court of Appeals show that the main issue was whether an automobile should be considered an inherently dangerous article. Prior to 1916, inroads had been made on the concept of privity of contract. The doctrine itself had been established in an English case back in 1842, *Winterbottom* v. *Wright*.[2] From 1842 until 1916 some exceptions to privity of contract had been made by courts in situations involving such items as food, drugs, firearms and explosives, all deemed articles of obvious inherent danger. It was therefore in this setting that the Buick attorneys argued to the Court that an automobile is not an inherently dangerous article and therefore privity of contract should continue to apply.

Justice Cardozo pronounced that in the State of New York at least, privity of contract would be abolished as to any items which in normal operation could be implements of destruction. He expressly held that the doctrine should be modified to fit "whatever the needs of life in a developing civilization." In making this sweeping restriction to the application of the privity doctrine in New York, Cardozo made only a passing reference at the end of his opinion to the issue which had been the basis of the Appellate Division's affirmance—the duty of the manufacturer to inspect a product supplied by one of its vendors.

After World War II the courts resumed what has become since a wholesale attack on the doctrine of privity of contract, resulting in its virtual abolition.

Coupled with this, there has developed an increasing tendency on the part of plaintiffs' attorneys to name as defendants any and all entities with even a remote connection to the product causing injury or property damage. An extreme example by way of illustration: a woman wearing high heels trips on a carpet in the hallway of a ten-year old public school, and thereafter sues the supplier of the carpet, the maintenance organization servicing the school, the school board authorities operating the school, the construction firm that built the school and the architect who designed the school ten years ago.

As a result of these developments, geometrically accelerating during the past twenty years, the importance of adequate defense organization by manufacturers is manifest.

B. Most jurisdictions have enacted strict liability under Section 402A of the Restatement of Torts.

In May, 1965 the American Law Institute promulgated Section 402A of the Restatement of Torts entitled, "Strict Liability." The full text is appended in footnote form.[5] Section 402A applies strict liability to both personal injury and property damage situations, but the courts in most jurisdictions have been unwilling to apply strict liability doctrines to property damage or to consequential damages. Section 402A expressly continues the abolition of the privity doctrine and abolishes any issue of whether the manufacturer has used all possible care. There are two caveats about Section 402A. It may not apply if the manufacturer knows that there will be a substantial change in his product before it reaches the ultimate consumer or user, and secondly, the ultimate consumer or user must still exercise some prudence in the use of the product. He may not unreasonably assume a risk by his own conduct, such as taking a turpentine spray can and spraying the product into his eyes.

Strict liability has been extended beyond food and drug to other categories such as automobiles, airplanes, insecticides, power tools, children's equipment, gas stoves and water heaters. Several states have statutes expressly applying strict liability to *all* product sales.

C. A manufacturer is subject to suit wherever his product is used or consumed.

So-called "long-arm statutes" involving service of process on a foreign corporation have in many instances been amended to include a provision that "Production, manufacture, or distribution of goods with the reasonable expectation that the goods are to be used or consumed in the state and in fact are so used or consumed (regardless of use of independent contractors, distributors or dealers) shall subject a foreign corporation to suit."

Furthermore, even the fact that product suits tend to be multi-defendant actions provides little comfort. The courts are increasingly willing to effect consolidation in one jurisdiction, especially in federal court where the new multi-district litigation rules have been applied with increasing liberality.

D. The education gap has fast diminished.

Immediately following the *Henningsen* decision, *supra*, as product cases proliferated, the record of the defense bar was impressive. The defendant manufacturing companies and their attorneys knew the product, had access to the experts, and enjoyed far greater sophistication than the plaintiff's counsel during pre-trial preparation and often during the actual courtroom proceedings. However, they quickly discovered the necessity of adopting trial preparation and conduct techniques applicable to the product involved in a particular situation. As a result, today the prudent manufacturer relies not on the inexperience or lack of organization of the plaintiff bar, which no longer pertains, but prudently looks to the experience and strength of his own structured organization for product liability prevention and defense. Such structured organization by the manufacturer will now be reviewed.

II—Organization of the Corporate Response to Product Defect Liability Exposure.

The manufacturer does not stand alone when he seeks to defend himself against liability for a product defect. Available to the manufacturer are the following entities, all of which he should utilize:

1. *The Insurance Carrier.* Most major carriers which underwrite comprehensive general liability are highly sophisticated in the organization of product liability prevention as well as product liability defense, and their expertise will be made readily available to the manufacturer upon his request, and often without his request, but at the insistence of his carrier. Insurance publications are available, as well as insurance briefings of the policyholder.

2. *Legal Counsel.* The manufacturer should utilize outside counsel knowledgeable in the defense of product liability litigation in order to establish product safety teams within the company, or should train one member of the house counsel staff in this area.

3. *Consultants.* Expert systems consultants in the product liability area are available to the manufacturer and offer both regional and generalized seminars as well as in-house particularized expertise. Lists of such consultants are readily available, through such organizations as the Defense Research Institute, ASSE, and many others.

4. *Testing Laboratories.* Testing laboratories are available for all stages of the product development and cover a wide range of specialties and product expertise. Although the competence and credibility of testing laboratories is subject to wide variation, cross-checks prior to retainage are not at all difficult and obviously should be accomplished.

5. *Trade Associations.* The manufacturer should make full use of any trade association that pertains to his product area, with respect to both its personnel and its publications. Trade association programs should be utilized where they exist and developed where they do not exist.

III—Quality Control is the Manufacturer's First Line of Defense Against Product Defect Liability

Section 402A of the Restatement of Torts in no way means that the manufacturer should abandon all efforts at quality control. It may at first glance appear discouraging that a manufacturer is strictly responsible for personal injury regardless of any standards of care he may use in making and vending his product. Nevertheless, if a manufacturer is to be subject to strict liability regardless of due care, then the only way in which he can decrease his exposure to litigation costs, and indeed to reputation damage, is to manufacture the best possible product it is within his power to make and vend. A satisfactory product in the last result is the only sure way of reducing exposure to claims.

It would be tempting to state that no expense should be spared in dealing with quality control. However, the sophisticated attorney is aware that the budget can only be stretched so far, and quality control is but one consideration. However, the general rule that should be applied is that quality control can never be made a department second best to any other department of the company. It must have high caliber people and must have a reasonable and adequate budget. Fortunately, it appears that today management is cognizant that the yardsticks just mentioned must be axiomatic.

The manufacturer should keep itself aware of standards being applied currently in the industry. Performance up to standards in the industry is not in itself protection in a suit. On the other hand failure to meet the standards of the industry can be very damaging indeed. Such evidence is admissible in a product liability action. So axiom No. 1—keep your quality control standards up to those in the industry and if possible, ahead of the average.

Secondly, develop a quality control plan and make it very comprehensive. It is not just eyewash, and as a matter of fact it can be damaging if you create such a plan and then do not accomplish it. The interest of the company and its concern for quality control is best shown by having the same type of organizational plan as prevails in other departments of the company. Such a plan might well contain the following items:

1. Organizational chart of personnel.
2. Job descriptions.
3. Operating procedures.
4. Quality control forms.
5. Quality control performance statistics.
6. Quality control costs.
7. Quality control progress reports.
8. A quality control manual.

One very important observation is that the function of quality control includes a check on engineering design correlation to engineer production. A simple illustration will suffice. Let us assume that an automatic fire sprinkler device fails in 1978 and its design becomes a significant factor. It will not only be embarrassing, but most injurious to defense of the lawsuit if the attorneys for the company find that the blueprints and other design drawings at the plant date back to 1960, have not been kept revised and are not in accordance with the actual design of the product. This may seem improbable, but it happens all too often. It is a responsibility of quality control to check the quality and currency of the blueprints kept in the files as well as the quality of the product itself. The work of keeping the designs current in the files will fall to the engineers, but the supervision and inspection of that work must be the responsibility of quality control.

There are many other areas falling under the responsibility of quality control, but perhaps none so important as quality checks on vendor-supplied components. A manufacturer will never successfully avoid responsibility by a claim that the component part which failed was not manufactured by him, even though installed in his assembled unit. Even as early as 1914, as noted above, the Appellate Division was ruling in *MacPherson* v. *Buick Motor Company, supra*, that Buick was responsible although the sole defect occurred in a wheel supplied to Buick by an outside manufacturer. The language of Justice Kellogg in the *MacPherson* case[6] remains very applicable today.

Justice Kellogg noted that the Buick Company had purchased the defective wheel from the Imperial Wheel Company, "a reputable manufacturer of wheels". When the wheel was received by Buick, it had already been primed with one coat of paint. The Court then observed:

> "The defendant made no examination of it (the wheel) when received, except to see that it ran true and that it had not been marred in shipment."[7]

The court noted that the coat of paint on the wheel did make it more difficult to determine the quality of the wood but also noted that Buick could have ordered the wheels to be delivered unpainted. The Court then made the following very significant quality control observations:

> "The defendant had no wood expert, and never examined the wheels when in course of manufacture, or made any examinations as to the safety of the wheel before it was put upon the car, but ran the car several miles on a trial test before it was sold, turning sharp curves and giving it severe usage. It had never known a wheel to collapse on account of the poor quality of the wood from which it was made. Its attention had never been called to the necessity of making any examination to determine whether the wheels bought by it were safe or not; it assumed that they were safe."
>
> "The evidence indicates quite clearly that many other automobile manufacturers, prior to 1909, exercised no greater care as to wheels bought by them than the defendant exercised with reference to its wheels, and that no accident had resulted therefrom. This evidence indicated, not that the defendant was careful, but that the manufacturer had been very lucky."[8]

The court added that a manufacturer of an automobile cannot be satisfied with the fact that he is buying a component part from a reputable maker. If it arrives in his plant in such condition as to make inspection difficult or impossible, he must have it arrive in his plant in some other condition or he must go to the plant of the manufacturer and inspect before the product is so altered as to make inspection impossible. The conclusion of the Court is stated as follows:

> "We hold that under the circumstances the defendant owed a duty to all purchasers of its automobiles to make a reasonable inspection and test to ascertain whether the wheels purchased and put in use by it were reasonably fit for the purposes for which it used them, and, if it fails to exercise care in that respect, that it is responsible for any defect which would have been discovered by such reasonable inspection and test."[9]

The same criteria apply today. The manufacturer should assure that his vendors are delivering quality products. Unless he knows that he can inspect the component part adequately at his own plant upon shipment, he should inspect the part at the plant of the vendor. Obviously if he experiences repeated difficulties with the component part, he is increasing his own negligence and his own exposure by continuing to accept the part.

With respect to testing, if, for economic or other significant reasons, he deems it impossible to test the vendor component at his own plant when it arrives, then he should either arrange for tests at the vendor plant or arrange for reports of such tests to be furnished.

One of the gray area issues is how much testing of a vendor component should be done. Obviously the attorney's recommendations will be to test every single item and product unit on the assembly line. With some highly critical products, this is feasible and is actually accomplished. With a majority, it is undoubtedly not accomplished, and tests are made on a sampling basis. There is no set rule, but obviously the protection increases with the amount of testing. It should be limited only for valid extrinsic reasons, and any decision limiting testing should be made with full consideration of the exposure risk entailed.

IV—Organization of the Product Saftey Committee

Product liability exposure extends to all stages connected with the product from the initial, tentative design through all design phases until final approval is given for prototype product development. The design area is in many respects the most hazardous area of product exposure, because attorneys representing plaintiffs often feel that if they are not able to prove or even plead a specific manufacturing defect, they might be able to hold the case in court by a vague allegation of design defect.

Product exposure of the manufacturer continues through development and testing of the prototype, and then into the manufacturing phase with the negotiation of contracts and purchase orders with suppliers of component parts. The exposure continues during manufacture and assembly of the final product, followed by packaging, to include labeling and use instructions, and then ultimately product exposure extends to the methods of promotion, marketing and distribution of the product, including warranty periods and service arrangements.

The exposure in all these areas is by no means limited to the manufacturer alone or even limited to his vendors. He may have retained an independent testing company to evaluate the product and he probably retained an advertising agency to promote its sale. Both of these entities can share responsibility with the manufacturer for product claims. Likewise, those in the chain of marketing and distribution are more likely than not to be joined as defendants in a product suit.

How does the manufacturer cope with this formidable exposure? Not by waiting until the company receives notification of a product defect claim. The processing of such a claim, and the defense of any litigation that ensues, will be made far less expensive and far less traumatic if manufacturer has already in place a functioning product safety committee.

Such a committee should be established to meet on a regular basis, at least monthly, and should contain representatives from five basic areas as follows:

1. Engineering and design.
2. Purchasing.
3. Manufacturing.
4. Quality Control.
5. Marketing and field service.

Delegates and alternates should be appointed from each of those five areas to ensure that each is represented regularly at the meetings. Scheduling of regular meetings serves to avoid an impression of *ad hoc* organization to meet emergencies, an impression which must be avoided.

In addition to the foregoing five types of representation, the committee membership should also include representatives of the financial, legal, insurance, and executive areas. These last four representatives need not attend every meeting of the committee and indeed it is preferable for many reasons not to have an executive present at the committee meetings. The chairman of the committee, often the Director of Quality Control, makes certain that minutes are kept of committee meetings and that these are forwarded to the executive for action, with all action items pinpointed and prominently identified.

Responsibilities of the product safety comittee are quite extensive, especially during its initial period of organization and functioning. It must first review all of the products of the manufacturer and must identify the critical components to which priority attention is accorded. It reviews all aspects of the critical items, from initial engineering and design through complaints from field service.

The work of the committee is best done through delegation of tasks to subcommittees. Special subcommittees can be established on the basis of need, but the following subcommittees should be established on a permanent basis, and assigned the following responsibilities:

1. *New product design*
a. Reviews all pertinent standards of federal, state or local agencies and private associations.
b. Evaluates hazards and the effectiveness of design and manufacturing safeguards.
c. Identifies critical components and arranges for such components to be given attention by all subsequent subcommittees.
2. *Vendor control*
Initiates and monitors a certificate of compliance program and with respect to critical items as previously identified, arranges adequate visitation and inspection programs applicable to vendors.
3. *Product modification records*
Maintains all blueprints and other documentation relating to the product and maintains historically accurate records showing changes made to the product and to its components.
4. *Quality control records*
Publishes the quality control manual in accordance with the items noted previously.
5. *Product publications, including catalogues and advertising material*

Reviews all catalogues for accuracy and current reliability, and monitors all advertising and promotional claims for accuracy and reliability.

6. *Field Service and Complaint Records*
This may be combined with the corrective action reports subcommittee or field service may be separated out from the complaint and corrective action responsibility. Effective field service is an increasingly stringent requirement for a manufacturer.

7. *Corrective Action Reports*
If this subcommittee is separated out from the field service subcommittee, then it restricts its responsibilities to handling the complaint area of field service to coordinate all corrective action and maintenance of records concerning such action.

The exact duties of each subcommittee in the areas just generally set forth will depend upon the particular problems involved with the products that the manufacturer markets. However, the role of the product safety committee becomes crucial in defense of product defect litigation and it would therefore seem worthwhile to particularize in some detail the operation of the committee in the litigation setting.

V — The Role of the Product Safety Committee in Litigation Defense.

The product safety committee plays a significant litigation role in three areas of defense development as follows:

1. Preservation or re-creation of the product.
2. Preservation of the pertinent files.
3. Preparation and preservation of fact and expert testimony.

The first priority of the product safety committee in its defense of product litigation is preservation; this means preservation of the product, preservation of the files, and preservation of testimony. Let us examine what must be accomplished in all three areas to provide effective product liability defense.

If it is obtainable for inspection, by compulsory discovery process or otherwise, the product should be inspected at the earliest possible moment and photographic evidence should be preserved. Testing and sampling will be required, so the product should be reproduced under conditions identical, or as identical as possible, to its original manufacture. Blueprints must be studied, and assembly line techniques reviewed and duplicated as fully as possible. The product should be reproduced in quantities sufficient for in-house testing, outside testing and for use as exhibits at trial.

If the insurance carrier is involved, its representatives will be taking adverse witness and party statements, at the earliest possible moment. Meanwhile house counsel is proceeding rapidly to obtain and preserve statements of employees of the manufacturer involved in production of the claimed defective product. Concurrently with the taking of such statements, an attorney-engineer team will be reviewing the files. This can range from a simple to an extremely complex task. There have been cases in which files examination at the manufacturer's plants has taken months, even longer than a year. In these cases, the attorneys are assigned a room that is considered to be the litigation room at the plant itself where they accomplish examination and reproduction of the documents. As a matter of course, the attorneys will retain the original files of the company in the litigation room under lock and key, and will provide reproduced files of use by company officials. Only by a thorough review of the files can the attorneys for the manufacturer evaluate the defense case, and be prepared for effective interrogation of their own witnesses as well as of experts that the plaintiff can be expected to retain.

As soon as the files' contents have been mastered, and often simultaneously with files review, the defense attorneys will interview all corporate officials and employees who possess any information relevant to the product or the claim. Such interviews normally will be conducted in a manner of a formal deposition. Questions will be transcribed by a court reporter and the transcript certified by the witness. This both helps to prepare each witness for the atmosphere of an actual deposition and also preserves sworn testimony in the event that a particular individual leaves the employment of the company either before his actual deposition is noticed or before the trial occurs. In addition, each witness will be asked questions of a cross-examination nature to fully prepare him for what can be expected when depositions will be noticed by the plaintiff's attorney.

Certain questions involved with product liability defense, such as effect on company morale and company finances, never will be resolved by criteria uniformly acceptable to all manufacturers. Only guidelines through experience can be offered. Nevertheless, the company that conceals the existence of a product suit is making a mistake. While there is no reason to publicize the suit, there is likewise no reason to employ any cloak-and dagger techniques in preparing the defense at the manufacturer's plant. Far more unnecessary interest will be aroused and far more commotion created if the purpose of attorney visits to the plant is misrepresented or concealed.

Obviously, the trauma will be greatly reduced if the particular manufacturing facility has become accustomed to the operation of a product safety comittee. Not only is the presence of an attorney on a fairly regular basis an occurrence that becomes commonplace, but the attorney has benefited by having developed a familiarity with both product and personnel of the particular manufacturer.

Finally, it is important to stress one significant aspect of product liability defense organization through a product safety committee. The manufacturer is well ahead of the plaintiff's attorney concerned with a general or perhaps even a negligence practice. The gaps are narrowing every month, but there still is a great advantage to the manufacturer which is difficult for the plaintiff to overcome, and that is an intimate knowledge of the product concerned. The effort of the defense team organized from the product safety committee is to take every legitimate advantage of that expertise, to organize it effectively and to make the strongest possible presentation, either for a low cost settlement or for successful defense against the claim.

References

[1]*Donald C. MacPherson v. Buick Motor Company, 217 NY 382, 111 NE 1050(1960).*

[2]*Winterbottom v. Wright, 10 M&W 109, 152 Eng. Rep. 402(1842).*

[3]*MacPherson v. Buick Motor Company, supra, note 1 at 391.*

[4]*Henningsen v. Bloomfield Motors, 32 N.J.358, 161 A.2d 69, 75 A.L.R.2d 1 (1960).*

[5]*2 Restatement of Torts* 2d Section 402A at 347-8 (1965):, 'Special Liability of Seller of Product for Physical Harm to User or Consumer.

(1) One who sells any product in a defective condition unreasonably dangerous to the user or consumer or to his property is subject to liability for physical harm thereby caused to the ultimate user or consumer, or to his property, if
(a) the seller if engaged in the business of selling such a product, and
(b) it is expected to and does reach the user or consumer without substantial change in the condition in which it is sold.
(2) The rule stated in Subsection (1) applied although
(a) the seller has exercised all possible care in the preparation and sale of his product, and
(b) the user or consumer has not bought the product from or entered into any contractual relation with the seller.'

[6]*MacPherson v. Buick Motor Company, 160 App. Div. 55, 145 NY Supp. 462 (3rd Dept. 1914).*

[7]*145 NY Supp. at 463.*

[8]*Id. at 463.*

[9]*Id. at 465.*

A Judicial View of Legislative Approaches to Product Liability

Honorable Warren W. Eginton

Editor's Note — This article presents a business management and insurance company approach to resolving the product liability "problem." It also provides some understanding of political realities relating to safety and liability legislative development. It is important that the safety specialist understand that safety law is not a hasty and arbitrary process, but is evolutionary, responsive to many societal demands, and is under constant debate, argument, and compromise. This was adapted by Judge Eginton and updated for this book from a speech he presented on this subject at a Federal Practice Conference of the American Bar Association in June, 1982 in New York City.

On June 16, 1982 the Consumer Subcommittee of the Senate Committee on Commerce, Science and Transportation, chaired by Senator Robert W. Kasten (R-Wisconsin), received for consideration Senate Bill No. 2631, introduced by Senator Kasten in behalf of himself and seven other senators. The bill, designed to reform product liability tort law, was reviewed and debated in the Subcommittee, and reported out on October 1, 1982 to the parent Committee on Commerce, Science and Transportation, chaired by Senator Bob Packwood (R-Oregon) and on the same date the full committee adopted Senate Bill 2631, which was thereafter sent to the Senate floor on November 30, 1982. The bill was not called up for debate or vote prior to the expiration of the 97th Congress, but will presumably be introduced during 1983 by Senator Kasten's and Senator Packwood's committees in substantially its present form for consideration by the 98th Congress.

In sponsoring this legislation, Senator Kasten, as he himself has stated, was hardly pioneering a new approach. In addition to the several bills introduced over the years in the House of Representatives, many can recall the initial senatorial effort of James B. Pearson of Kansas.

Historically the Congress of the United States has directed its attention to two primary areas of legislation, meeting with far more success in one than in the other. Senator Pearson several years ago joined with other federal legislators in promoting a reinsurance concept, and those early efforts culminated in the passage of the *Product Liability Risk Retention Act of 1981, Public Law 97-45* of the 97th Congress. Since that legislation will not affect the judicial approach to product liability litigation, it is outside the scope of this presentation.

More significant to the judicial process was the spearheading effort of Senator Pearson to persuade the Congress to enact a federal product liability and tort reform law. During the course of that protracted effort, he received a liberal education in the complexities of drafting legislation satisfactory to a plurality, let alone a majority, of individuals and entities affected by the product liability explosion. As he advised the author in a philosophical letter just before he resigned from the Senate, he had found the problem virtually impossible of solution and looked with some relief upon the then burgeoning efforts of the Commerce Department's Victor Schwartz to draft a model and hopefully uniform product liability act for adoption by the states. Following the Schwartz interregnum the spotlight has again returned to the congressional efforts to enact federal product liability legislation.

Development of the law respecting product liability is hardly limited to one arena. The activities are so prolific and so varied that even the traditional three-ring circus arena would be insufficient to display all of the acts. Most experts will agree that the origin of legislative attacks lies in *Henningsen v. Bloomfield Motors*[1], the 1960 New Jersey Supreme Court decision that, coincidentally with a spate of California decisions by Justice Traynor, breached, apparently permanently, the long-protective privity barrier.

Debate and discussion among advocates of the various organizations and interests have been and are continuing to devote considerable time, attention and energy to promoting various solutions. Senator Kasten, as his predecessors, has no dearth of input from such organizations as the Association of Trial Lawyers of America on the plaintiff's side, the Defense Research Institute on the defense side, insurance organizations such as the American Insurance Association, corporate counsel, eminent scholars and professors, and representatives of various government task forces. To date, no one would seriously urge that any solution alone, or taken in combination, has accomplished the goals of these interested parties, a development hardly surprising in view of the diversity of objectives and aspirations.

Congress was not the first to test the temperature of the water. Long before Senator Pearson took the legislative plunge, President Lyndon B. Johnson on March 27, 1968, appointed the National Commission on Product Safety. That commission labored for two years, issuing its findings and conclusions in June of 1970 with an admonition that priority must be given to the protection of consumers from "unreasonable product risks." A response from federal and state authorities could be anticipated from the commission report, although it has not turned out to be the uniform response that the Commission recommended.

A major finding of the Commission was that legislation on the state and local level presented a "hodgepodge of tragedy-inspired responses to challenges." (This thesis assumes even more validity in times of fiscal belt tightening such as the nation is currently experiencing.) The commission urged that federal authorities exercise "central leadership" in providing guidance to state and municipal governments for the enactment of appropriate legislation. Specifically the commission found "a need for a major federal role" in the development of product liability legislation.

Some of the offspring of the Commission were not stillborn. From the recommendations of that Commission came the establishment of the Consumer Product Safety Commission in 1973. Thereafter, Congress enacted the Magnuson-Moss Warranty-Federal Trade Commission Improvement Act. However, the application of these acts was quite limited in scope, basically covering consumer products and express warranty provisions. It accordingly became obvious to concerned legislators such as Senator Pearson that treatment with a broader brush would be required. Hence for the past decade bills have been fed into the hoppers of Congress in the areas of reinsurance protection and general tort reform.

In 1976 the Federal Interagency Task Force on Product Liability was created, chaired by Victor E. Schwartz of the Department of Commerce. Following its report, published in November, 1977, the comment draft of the Uniform Product Liability Act (UPLA) was published in January and reissued in final form in October, 1979. UPLA was intended as a model to be enacted, hopefully without major variations or omissions, by state legislatures. The Kasten Bill (it will be so designated for shorthand in this paper) is to be federal legislation, although it specifically is not intended to add any burdens to the already heavily burdened trial courts in the federal system.

This author has previously noted, with some specification, the problems he envisions for the judiciary from the provisions of UPLA.[2] This paper will supplement that earlier review with an examination of problems for the judiciary which may be created by enactment of the Kasten legislation.

Comparison of Kasten to UPLA

As a starting point, let us compare the purposes and goals of UPLA and Kasten, as they impact upon the judiciary. The goals of UPLA, six in number, were clearly set forth in Section 103 (C) of the Act. *There was an understandable desire to place the incentive for loss prevention on the party best able to accomplish such a goal, and a desire to expedite the reparations process from the time of injury to the time of payment on the claim.* There was an equally understandable desire to minimize transaction costs. There was the typical legislative desire to use statutory language that would be "comparatively" clear and concise. However, the critical goals from the standpoint of a trial judge were the first two enunciated in Section 103 (C). The first goal was to insure on the one hand that injured parties would receive "reasonable compensation" for their injuries. This laudable desire conflicts squarely with goal No. 2, which is to insure the availability of "affordable" product liability insurance with "adequate coverage" to protect product sellers. Obviously the legislation embodied in the Product Liability Risk Retention Act of 1981 will help on that score, but inevitably the obligation will rest with the trial judge or jury to perform the balancing task and to weigh the applicability of the quoted modifiers whenever those first two goals come into conflict, which situation will presumably pertain when any serious dispute is involved.

The goal of Kasten, as stated by its author in an interview with Representative Broyhill (R-NC) contained in the *Enterprise* (magazine of the National Association of Manufacturers) issue of December '81/January '82, is for the most part the same as that of UPLA. Representative Broyhill observed that the bill should be one that "balances the rights and obligations of consumers and product sellers." He also stressed the need for uniformity. Senator Kasten noted an effort to use "clarifying language" understandable to "non-lawyers as well as lawyers."

Senator Kasten also mentioned an area in which the bill appears to be more successful than was UPLA. Senator Kasten noted a desire in his bill "to draw a clear division between tort and commercial law, the absence of which has been a primary source of conflicting rules in the states."

This writer called the attention of the Commerce Department to an element of confusion which he discerned in the provisions of UPLA. Although UPLA's scope was not to include direct or consequential economic loss, which would be left to the provisions of the Uniform Commercial Code (see UPLA Section 102 (F) *Harm*), the language of UPLA did not clearly indicate how a court was to deal with injury to or loss of the product itself. In the official analysis issued by the Commerce Department, it was noted that Section 102 (F) "includes damage to the product itself", but in the analysis of Section 103 *Scope of This Act*, it was noted that the Act covers damage to property "other than the product itself."

In any event, the language of Kasten is admirably clear. It notes that "harm" means "damage to property other than the product itself." (Section 2 (5)). In addition Section 3 (b) states that a product liability action does not include any claim for harm "caused to a product itself."

The clarity of the separation of applicable law in Kasten still leaves the courts, both state and federal, with the same problem that this author has criticized about UPLA. It ought first to be conceded that the entire field, as Senator Pearson had commented, is so complex and so controversial that it is virtually impossible for the legislature to enact a comprehensive governing law. It then ought to be conceded that judges are accustomed to being required to apply different laws to different counts of a complaint and to different parties in a civil action. Nevertheless, in the extensive experience of the author as a trial attorney and in his more recent time as a trial judge, *this application of differing standards to essentially the same set of facts in a given case is one of the primary culprits of extended trials and confusion, especially when lay juries are involved.* It often leads to conflicting results in the same case, which induce heightened expectations on the part of a losing party that an appeal may indeed be successful. In some cases the application of the different standards leads to a party being both a winner and a loser in the same case, so that an appeal is almost guaranteed on the part of every party involved.[3]

Section 104 of UPLA has become Section 4 of Kasten, and the problem which the author found for the judiciary in Section 104 carries over to Section 4. Section 4 (a) (2) of Kasten Staff Draft No. 1 provided: "A court may not submit as product liability action to the trier of fact unless the court has determined that sufficient evidence has been admitted to allow a reasonable person, by a preponderance of the evidence, to make the determinations" as to any or more of *the four bases for liability, which are the time-honored yardsticks for product liability: unsafe construction, unsafe design, inadequate warnings or instructions and failure to conform to an express warranty.* In addition to reviewing those four elements, the judge would have to determine that there was a sufficient quantum of evidence as to manufacture of the product by the defendant and as to proximate cause.

Kasten's initial draft apparently contemplated, as did the authors of UPLA, a procedure similar to that of a motion for directed verdict at the close of plaintiff's evidence. If indeed Senator Kasten shares the approach of Professor Schwartz, then it seems obvious that the judiciary was not initially consulted as to whether this language was required in the statute. Courts traditionally entertain motions for directed verdicts at the conclusion of a plaintiff's case with no specific authorization other than the provision common to the Federal Rules of Civil Procedure and to procedures in any state court. *No judge will permit a case to go to the jury if he finds failure to prove a prima facie case and if the defense makes a proper and timely motion.* If, on the other hand the language of Sections 104 of UPLA and initial Section 4 of Kasten were an effort to modify that routine procedure of a trial court, then the legislative language may indicate a desire that a judge make a threshold finding as to defect and proximate cause. Since no guidelines were furnished on this issue, it would seem to this author obvious that a prudent judge would hold a mini-hearing and thus cut down the burden of an extended jury trial (and most product cases are extended). Such mini-hearings are common on issues involving prejudgment attachments in almost all state courts and are common in claims for injunctive relief. Presumably many judges would be tempted to combine the preliminary and final hearings in a product case, as so often is done in hearings on temporary injunctions. This presents no problem if the product case has not been claimed for a jury trial, but in fact most such cases will be so claimed.

In any event, this commentator could not see the need for the referenced provision contained in Section 104 and in Section 4 of the initial Kasten Draft, since it appeared to call for a procedure uniformly applied by the courts in any civil jury trial. Apparently others shared this view, or at least this portion of the first Kasten Draft must have been questioned, because in both a later draft of March 1, 1982 and in the bill as introduced on June 16, 1982, the language of Section 4 was modified to eliminate any reference to a threshold determination by the court. The Section 4 (b) language now reads in positive fashion to the effect that: "The claimant must introduce sufficient evidence to allow a reasonable person, by a preponderance of the evidence, to make the determinations" respecting the four bases for liability. This modification, in the author's subjective judicial opinion, constitutes a significant improvement over the language used in UPLA and in the first Kasten Draft, insofar as it embodies the normal prima facie case requirements.

Sections 4 through 7 of Kasten provide the heart of the legislation. These sections need not dampen the spirits of the army of consultants who have found product liability havens over the past decade. Even a cursory review of Sections 4 through 7 indicates *several prime areas for expert confrontation; 1) Whether a reasonable prudent manufacturer in the same or similar circumstances would have used the particular design; 2) Should the manufacturer have adopted a safer alternative design and would that design have prevented the particular harm; 3) If so, were there adverse effects that the alternative design would have caused to the utility of the product (and this in turn depends upon the social desirability of the product in its intended function); 4) Was the safer alternative design within practical technological feasibility at the time of manufacture; 5) Was the product unavoidably dangerous, in which case again a balancing act as to social utility comes into play; 6) Were the warnings or instructions adequate or, if there were no such adequate warnings or instructions, what would such adequate standards have been in this particular case and would they have avoided the particular harm, and finally; 7) Was the product misused or was the product altered or modified in a manner not to be anticipated by the manufacturer after he had parted with the product.* The mind boggles and the trial judge watches his docket grow longer and the backlogs increase.

As for the balance of Kasten, it omits some of the provisions of UPLA that had caused comment and controversy, especially among the segment of the Bar most closely involved with product liability claims and litigation. For example, Section 107 of UPLA, which this author has termed "state of the art camouflage," is entirely eliminated from Kasten and the only definition guidance retained from UPLA is found in Section 2 (8) wherein a definition of "practical technological feasibility" is provided.

Perhaps the Kasten Bill language is a recognition that, regardless of what terminology legislation may provide, experts are still going to testify in terms of the "state of the art" and the courts are still going to apply the balancing act that was provided under Section 107 of UPLA[4] whether it is authorized or not. In fact, balancing authority is expressly afforded federal judges by Rule 403 of the Federal Rules of Evidence.

Another section of UPLA that has been perhaps wisely omitted from Kasten is Section 109, which this author has termed the "birth of a professional liability area."[5] Kasten does not mandate any responsibilities upon attorneys on either side of product liability litigation, and hence imposes no penalties that could accrue to those attorneys, or sanctions that could affect their clients. Likewise, Section 115 of UPLA[6] has been omitted from Kasten, eliminating another sanctions area probably not required to be set forth in legislation, so long as it is not expressly prohibited by the legislation.

Finally, a section which this author is pleased to see eliminated from Kasten is Section 116 of UPLA, which attempted in somewhat ambiguous fashion to impose upon the parties (with the concurrence of the court) arbitration in suits of less than $50,000.[7] This section was inserted at a time when many professionals of optimistic bent believed that the federal arbitration program might be a success and therefore should be encouraged. As one of five active federal judges in Connecticut who last year unanimously and enthusiastically voted to terminate the arbitration program in Connecticut, I can only applaud its elimination from the Kasten Bill. Unless and until the applicable provisions of the Constitution are repealed, *the absolute right of jury trial will mean inevitably that the arbitration program is a trial balloon for an expensive round of discovery without exposing a party to the risk of a losing verdict.* Arbitration as provided in UPLA means for the judiciary a prospect of duplicate litigation proceedings.

The Kasten Bill provides for a statute of limitations and a statute of repose. Kasten mandates a two-year statute of limitations from the time of discovery of the harm. With respect to the more important statutes of repose, Kasten proposes a flat 25-year repose, with an alternative 10 year presumption with specific exceptions for fraud or prolonged exposure (e.g., asbestos) tacked on in an effort to avoid obvious Constitutional problems.

As to punitive damages, Kasten provides that a court rather than a jury should determine the *amount* of punitive damages, once the jury has made the finding as to whether punitive damages should be awarded at all.

CONCLUSION

Kasten, as did UPLA, appears to represent a step forward in a highly contentious field of increasing importance to litigants and to the courts in which they litigate. This author espouses the common goal of decreasing transaction costs and decreasing litigation docket burdens. The only firm conviction which the author has held for many years is that *all* aspects of product liability, including direct and consequential economic loss, should be included under the provisions of the Act. If all of the state product liability laws can be wiped out by this federal legislation, why not at least make an effort toward combining the commercial aspects of UCC with the tort aspects of Kasten and of UPLA? Certainly anything that can be done to minimize the burden of the trial judge in applying different standards and different guidelines in his charge to the jury would be a consummation devoutly to be desired.

Aside from that, so long as all parties involved realize that no legislation is likely to reduce the traditional necessity of retaining expert testimony, then the legislation can be viewed as enhancing communication in a difficult problem area. For that alone, just as I extended tribute and empathy to Victor Schwartz and his colleagues in previous years, I extend the same to Senator Kasten and his colleagues as they enter the fray.

References

[1]*32 N.J. 358, 161 A. 2d 69, 75 A.L.R. 2d 1 (1960).*

[2]*Eginton, An Unofficial Overview of the Model Uniform Product Liability Act 10 INCL Journal 4 (June 1981).*

[3]*For details of such a horror story in which the author participated see pages 5–7 of the INCL article cited in footnote 2, under the heading "Problems of Coverage Interrelationships."*

[4]*"If the court finds that the probative value of such evidence substantially outweighs its prejudicial effect and that there is no other proof available, this evidence may be admitted for other relevant purposes if confined to those purposes in a specific court instruction. Examples of 'other relevant purposes' include proving ownership or control, or impeachment."*

Product Liability Prevention for Small Businesses

Louis P. Geoffrion, P.E., CQE

Mr. Geoffrion is Director of Quality Control for the Royal Electronics Division of ITT Corp., Pawtucket, R.I. This article is reprinted by permission, originally from the 11th Product Liability Prevention Conference Proceedings, September, 1980, American Society for Quality Control, and later reprinted in the March 1982 issue of ASSE's Professional Safety Magazine.

The problems of product liability in contemporary society are experienced by large and small firms alike. In the viewpoint of the law, the so-called small business person has equal responsibility as General Motors-sized organizations, since whatever the size of the manufacturer, an injured consumer brings suit under the doctrine of strict liability, claiming the right for redress of injury. This article presents some generic guidelines and suggested techniques to allow the small businessperson to develop a product liability prevention system which can be economically and efficiently utilized by a firm with limited resources in people and funds.

The last several years has clearly demonstrated the importance of product liability and product safety in this country and, to some extent, in the world. Large companies that have been subjected to product liability lawsuits have developed effective product liability prevention programs, because of their broad breadth of management and management knowledge as well as their engineering disciplines and the insurance risk management responsibilities of their insurers.

Product liability problems occur in small business, as well as large. The potential magnitude of product liability problems may be disproportionately large for a small businessperson, since larger firms have many more alternatives for the absorption and conversion of expenses relative to not only the prevention of product liability problems but also the financial judgments associated with liability lawsuits. These resources may be totally unavailable to a small business.

Nevertheless, the responsibility of management, large or small, for addressing product liability prevention is clearly demonstrable to any person who is at all current with recent activity in the courts of our land. Fiduciary responsibilities of any owner to the viability of the small business require addressing this problem appropriately. At the same time, the small businessperson often has limited resources to devote to product liability prevention. These limited resources may initiate, in the manager or owner of a small business, the thought that, with all the other problems and demands on available personnel, including the owner or manager himself, nothing can be done; and therefore, nothing is done.

Over and above any economic imperative for addressing product liability prevention, legislative imperatives exist, in the area of consumer products, through the Consumer Product Safety Act and through the operations and activites of the Consumer Product Safety Commission. The Act does not distinguish between large and small companies. It only addresses consumer product safety.

I am sure that many are familiar with the economic dislocation and burdens imposed on small textile manufacturers several years ago, following the flame-retardant, cancer-scare hearings. The popular press and business magazines covered the subject in greater or lesser detail. I attended Congressional hearings and heard small business owners describe to a panel of Congressmen and the media, how they had been put out of business by attempting to comply with government safety regulations with which they had no financial or management resources to comply adequately.

I maintain that it is possible for a small businessperson to adequately develop and operate a product liability prevention program with a concern for scale and resources. It will still provide the desired prevention level that can be economically derived — certainly in the long term, if not in the short. The product liability prevention program can best be operated, in my opinion, within the context of an adequate quality assurance or quality control system. Again, this is a system which is vital for the achievement of profit and can be operated even within a very small organization with limited resources.

REQUIREMENTS FOR THE PROGRAM

Certain basic things are required for any program such as a product liability prevention program. I shall enumerate them, discuss each one briefly, and give some specific information indicating the utility of each part of the program.

The first part of developing a good product liability prevention program is for the head of the firm to clearly, simply and as a matter of record, enunciate a statement of policy. This statement should cite the reasons that necessitate the development of a policy, including any statutory or financial obligations, as well as any ethical or moralistic beliefs, which are often appropriate to statements of broad policy. The policy must be very clear in its placement of product safety as the overall guiding principle of the design, development, production and distribution of the products that the firm produces. Applicability of this policy to all aspects of the company's operation, including sales, engineering, etc., should also be stated. In addition, a reference to emphasis on product safety and product quality should be made to vendors and suppliers. This statement should be publicized through all parts of the organization, and can serve as a basis for subsequent planning.

Often, people who have been in business for a while have been exposed to various policy statements within their own firms or at customer or vendor firms. Many times, whatever it applies to — whether it's equal opportunity in employment, the importance of the customer, personal integrity of employees, etc. — it is perceived as being mere platitude or camouflage. This is perhaps because the statements often are not reflective of the personality or needs of the particular organization in question.

A policy statement can be very simple and very short, and, for the small firm, should probably be just that. If there is no statement of policy, and especially, if there is no document called a policy statement, everyone is unsure as to what the policy is. Members of the firm, customers, government regulators, and competitive attorneys cannot describe or refer to any document. In defending a product liability case, the owner of the firm would have to rely on verbal statements which often have minimal impact in a courtroom situation. Anyone who has written a policy has already discovered that the mere process of thinking about the policy often reveals problems, structural arrangements which may cause problems, and voids in control measures, all of which often would never have been revealed without the mental exercise of putting words to paper.

ORGANIZATION

The organizational requirements of small business for the control and administration of a product liability prevention program are, on the one hand, much simpler than for a large business. And yet on the other hand, are sometimes more difficult, since, as stated above, many of the functions that are required for any product liability program may be performed by one or two individuals. Therefore, it is difficult to provide a hard and fast structure or organization for a small business, although there are some certain and simple guidelines which should be followed.

One of the simplest ways for a small business to organize is to utilize the concept of a product liability or product safety advisory committee. (See Figure 1.) This is a universal outline which would be applicable to a large or a small firm.[3] You will note that the headings of the various functions are: (1) sexless and (2) broad descriptions of function and responsibility. This structure may actually be represented by one person.

In a specific recent consulting experience, I assisted a very small business which was composed of one energetic, bright engineer, his wife, and four high school students. They had embarked on the fabrication and distribution of a tool which enabled people who had undergone cataract lens removal operations to easily insert and remove contact lenses. Due to his previous employment with a large firm, this individual was well aware of product liability problems and knew that he must do something to prevent and anticipate problems within his firm.

For the moment, let us assume that a small business has a few more employees and performs the basic functions of defining a market need, establishing a product design, developing a method of manufacturing the design, accomplishing the manufacturing, evaluating the capability of the product to meet its design objectives through testing, inspection or other assurance activity, and, finally, accomplishing distribution of the product to the consumer.

Perhaps the first figure is too limiting, even for a small business. Perhaps the next figure helps to outline what I have in mind. (See Figure 2.) The functions are the predominant elements in the figure, and I have added, parenthetically, labels which may help the reader in associating this conceptual outline structure to his or her own organization. Depending on the size of the organization, the ultimate authority could possibly be the only person charged with execution of the product liability prevention policy of the company.

In a somewhat larger organization which has individuals filling the various slots that I have presented, some other individual may have that responsibility as a delegated, specific task. I suggest that this responsibility may be adequately delegated to the head of the quality assurance or quality control department, since one of the fundamental quality characteristics of a product is that it be safe in its operations.

Whatever organizational structure is decided upon by our small businessperson, that structure and the responsibilites of the elements of that structure should be formalized in writing and made available to all of the personnel involved in this matter.

An immediate question, important to any organization, may be, "What about costs?" Certainly, if nothing has been done to develop an organization's response to product safety needs, costs will then have to be incurred, whether they are measured directly in dollars and cents, or whether they are equated in terms of man-hours or resources available from a limited resource base. Total avoidance of product liability problems is difficult in today's marketplace. "Costs now or costs later?" may be the question which must be answered by the small businessperson in deciding whether or not to undertake a product liability prevention program. A program which is structured around contemporary ideas of quality assurance practitioners will

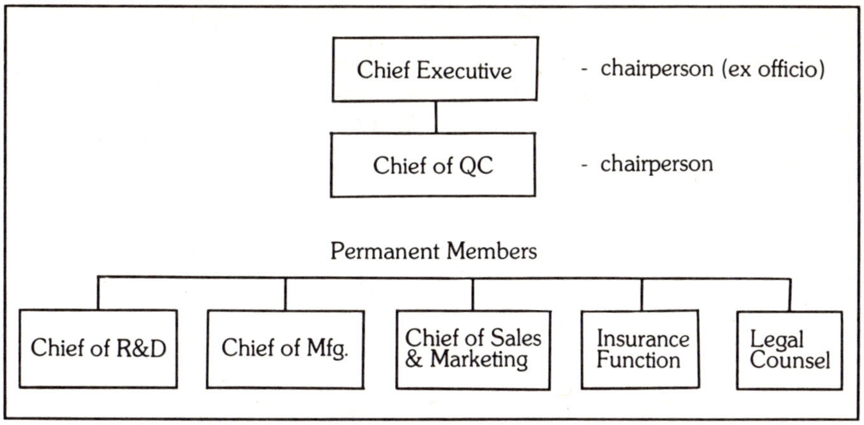

Figure 1 Product safety advisory committee

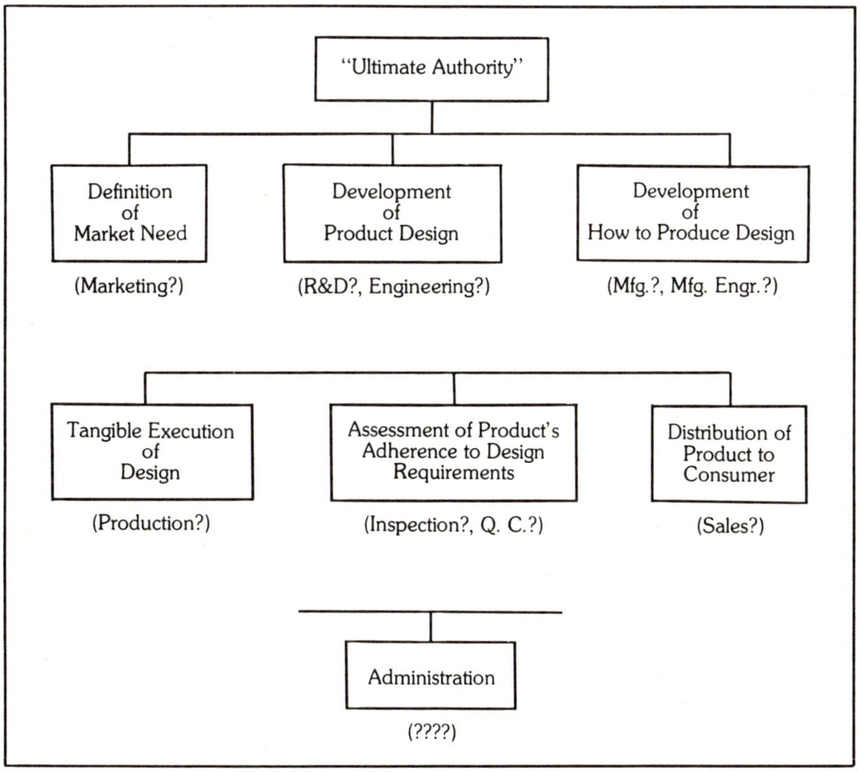

Figure 2 Product safety functions

hopefully produce the profit results which will help justify this program.

COMMUNICATION

Depending again on the size of the organization, the policy and organization decisions must be communicated to the people in the organization who are responsible for carrying out the policy. Education and training in the mechanics of program administration must be an on going activity of the members of the firm, since the state of the art in product liability is changing frequently, as, of course, is the state of the art in new product design in most industries. The level of sophistication of any communication or training is clearly a function of the size of the organization, and, I don't believe that it is important to discuss it significantly at this time.

There are many aspects of the implementation of a prevention program applicable to small business. Quite a few of them can be equated with other operational programs. I will discuss only those which have some specific merit for the small businessperson.

PRODUCT DESIGN

Product design is the most significant aspect of product safety. Safety begins in a thought process, not in a product. This thought process is that of the initial designer. It occurs before pencil point touches drafting board. The initial considerations which are applied to that process known as creativity must be influenced by product safety considerations. For guidance in this area, I refer the reader to the many publications available on the topic of product design, including the recent work by Messrs. Weinstein, Twerski, Piehler, and Donaher[4] and the excellent pamphlet by M. F. Biancardi.[5]

The most effective method of insuring that the product design function includes safety, is to accomplish a formal design review prior to the production of the item designed. The technical literature adequately discusses what design reviews should consist of. A quick summary here provides for:

(1) The identification and evaluation of potential safety risks which may derive from the use or abuse of the product. The risks must be evaluated against criteria defining such things as age of the user, environmental considerations attendant to the product's normal or abnormal use, and other relevant items.

Those risks relating to injury should be carefully segregated from the risks associated with product nonperformance or product nonfunctioning which may produce an uninjured but dissatisfied consumer. This is, after all, a design review with product safety as its prime function.

Other characteristics may be secondary, though integrated for economy of resources. The design review must be performed by someone other than the designer to insure objectivity and unbiased viewpoint.

(2) The design review must be documented and preserved as a matter of record for any future litigation possibility.

Following the establishment of a product design, it is important that the firm establish a system of control which insures that the design is produced as desired. This is normally provided for by the use of a so-called drawing and change control system. Appropriate specifications, drawings, procedures, methods sheets, and other instructions to the production personnel must be maintained, following normal good business practice. Changes to the original design and careful documentation must be preserved. An additional element of this documentation should include a discussion of the reason for the change.

Whenever elements of the product must be purchased from sources outside the small business, carefully detailed purchase orders (or preferably purchase specifications) should be utilized for all procurement activity. Certainly, most firms, large or small, have a formal method of contracting for obligations for materials.

Those elements of a product's design which are controlled by other than company people, should be adequately controlled through use of clearly defined specifications. In addition, purchase documents should establish the need for such inspection records as finished product test data, certificates of compliance, and other indications of vendor decision-making as to product suitability. Certainly, each vendor should be formally advised of the need for safety in the products delivered to the small business.

We could devote days to the discussion of the many ways that product safety or product liability prevention could be implemented during the production of the product. There are certain things which must be considered, such as control of materials, control of semi-finished assemblies and other aspects of process control. Though they may be very simple in nature, appropriate work instructions are a necessity and documentation is required to insure that the integrity of the design is maintained.

If the product requires special processes that generate characteristics with difficult assessment requirements, the employer should consider the introduction of personnel qualification methods, for example, specific welding techniques or NDT processes. Due to economic considerations, the inspection activities, which define the product conformance, may not be inclusive of all special processes. Whatever activities are performed in the area of special processes should be recorded and made a part of the firm's records to substantiate the state of control of the process.

QUALITY ASSURANCE

The quality control or quality assurance function is generally understood by most individuals today to include those activities of a manufacturer which determine the suitability of a product against certain criteria. Again, volumes are available to discuss specific QC activities. The small businessperson should insure that at some part of the manufacturing/distribution cycle, a specific quality determination against criteria be performed and most importantly, be recorded to help provide adequate documentation of the activity. Again, this documentation may be vital for future litigation.

Where the quality verification activity includes

the use of sample testing or other statistical methods, there should be, within the quality instruction, a statement and understanding of the need for sampling and the basis upon which the sample plan was derived.

Business, large or small, does not perform perfectly all the time. Production often will produce items which do not conform to the design requirements. The quality verification function must provide a positive control to insure that non-conforming material is removed from the stream of production, that the non-conforming material is made acceptable or is discarded with appropriate safeguards, and, most importantly, that the cause of the non-conformity is determined and corrected. Again, documentation, evidence of control, is important.

In my experience, one aspect of quality activities which is often overlooked by small business is the necessity for calibration of instruments and measuring devices. It is often uneconomical for a business with limited staff to attempt calibration with internal resources. There are many companies who provide contract calibration services which a small businessperson can profitably utilize.

Two criteria are important in the selection of any outside calibration service. The first is sufficiency or traceability to the National Bureau of Standards on the part of the calibration. The second is some good system of instrument control, status indication, recall notification and calibration record system. Without this paperwork, the activity will be compromised if litigation research ensues.

DISTRIBUTION

When I use the term, "distribution," I refer to a much broader concept than the classic notion that distribution is related to shipping and warehousing. By distribution, I am attempting to encompass all of the aspects which interface the producer and the consumer. Yes, shipping, warehousing, packaging, are all parts of distribution, but, in addition, I consider sales or sales administration, field engineering, distributors, and so forth, to all be part of that generic term.

Some parts of the distribution process, which a small businessperson must consider from the product safety viewpoint, can start with packaging. Adequate packaging methods and materials, which will insure the protection of the product from the shipping environment, are essential. The selection of these materials should be a part of the design process and should not be left to the judgment of the technician at the shipping door.

In addition to these simple considerations, the package should include protection against anticipated deterioration. For example, you may wish to require a desiccant be made a part of the pack to prevent corrosion. If the product has a shelf life, labels indicating this shelf life should be made a part of the package design. If there are specific environmental requirements for storage, then care and consideration should be given to the method of communicating the storage requirements to insure that they will be followed.

Handling methods, which can reasonably be expected to be used during the shipping process, must be anticipated to prevent damage during shipping. Provisions for the inclusion of any assembly or installation instructions and the verification of their presence comprise another part of the distribution system.

There is another part of distribution which I call consumer communication links. These links may include customer service functions; they may also include distributors, field sales personnel, order-entry sales administration personnel, or other types of people who have direct or indirect links with wholesale retailers, or ultimately, with end-use consumers. These people are an important part of the distribution system, because they may initiate the business and certainly, often have the only way of determining the consumer's true needs for product capability.

Mechanisms for capturing and documenting this consumer information should be a part of any small business, since one of the elements of implied warranty (that is, fitness for use as defined within the Commercial Code) is based on a seller's knowledge of the user's intended use environment or the purpose to which the user will subject the product. With this knowledge, the sale creates an implied warranty. Therefore, it is important in the product liability prevention format to also consider commercial liability. That is, although the product may not produce an injury to a person, it may not function adequately, thereby generating a claim against the producer, which may also require extensive legal expense and effort.

Other types of communcation which must be carefully documented fall under the broad category of customer complaints. A method for detecting, recording, and analyzing complaints, and a feedback mechanism should be established to insure that any customer-generated observations, which indicate either an inadequacy of product to perform or any hazards associated with the product, are communicated to the responsible parts of the small business organization as rapidly and as efficiently as possible. An early detection system has saved many a manufacturer from extended and expensive liabilities by quick reaction to the first indications of a possible problem related to safety.

Here, as in other parts of a small business operation, simple uncomplicated forms can be utilized by personnel who are handling the customer's communication effort, provided that they understand the needs and a mechanism is provided allowing them to use the information efficiently. Once again, for practicality and whenever possible, the focus for all of the information processes can be the quality assurance function within the organization.

ADMINISTRATION

The final part of our theoretical organizational structure is labeled "Administration." There are a lot of question marks here, because this is an area which has the most potential for variability in a small organization.

I am sure that in many small organizations, administration is handled by the secretary to the company. In other, somewhat larger companies, we may have an office manager who takes care of everything, including the contract for the trash collection. Whoever in the organization coordinates such things as insurance, the activity of attorneys, consultants, and so forth, probably should have the additional responsibility of integrating any product liability interface requirements. Since this area is so variable, I will leave it to the reader to recognize that the liaison must be done and to devise appropriate methods applicable to the specific requirement.

DOCUMENTATION/RESPONSIBILITY

I have attempted to address some of the basic concerns for any product liability prevention program, by focusing on my understanding and experience of the needs of the typical small business. Obviously, some of the material that I have presented is appropriate to a large firm as well, though complexity and personnel availability certainly generate a different response to the implementation requirements of a program. In summary, I believe that adequate documentation and assignment of responsibility, combined with the careful attention to product safety in the design stage, will provide the small businessperson with reasonable protection against product liability problems.

There is one area which I believe is important to call to your attention and which I feel is difficult for the small businessperson to properly respond to — that is, the necessity to remain constantly alert to changing conditions. We know that there has been recent legislation affecting product safety in a number of states.[6]

It is difficult for a small businessperson to remain current. The normal firm is too small to allow the luxury of having one individual be assigned the responsibility of keeping tabs. Nevertheless, it is important to stay current. Membership in and participation in the educational activities of professional societies at the local level are useful and effective ways of learning.

References

1. *Ungles, William H., Product Risk Management for Small Business, 1971*
2. *Scerbo, Ferdinand A., Product Liability Prevention Techniques for the Small Manufacturer, 1973*
3. *Geoffrion, Louis P., "Contribution of Q.C. to Product Liability Risk Aversion," 1978 ASQC Technical Conference Transactions*
4. *Weinstein, Alvin S. et al., Products Liability and the Reasonably Safe Product, 1978.*
5. *Biancardi, M. F., "Design for Product Safety," Society of Automotive Engineers, 1970*
6. *Jacobs, R. M., "Effect of the Model Uniform Product Liability Act on Quality Assurance," 1980 ASQC Technical Conference Transactions*

What to do About Product Liability

George A. Peters, J. D.

Most of Mr. Peters extensive litigation experience is in the product liability area. Here he offers some practical hints to manufacturers on product safety and its impact on product liability. This essay is reprinted by permission from the September 1980 issue of Professional Safety Magazine.

During the past 20 years, we have seen a series of major changes in the law regarding product liability. The number of lawsuits and the amount of damages awarded have rapidly escalated. Insurance premiums have reflected these rising costs; appropriate insurance coverage has become more complicated. Risk management has become something of an art. Cries for tort reform blamed the legal system, the insurance system, or consumerism in general. Gradually, what seemed to be simple causes and quick solutions have been transformed into more substantive understanding and realistic appraisals of what to do about product liability.

Some industrial enterprises have become entrapped by product liability, despite vigorous and sometimes costly efforts. We have seen other companies seize upon affirmative responses, place their competitors at an economic disadvantage, gain marketplace penetration, and even reduce the production costs. Rarely did this occur as a result of routine stratagems. It seems that a very specific, tailored, and innovative approach is necessary.

Background

Much of product liability involves third party actions for workplace injuries. The Occupational Safety and Health Act of 1970 was debated and enacted by Congress because there were too many workplace injuries. OSHA has had about nine years to promulgate safety regulations, impose compliance, inspect and penalize, threaten and educate, at great direct cost and indirect economic burden. Injury rates and product liability actions for industrial products have not declined. But I believe that OSHA has scored some small successes and that the real lesson to be learned is that safety is not simplistic nor can it be legislated or delegated away.[1]

The Consumer Product Safety Act was enacted in 1972. If it had worked as intended, product liability for consumer products would have declined. Instead, it has increased. Perhaps too much was expected from those who are not directly involved in the design, manufacture, and marketing of products.

In terms of automotive product liability, in 1978 the National Highway Traffic Safety Administration announced the recalls of nine million motor vehicles and nearly 15 million tires, in 270 recall campaigns. While consumer activists complain about what is being done by the NHTSA, the automobile industry complains of the excessive costs, burdens, and loss of innovative technological progress associated with such efforts at accident prevention. Injury rates and product liability actions remain intolerably high for automotive vehicles.

We do not have a "national policy" on safety nor liability, only fragmented approaches. However, there is one type of consolidation that is important. We are witnessing attempts to obtain a more uniform, predictable, and simplified set of product liability laws on a national basis in the United States, between nations in Europe, and, to a lesser degree, among all industrialized nations involved in international or worldwide commerce and industry.[2]

Non-uniform laws open the door to marketing pressures relative to competitive selling price, perceived regional needs, as well as targeted dumping and selective disposal of discrepant items likely to cause harm. Uniform product liability laws would provide the assurance of predictability and easier translation of the law (in terms of product requirements for safety). Obviously, better knowledge of the legal requirements would significantly eliminate the cause of the losses; because, quite simply, no injury means no loss. Fewer injuries, fewer lawsuits. The less the perceived safety problem, the less the perceived need for laws and regulations. Relative to the development of uniform product liability laws, it appears that the learning processes involved in compromising or balancing *all interests* suggests that some form of strict liability in tort will become the worldwide basis for formulating product design and quality assurance criteria.

In essence, the ultimate remedy for product liability does not rest upon development of safety standards nor their use in defense, it does not rest with regulatory agencies even if they attempt to be supportive, nor is there salvation in some simple remedies. Uniform product liability laws alone are not likely to ease the stress, even through they promise great benefits to many companies with sophisticated product liability prevention programs.

Product safety programs

Different companies have adopted different product safety programs. For example, the general philosophy of one illustrative effort has the following seven elements:

1. *Programmatic*. Identify the legal requirements for safety, then negotiate an implementing document or abbreviated set of program objectives for each function involved, and then monitor and audit to assure that the tasks are being performed in a cost-effective and results-oriented manner. The philosophy is that a vague program produces vague results; whereas, a clearly defined program can be assessed, modified, and eventually converted into something that is meaningful and productive. If possible, avoid unnecessary procedures and formalisms; keep it simple, so that the ultimate objectives do not become clouded and lost.

2. *Feedback*. Establish a means by which the lessons learned, both historical and on going, from diverse sources, can be utilized and brought to focus on critical decision-making in a timely fashion. Relevant facts should be in some tangible form, not held only in the fallible minds of opinionated transitory personnel. Keep the expert knowledge of other people available in terms of relevant books, manuals, articles, and brochures on competitive products. Consider using a consumer appeals board for complaints and feedback to supplement dealer and service representative information.

3. *Emphasis*. The early identification of all probable hazards is necessary if there is to be appropriate risk reduction and control. It is too costly to focus primarily on accidents or losses as they occur; that is, after-the-fact corrective and defensive tactics. The emphasis should be predictive and preventive.

4. *Analysis*. Risk assessment necessarily includes, at the very least, some brief analysis of facts relating to the frequency and severity of accidents, the cost and technical feasibility of reducing the risk of harm, and the need or utility of the item. Otherwise, decisions on whether something is safe or unsafe may be hurried, based on ill-informed personal opinions; opinions lacking any substance in terms of real facts or balances between competing considerations. The true risks and considerations associated with each hazard should be made known for management decisions. Engineers should "sign-off" personally to certify the safety of the item or process.

5. *Scope*. The safety of products should be assessed for the predictable uses, the range of anticipated users, for each stage of its manufacture, and for wear out, malfunction, failure, and ultimate disposal processing. It should consider manufacturing defects as well as design defects, warranties and representations; and be from cradle-to-grave.

6. *Testing*. There should be appropriate testing to demonstrate the absence (or risk control) of hazards, in the service environment, and the testing should involve those likely to use or be harmed by the product. Where possible, safety tests should be verified by external or independent laboratories.

7. *Recordkeeping*. Keep records to prove that safety analysis and testing were in fact performed, provide for product identification and traceability consistent with recall or modification planning documents, provide supplemental descriptive information for future briefing of counsel and outside experts, do not destroy records in the immediate future. Maintain a list of standards that apply to the product and indicate compliance.

Liability mitigation

A product liability mitigation program might include the following five elements:

1. *An Accident Reporting System*. If any employee becomes aware of an accident, he is to telephone a 24-hour central station in the legal department. The responsible department receives an accident report and within 24 hours a decision is made whether to investigate. A minimum sized accident team departs for the accident site the next day, and a separate investigation, data gathering, and reconstruction are conducted. All stages of the accident investigation process are pre-planned, personnel trained, and the team rehearsed. (Incidentally, some companies have found it more appropriate to create an accident reporting system that relies heavily on their independent distributors, despite problems of re-education and information transmittal because of customer contact with proximity.)

2. *Education*. If a claim is filed, the legal department receives everything regarding the equipment such as operating manuals, engineering drawings, and trouble reports. A special file for this purpose is to be maintained on every product designed and manufactured. Education of outside defense counsel occurs prior to discovery. There is training on legal theories and courtroom demeanor for key employees.

3. *Designated product safety representative*. He maintains a list of in-house and independent expert witnesses. Assists outside counsel in selection of expert based on suitability for local juries. Coordinates internal discovery process, including contact with different sources of information, screening for compatability, and integration of responses.

4. *Document review*. Language on report forms should be legally appropriate and not misleading; no room for cursory remarks on report forms, and a patterned system so nothing goes unresolved.

5. *Recall*. Recalls should be preplanned, documented, and exercised in the form of mock recalls. There should be up-to-date information on types of recall, with options and costs.

Product safety techniques

A product safety engineer may assure that certain safety principles are applied in the design of a product, or a consultant might be retained for an occasional safety assurance review. This assures application of fail-safe features (such as fail-off, fail-slow, and fail-with-warning). It includes such design-for-safety principles as fault tolerant design, warning devices, dual load path, derating, environmental insensitivity, debugging, suppression isolation, shielding, part deactivation, part-out capability, redundancy, crashworthiness, seaworthiness, fireworthiness, and escapeworthiness. The problem is not in the availability of design safety concepts, but in their imaginative application at low cost. Design review procedures and technical audit of processes and procedures may be desirable. Remember, this is specific self-help technical prevention of future product liability lawsuits!

There are several commonly used design analysis techniques to assure a systematic identification of all probable hazards and for risk assessment. First, some version of a failure mode and effect analysis. Second, a fault tree analysis. There are several other types of specialized hazard analysis techniques, criticality analysis, and sets of risk classification criteria. The point is that there are organized ways to discover and eliminate potential product liability lawsuits during the early design process.

Defect criteria

According to product liability law, there are two types of design defect or near-objective criteria as to whether something is safe or unsafe. The first is "ordinary consumer expectations"; that is, the product may be found defective if it failed to perform as safely as an ordinary consumer would expect. Thus, we are concerned with discovering these expectations and not creating expectations that set the stage for lawsuits. The second type of design defect is "excessive preventable danger"; that is, that the risk of danger outweighs its benefits. This means that we perform a risk benefit analysis considering and balancing the following factors: (1) the likelihood or probability of injury, (2) the severity of the injury, (3) the technical feasibility of remedies, (4) the cost of an improved design, (5) other hazards and risks created by the improved design, (6) the utility or social usefulness of the product, and (7) the availability of a safer substitute. The risk benefit analysis is important; it may be required testimony on the part of your defense expert in a product liability trial and it provides meaningful risk assessment information for management.

In terms of manufacturing defects, the quality assurance engineer is faced with three independent definitions. First, the old specification conformance definition of a defect. Second, the newer user requirements definitions. Third, the brand new deviation from the norm or maverick product definition.

Significant trends

There is also a decline in the contributory negligence defense and a transition to pure comparative negligence, wherein each party pays according to his degree of fault. This comparative responsibility doctrine has two important ramifications for the product safety engineer. First, his accident investigations should not determine who is at fault, but rather the proportionate fault of all those responsible; so he must think in terms of multiple causation. Second, this emphasizes knowledge of human fault, already emphasized in legal concepts of liability for predictable human misuse, abuse, improper servicing, inadequate repairs, and failure to understand warnings and instructions. Thus, testing with human subjects is increasingly important, but he must understand the informed consent and ethical obligations relative to human research.

Once a lawsuit is underway, your primary guidance and counsel should flow from the local defense counsel, although larger companies are broadly expanding the scope, function, and experience of in-house counsel. Avoid commonplace misunderstandings of the nature of the adversary process and the role of its participants. I have noticed that, of 1,572 lawsuits going to jury verdict in Los Angeles during the past five years, there have been verdicts for the defense in 39% of the cases overall and with no significant trend (i.e., 39.3 ± 3.7% per year). This suggests that discovery and settlement are working well in Los Angeles. Hopefully, elsewhere, there is open discovery (sunshine) and settlement (business-like compromises based on claim evaluation and risks prior to the expense and uncertainties of trail).

Conclusion

Those who are now vulnerable to product liabiity lawsuits are those who remain ignorant of the applicable law, who are antagonistic to our system of law in either an antisocial or asocial manner, who attempt to apply quick homemade palliative adhesive bandages to safety problems, who fail to institute a systematic effort to comply with the law, or who fail to seek competent assistance to help solve technical and managerial problems related to safety.

In essence, there is no secret as to what the law requires in terms of product safety, the methods and techniques to achieve those requirements are known, so vulnerability to product liability has to become a matter of choice and appropriate financial risk management.

Footnotes

1. It can be argued that reports of increased injury frequencies should be adjusted to reflect increases in the work force. However, an opposite adjustment would be appropriate for the decreases in injury normally expected from sources unrelated to the actions of government agencies. For example, technological improvements relating to safety, better knowledge and training concerning accident prevention, improved loss control services by insurance carriers and higher premiums, the effect of labor union safety programs, the increasing professionalism of safety specialists, the effect of significant changes in media communications and general sensitivity to safety engendered by consumerism, the effects of lawsuits and court orders, and the role of the National Safety Council and other safety organizations. Perhaps, after all adjustment or balancing, the "bottom

line" for the taxpayers would be how much it cost per life saved or injury prevented, for each of the various alternative programs. Regardless of approach, the balance shows either a statistically negative or socially insignificant accident prevention result. Comparisons are then made to the recent experiences in England that suggest that a citizen's blue ribbon panel evaluation might find remedies that could produce dramatic reductions in workplace injuries at less cost. Whatever the truth of the matter, the bottom line results have been disappointing and alternatives should be studied and considered.

2. Dr. Leo Greenberg of New York has been engaged in comparative studies of safety programs in various countries, their characteristics and effectiveness, and their relation to national safety policies expressed or implied. Results of these studies will be available.

New Dimensions in the Tortious Failure to Warn

Harry M. Philo, Esq.

This article on the latest developments in the emerging problems of warning signs and labels is reprinted by permission from Trial Magazine of the Association of Trial Lawyers of America, and from the author. Mr. Philo, an ASSE member, is a prominent product liability attorney who is associated with the Detroit firm of Philo, Atkinson, Steinberg, Walker and White. He is past president of ATLA.

On January 15, 1969, the National Machine Tool Builders Association mailed out Accident Prevention and Safety Bulletin No. 69-4 which said in relevant part:

"The Metal Forming Subcommittee of the Association's Accident Prevention and Safety Committee has concluded its evaluation of a warning sign for use by this segment of the Machine Tool Industry. The Committee believes that the use of *warning signs can be of prime importance in helping to eliminate accidents. The proper use of warning signs can also reduce possible exposure to product liability suits.*

"The signs have been designed to afford adequate and readable instructions to the operator of the machine on which it is installed.

"Embossing of the sign provides a three-dimensional appearance to improve readability. The three colors used, black, white and red, are in accordance with guidelines found in U.S.A.S.I. Standard Z-35." (Emphasis added.)

The Bulletin is particularly illustrative of many points this article will seek to make:

1) The year 1969 represents the approximate turning point in the recognition of what products liability means to product safety; the social purpose of tort law is accident prevention. The tort law, which historically had given business a legal license to kill and maim, was beginning to eliminate that privilege in sufficient degree as to be recognized by a major association of manufacturers.

2) The preparation of a warning is very sophisticated business.

3) Warnings are of prime importance to the elimination of accidental injuries and deaths.

4) Warnings require standards and conformance to standards, and standards were in existence.

5) Warnings must be on the product or machine itself.

6) The low level of safety consciousness of industry generally required that an industry association remedy the failure of the individual companies and even produce subsequent modification signs. The signs, which were aluminum and which cost from 40 cents to 70 cents, were intended for placement on machines which sold in six and seven figures.

THE TRIAL LAWYER'S ROLE

The design engineer *who has done a proper failure mode and effect analysis* and recognized the hazardous uses of a product, evaluated the risk of injury and understood the gravity of that risk, and further determined that the risk was unreasonable and unacceptable often is in the position that neither the hazard not the risk can be eliminated reasonably by guarding, interlocking, fail-safe-ing or nontoxic substitutes. There remains a risk of serious injury or death. Reasonable prudence requires a warning which describes the hazard, alerts of the grave risk, states the safety engineering alternative and often details emergency treatment, if injury occurs. Let us then examine the purpose, the history of, and the quality of necessary warnings.

We must do this because no one else has. Just as trial lawyers are forced every day to redesign products for safety and discover the etiology of chemical insult, so too are we forced to bring together the work of all the various disciplines concerned with warnings and their adequacy.

The prudent preparation of the warnings so necessary for societal safety combines the expertise of:

1) The safety engineer who is trained in the recognition of hazards and risks through use of the tools of the safety profession;

2) The psychologist or the human factors engineer concerned additionally with understanding the lack of hazard and risk recognition of those with simple "common sense";

3) The semanticist who understands that the intended meaning of a writer does not necessarily coincide with what is the understanding of the reader; and

4) The graphic artist trained to recognize the color combinations, signal words, kind of type, size of type, attaching mechanisms, etc., to meet the purpose of a warning.

While trial lawyers often have the luxury of hindsight, the prudent design engineer must either combine the aforementioned skills or employ consultants with the necessary sophistication.

When the trial lawyer seeks to understand the

history, purpose, and scope of warnings, it becomes obvious that neither lawyers, judges, nor the law are as yet with it when it comes to the law and warnings.

HISTORY

Accident prevention signs probably have been used longer than any other safety device or piece of safety equipment. In fact, they were probably used even before 1450, when Scotland enacted the first statutes governing product hazards. The first American standards governing warning signs appeared in 1914 in a book titled *Universal Safety Standards*. One chapter or section was called "Standards For Danger And Safety Signs." The concepts, approaches, and specifications are similar to what we have today in the American National Standards Institute's Z35.1 Standards.

Many American industries have made some good faith efforts to prevent accidental injuries and deaths by use of warnings. The only industries to deliberately violate everything that has been learned historically about warnings are the pharmaceutical and cosmetics industries which hide and obscure the necessary information about the dangers or inadequacies of their drugs and cosmetics. They, as one might expect, have been given the broadest license to kill and maim by backward common law decisions which grant them protection against paying damages for much of their culpability.

We have long had standard specifications for industrial accident prevention signs. The Manufacturing Chemists Association first published its *Guide to Precautionary Labeling of Hazardous Chemicals* 36 years ago, and it became an ANSI Standard in 1976. The *Uniform Traffic Control Device Manual* of the federal government, detailing the color, shape, placement, and purpose of every highway device, has been incorporated by reference in the statutes of each state for decades. It includes the warrants for and details of railroad grade crossing warnings. It has for more than 15 years described the kind and quality of highway construction warnings. The Federal Caustic Act of 1927 covered mainly the labeling of some caustic corrosive chemicals intended for household use. The Pure Food, Drug and Cosmetic Art of 1938 was passed with the pretense of requiring adequate warnings on the labels of all drugs. The Federal Insecticide, Fungicide and Rodenticide Law of 1947 mandated labels with warning statements on economic poisons. The Interstate Commerce Commission (ICC) by regulation requires particular warning labels on explosives and dangerous materials when they are shipped in interstate commerce.

The United Nations, through UNESCO and the International Labour Organization, has been attempting with some success since 1955 to get international signal words and symbols with universal recognition.

The Consumer Product Safety Commission (CPSC) has attempted to mandate and has also suggested warnings for such diverse products as water slides and football helmets, among other things. It has jurisdiction over conformance with the Federal Hazardous Substances Act which governs warnings on products which may foreseeably be used in the household.

When one understands the extremely low level of safety consciousness in the United States and the absurd level of attempted warnings which have been given historically, it is readily recognizable that there is presently a climate which underestimates the tool of warnings as a major accident prevention device. There is, however, an unconscious recognition that exhortations to "be careful," "operate your machine safely," and "drive safely" have caused more injuries and deaths than they ever prevented. Warnings constitute a much higher level of sophistication in communication. A failure in communication is near-conclusive evidence of negligent design.

We have had safety color codes for marking physical hazards since 1945. There has been a separate code for warning tags since 1966. There has been national recognition of the safety movement in the United States since the first national conference on industrial safety was held in 1912. All participants in the safety movement at that time used safety signs.

We have long had scores of companies producing safety signs and decals and buying booths at the scores of conferences and seminars.

THE PURPOSES OF WARNINGS

In examining the purposes of warnings, it may first be desirable to detail what warnings are not.

1) In safety engineering a warning is never enough if one can do better. If the hazard can be eliminated reasonably, then it must be eliminated. Zero danger results. If the risk can be eliminated reasonably, then it must be eliminated. Zero danger results. If the hazard can be reduced reasonably, then it must be reduced. If the risk can be reduced reasonably, then it must be reduced.

The next step in safety engineering is instructions for safe and effective use and warnings against risks that may cause injury and death.

2) An inadequate warning is no warning at all.

3) A warning is not a statement for the sole purpose of avoiding liability. Disclaimers seek to avoid liability. Warnings are aimed at preventing accidental injury and death. Obviously, misrepresentations that interfere with warnings should not be used.

An important concept in safety engineering is that of the banned product. The remaining risk is so great that no warning is sufficient. The product must be banned by statute or regulation. If not, the common law court can find it should have been banned.

Proper warnings can fulfill any or all of a number of purposes.

1) An *informed choice* for the *entity in charge of the environment*—the employer, the farmer, the parent, the athletic director, the equipment purchaser is alerted to the fact that a manufacturer or one initiating an activity could not get zero risk, and there remains a risk of serious injury or death so that the new entity having been adequately informed of the gravity of the risk may decline the risk entirely.

- The employer may not buy the machine.

• The farmer may not buy the switch that has not been explosion-proofed.

• The mother may seek a non-toxic substitute.

• The athletic director may abandon football rather than have the players play with inadequate helmets to protect against brain damage and spinal cord injury.

2) An *exhortation* with the intensity required to alert the *entity in change of environment* of the nature of the hazard—the gravity of the risk so that the hazard and risk may be further reduced.

• The employer may use die guards to limit access when the machine builder did not guard point of operation.

• The farmer may use a big round bale clamp on the front end loader when loading such bales.

• The mother may prevent access by the child to the poisonous household chemical.

• The employer may provide chemical goggles and emergency equipment to workers working with aqua ammonia.

• The coach may start teaching football play in a way to minimize the number and severity of blows to the head.

3) An *informed choice for the user.* The user may well choose not to undertake the risk at all—zero danger/zero injury.

• The young woman may decline taking birth control pills with the very high probability of death, thrombotic stroke, blood clots, cancer, or defomed children.

• The farmer may decline to use the particular pesticide.

• The student may forego use of the trampoline.

• The car purchaser may want more fireworthiness than given by some models such as the Pinto or more crashworthiness than some motorcycles.

4) An *exhortation to the user* with the intensity required so that the user will take further steps to minimize the hazard and risk.

• The worker may not weld on the empty drum.

• The vehicle owner will not crank the engine while spraying quick-start into the carburetor.

• The motorcyclist may not drive the motorcycle up a hill with a passenger in the first 500 miles.

• The window washer may use a safety belt and independent safety line rather than rely upon the powered scaffolding.

• The painter may not use a ladder to paint from and insist upon a scaffold with guard rails.

5) A *reminder* to someone who already knows:

A very important purpose of a warning is to remind one who already knows the danger but whose attention has been diverted or arrested by competing circumstances, competing tasks or heat, light, noise, etc.

6) To *assure safe disposal* of containers whose contents were toxic, corrosive, caustic, etc.

7) To *minimize the injury.* A major purpose of a warning is the minimizing of the extent of injury, i.e.:

• There may not be movement of the paralyzed person without a spine board.

• The poison insult may be lessened with an antidote.

• There may be immediate massive flushing of the eyes where there has been alkali splashed into the eyes.

• The exposure to vapor may be minimized.

• The spillage may not cause fire.

8) To *assist a recall campaign.* Warnings subsequent to sale are becoming commonplace for all the above reasons. They are regularly used by industry to hasten calls. The Department of Transportation, the Food and Drug Administration and the Consumer Product Safety Commission have all been part of warning campaigns in the last 15 years. The *Product Liability Portfolio* by Man and Manager Inc., a major industry management advisory service, has helpful material for the trial lawyer seeking to find evidence of reasonable prudence in these kinds of policies and procedures.

There are, of course, times when reasonable prudence might be met by warning campaigns less than recall. This is a major question in the conduct of Ford in its park-to-reverse transmission problems.

THE BACKWARDNESS OF THE LAW

The A.S.A. Z35.1 Code which was adopted 40 years ago pursuant to directions from the American Standards Association and the National Safety Council as to their scope:

"Design, application and use of warning signs ... intended to indicate and insofar as possible to define specific hazards of a nature such that *failure to so designate them may* cause or tend to cause accidental injury to workers or the public or both.

If there is a failure to warn, then in every instance that failure is a cause of the injury or death complained of unless the injured person was attempting suicide, was blind or blindly intoxicated, or was intentionally undertaking an unreasonable risk. In every instance where there was a failure to warn reasonable prudence would have alerted the defendant that harm could result unless one of the exceptions existed. This is so because the activity engaged in or the use of a product was unreasonably risky. The *hazard* presenting the unreasonable or unacceptable risk *caused* the injury. The hazard and risk could only be made acceptable with a warning.

The law has put the cart before the horse. It has been deficient in several respects and ill serves society as heretofore expounded.

Causation. It is absurd to have a jury groping and speculating on failure-to-warn causation. If a product can only be made reasonably safe with a warning, then it is not the failure to warn which causes injury. It is the unreasonable exposure to the hazard which is a cause of the injury. Unreasonable exposure occurs with a combination of hazard (an objective condition or changing set of circumstances) and risk (probability of a particular untoward result). All the erroneous jury instructions need to be corrected to reflect the true situation and eliminate the artifical testimony, "I would have obeyed that warning."

Burden of proof of causation. It is equally absurd to place the burden upon the plaintiff who has been injured after having been subjected to an unreasonable exposure to a hazard.

Once the plaintiff proves that a warning was necessary, the only logical and just method of handling this is to allow the defendant to prove that:

1) The defendant gave an adequate warning;

2) The plaintiff was attempting suicide;

3) The plaintiff was consciously exposing himself or herself to a hazard as a thrill seeker knowing the gravity of the particular risk; or

4) The plaintiff, either because of a blind drunkenness or mental incapacity to be helped by a warning, could have not been exhorted or reminded in a way to prevent injury, and there is no other way that the defendant, acting reasonably, could have prevented the particular unreasonable exposure.

Texas and Indiana are the only jurisdictions which have definitively shifted this burden.

Ordinary Consumer Expectations. The safety and design engineering principle—so crucial for accident prevention—*Any Risk of Serious Injury or Death Is Always Unreasonable and Always Unacceptable If Reasonable Accident Prevention Methods Would Eliminate or Minimize It*—does not limit protection to the ordinary consumer, but rather to anyone who could reasonably foreseeably be injured because of lack of warning. It is in the economic and moral interest of society to protect "the worst damn fool" when that can be done. The test then is simply scientific and economic feasibility of warnings.

Limitations on supplier's knowledge of danger. Just as strict liability is a shortcut based upon social reality (it is *fault* if you sell a defective product), so it is also necessary for the law to understand that a prudent failure mode and effect analysis in the design of every product will document every way the product can fail (or the inadequacies of testing), and the law should conclusively presume the necessary knowledge by a defendant of hazard and risk, and lack of risk recognition on the parts of users and the safety engineering alternative.

No duty to warm patient. Because of a succinctly stated special privilege, drug dealers have no duty to warn the patient if the physician has been adequately warned. It denies patients an informed choice and belies the reality that injury preventions can be greatly enhanced if patients know the ways to avoid unsafe drugs, avoid injury by understanding contraindications, and minimize injury with correct dosage, etc. It is constitutionally unreasonable privilege to give immunity to drug dealers dispensing such products as birth control pills which emphasize patient choice of contraception rather than a doctor's decision.

No duty if the danger is open and obvious. If there has been an expression in law comparable to, "The moon is made of green cheese," it is, "The danger is open and obvious." It was a stupid expression when first opined in *Campo v. Scofield*, and it was equally stupid in each subsequent expression. When Mrs. Campo put her hand into the jaws of the onion topping machine, one hundred thousand workers were putting their hands into the jaws of a machine some eight hundred times that day, and not one of them considered it an unreasonable risk. The question is not whether there is a recognizable hazard, or whether the user will recognize the percentage chance of injury, or whether the user will recognize the gravity of the risk or recognize the safety engineering alternative. The real question is: "Has the risk of injury been reduced as much as reasonably possible?"

If it has, the defendant should be relieved of liability; if it has not, the defendant should remain liable for that failure which results in injury.

Modification of the product. If there is anything that is foreseeable to a designer it is that the product will be modified. If there is anything foreseeable in safety engineering, it is that employers will remove guards. This has been important knowledge for at least 100 years. Products are modified proportionate to the inadequacy of the design. Guards are removed because of negligent design. Negligent design includes the failure to warn against modifications and its dangers.

Hiding subsequent warnings from the jury. There is a general maxim in science, philosophy, and law that one has adopted the wrong principle if the principle has multiple exceptions. Such is the immoral rule that a tortfeasor can hide its subsequent warnings from the jury in certain instances. The general rule is subject to exceptions which make the subsequent warnings admissible for showing control, scientific feasibility, economic feasibility, impeachment causation, prior knowledge and modification by others. Maine recently has corrected the problem by court rule, and New York and California did so by common law decision in confused ways. Illinois correctly abolished the rule by condemning the erroneous and immoral rationale from the rule. Subsequent modifications should be admissible for all purposes. There should be little solace to those who complain that they would subject society to unreasonable risks but for the general rule.

Conformance to warning standards which were less than reasonable prudence. In real life there has yet to be a safety standard adopted that rises to the level of reasonable prudence. As legislatures rush to reinstate the unreasonable privilege eliminated by the common law there are all sorts of attempts by industry to excuse negligence by showing compliance with government warning standards which are totally inadequate. If the courts allow this ploy, the law is an ass.

This article has purposely not taken space either to cite or to quote from the reported decisions. They are very adequately reported in the *ATLA Law Journal*, the *ATLA Law Reporter*, the *Appendix* to the *Restatement of Torts 2d*, and by James B. Sales in an excellent rationalization for the backward law in the Defense Research Institute's *Monograph*. As lawyers on the side of people, we have only come a third of the way in righting the law of warnings. Sophistication in accident prevention needs and concepts and perseverance will get us the rest of the way.

CONSIDERATIONS IN DESIGN

1) *Durability* — The warning must be on the product and be effective for the life of the product.

If the machine is to be used for 100 years, then at the end of the 100 years the warning should exist and be as easily read as the manufacturer's name plate (so well designed because it is an advertisement for replacement parts).

2) *Signal word* — A signal word such as "Danger," "Caution," "Warning," or "Poison" classifies immediately the kind and character of the hazard and the gravity of the risk. For example, "Danger" indicates immediate and grave peril and by itself communicates that there is a hazard capable of producing irreversible injury. The signal word is the attention getter. The signal word for different risks is governed by the most grave risk.

3) *Color combination* — Warnings operate upon the unconscious mind as well as the conscious. Warning signs speak a language of their own and operate together with the corresponding signal word to convey the extent of the peril in order to achieve virtually instantaneous recognition of the existence of the hazard and the gravity of the risk. Uniformity in design crosses language and literacy barriers in that it alerts the user of the necessity of getting further information before action.

4) *Size of warning sign or tag* — The size of any warning and the panelization within the sign is an integral part of the exhortation to prevent injury and depends upon standards, viewing distance, illumination, length of message, etc.

5) *Size of type* — Type size should be large enough to permit easy reading at the viewing distance reasonably foreseeable. Emphasis may be achieved also by a limited number of capital letters, underlining or bold face or italic type.

6) *Message* — The message must detail the hazard — the gravity of the risk and the safety engineering alternative. It should be done with a strong active voice with short, simple sentences and active verbs. It should contain no surplusage. It should be in the number of languages reasonably foreseeable. It should depend in part on the time to view. *It should not be ambiguous.* Words and phrases necessary for communication should not be left out unless the designer is assured that an abbreviation or sign will be understood. Research indicates even well-designed symbols require some 50 practice trials. The designer can ill afford the luxury of 50 dry runs. The reason for precautions should not be buried. Inverted sentences are desirable.

7) *Sign placement* — Warnings must be placed to inform and exhort in sufficient time for appropriate action to be taken. They should be legible and not be competing with distractions. Potential blockage of the sign should be foreseen.

8) *Sign illumination* — Warning illumination is an important consideration and may require the warning to be of a particular color or require reflective material, emergency lighting, etc., since a foreseeable need for the warning may be during power failure, blackouts, fire, etc.

If one thinks of warnings as a vital component of accident prevention, then one is appalled at the disclaimers or liability avoidance statements on such things as diet pop cans where the risk of cancer is buried in verbiage, or football helmets where the tiny decal warning of paralysis, brain injury, or death is buried beneath the padding, or worse yet in the small print of the *Physician's Desk Reference* by the drug manufacturers. These schemes exist and flourish because the law has given and does give legal license to kill in that it is still so woefully underdeveloped in the protection of lives from injury.

Science and engineering in this area have not failed; it is our social policy, as reflected in the law, which continues to be the problem.

(See Appendix D, p. 133)

The Safety Specialist as an Expert Witness

Gerald S. Burko, P.E., CPSM

Editor's Note — Mr. Burko is a long-time safety and health consultant with long experience in expert witness and court testimony work with attorneys in product liability and hazardous materials matters. He is associated with the Cleveland firm of Saf-Con Inc. and is a member of the Society's Consultants Division.

Safety consultants are playing a more significant role today through the increasingly urgent concern with occupational safety, product safety, and injury prevention in general on the part of the public, the courts, the legal profession, and government. Government legislation and court decisions have steadily broadened the scope of liability of employers, manufacturers, distributors, vendors, for harm allegedly caused by improper working conditions, defective equipment, unreasonably dangerous products, unsafe areas, or unsafe procedures and practices.

When an individual is injured he may go to a lawyer for recovery. The lawyer contacts the other parties who contact their insurance companies. The insurance companies in turn retain attorneys. Attorneys often seek expert advice to support their cases.

WHO IS AN EXPERT?

With increasing frequency, attorneys for all sides are retaining safety professionals, who thus become expert witnesses. What is an expert witness? Webster's Unabridged Dictionary defines as follows:

expert – *having a special skill or knowledge derived from training or experience.*

witness – *one that gives evidence regarding matters of fact under inquiry; one who testified or is legally qualified to testify in a cause or to give evidence before a judicial tribunal.*

In *Black's Law Dictionary* a definition is:

> one possessing, with reference to a particular subject, knowledge not acquired by ordinary persons.

WHAT DOES THE EXPERT DO?

In practice a safety professional as an 'expert witness' reviews the facts and consequences of an incident as presented to him and offers an opinion drawn from those facts. The expressing of an opinion by an expert witness is usually a two-step procedure. First, it is expressed in the form of a written report to the attorney. The second is usually a deposition (a statement given under oath) to the opposing attorney. On occasion a third step may be added, to testify in court.

When you are contacted by an attorney you must determine, in your own mind, whether or not you are qualified to testify on the subject in question. To make this judgment you must get as complete a description as possible of the problem and its background. If possible, talk to the attorney and have him describe the incident. If this is not sufficient information then ask for written material describing the occurrence. From these two sources you should be able to determine if you are qualified to work on the case.

FEES FOR SERVICES RENDERED

If you accept the assignment an explicit agreement should be drawn up detailing your charges, when payment is expected and exactly what you will do for this fee. It is vital to reach a compensation understanding with the attorney or client up front. Compensable activities usually include material review, research, site visits, conferences with the lawyer, report preparation, travel, etc. You would not be remiss in requiring a retainer against which these expenses can be applied. The only way to be sure that this is understood is to have a dated and signed agreement. In this agreement it should be stipulated when billings will be submitted and when payment is expected. The agreement should also spell out what the attorney is paying for and whether you will give a written report and/or be available for a deposition and/or court testimony. The agreement should define what activities will be reimbursed and compensated and what will not.

There are a couple of things to watch carefully. One is that a demand for payment should be made *after* the written report is submitted, with no further work to be done until this part of the fee is paid. It should also include the statement that the fee is *not* contingent upon the filing of a case nor predicated upon the outcome of the case, and that out-of-pocket expenses will be billed separately, as they occur, and payment made upon presentation of the bill.

The recommendations listed above may seem unnecessary and are not a problem in *most* instances. But, if the attorney goes to court and gets absolutely nothing for his trouble, payment to a safety consultant may be delayed or possibly disputed. Can you afford to present a bill for $2,000 plus expenses (phone bills, research, travel) and then have the attorney say "Since I didn't get anything I'm not going to pay you"? Can you afford to work enough hours that will add up to a couple of weeks work, then not get paid? What happens if you submit a report and then there is a change of attorneys? Be prepared to meet these unusual but difficult contingencies. Do not reduce your fee under the promise of additional work. If you do, it means you've charged too much.

RESEARCH

Time is a very important consideration. Before you accept an assignment, be certain that you have the time to do the work. It is not unusual to get a call expecting a report that may take weeks or months to prepare, then be told that the trial is in three weeks. If court testimony is to be required, find out when court appearances are scheduled. Obtaining data for your report often takes hours of research just to find out what information is available. The injury may have occurred several years ago. Perhaps the product was made years before the injury occurred.

1. Was the injury forseeable or predictable under ordinary use by those having reasonable access to it (a knife in the hands of a child is predictable)?
2. Were there ways to either prevent or warn those expected to have access to the item from being injured (a knife in the hands of a small child is not preventable by the manufacturer)?
3. Would the guard make the item economically impractical, hinder its use, or be unacceptable to the user?
4. Would the guard have created a greater risk?
5. Has the item been modified by the owner and caused it to be unsafe?
6. Was there a written notice on or with the equipment to warn the user of any possible unsafe conditions or limitations of the product?

For many consultants, the first step is to examine the appropriate written standard to determine if the item complied with the standard. Often the item does not comply — but the product was made 18 years ago. How can it comply with the current standard that was revised two years ago for the third time in twenty years? Methods, materials, and expertise is available today that may have been unknown ten or even five years ago. A product should be compared to standards that were available at the time of its manufacture.

It may be necessary to show that the 'state of art' at the time of the incident was advanced to the point that a method was available to prevent an injury to a reasonably prudent individual and that not only was this method available, but that it was economically feasible. This can be accomplished by referring to material commonly available to those manufacturing this type of product. This could include publications from recognized safety organizations such as American National Standards Institute, National Fire Protection Association, American Society of Safety Engineers, National Safety Council, etc. You must also be able to locate references published in various trade periodicals relating to the subject. There are also recommendations of trade associations to which the defendent belonged or could have been a member. On occasion it may be necessary to review the manufacturing plans and prints (both current and previous) or specifications and any notes available to determine if the company did indeed attempt to provide a safe product. You should determine if the company has made an attempt to manufacture a safe product and then incorporated new knowledge into the product. It may be that the product was safely designed but was not manufactured or assembled according to plan. It may be necessary to review quality control procedures, reject information, complaints, correspondence, and company memos for this purpose. All of this often takes considerable time and effort.

ADDITIONAL INFORMATION

After you have received the agreement, discuss in detail with the attorney the cause of injury or damage and exactly how he proposes to handle the case. Remember, it is his direction you must support. Obtain copies of all information he has such as, depositions, interrogations, sales literature, and references to similar cases. If similar cases have been tried, review any expert testimony used to *see* if you agree or disagree with the conclusions, or if you can use them as a reference source, or somehow incorporate them into your work.

It is not only the standard of the industry which you can use as a basis for an opinion, but also *common practice* in an industry. What General Motors and Ford do is not necessarily the standard of the industry. For example, large companies have metal stamping plants, but by far the greatest majority of stamping done in this country is done by independent companies with relatively few employees (100 or less). What may be commonplace at larger companies may be virtually unknown by others.

If there were no written standard to safeguard an individual from a particular hazard, you must check to see if there were articles published in widely read and easily available publications that discuss the problem and offer reasonable solutions or preventive procedures. Examples of such publications are: The *National Safety News* and *Occupational Hazards* and similar magazines; trade association publications from American Society of Safety Engineers and American National Standards Institute standards or Underwriters Laboratory standards or reports. These are readily obtainable and tend to show that information regarding the state of the art was available and could have been used. OSHA standards, particularly those detailing what they are based on, are good sources of information. The OSHA standard may be based on an ANSI or other standard. This standard in turn may be based on an even earlier standard which was in effect at the time of manufacture.

REPORTING YOUR FINDINGS

When it comes to writing the report, be as detailed and complete as possible. When referring to a specific standard or article, cite the example by title, page, paragraph, author, published date, etc. Quote the pertinent portions in the body of the report. No matter how you write the report, be prepared to re-write parts of it to suit the particular attorney receiving it, in terms of emphasis or choice of language for the *legal issues involved*. When you submit a report to the attorney include a copy of the signed original. The copy will be forwarded to the opposing attorney.

In the first section of the report include your curriculum vitae. This details your expertise on the subject in question and is used to *qualify* you as an expert in the eyes of the court. It must be clear that you are not only an expert in safety but have sufficient knowledge of the particular field or a closely related field to render an opinion on the incident. Keep this separate from the rest of your report. The attorney may feel that he does not need to qualify you with the submission of the report.

The next section should state all facts known. Describe the manner in which the injury occurred and everything that surrounded or was involved with the occurrence. If there was an amputation state:

1. *the equipment involved*
2. *the exact part of the equipment involved*
3. *what the plaintiff was doing*
4. *the intended use of the equipment*
5. *where the individual was standing*
6. *who the injured individual was – all pertient information a. age b. sex c. height d. weight e. etc.*
7. *age and condition of the equipment*
8. *manufacturer of equipment*
9. *dimensions of equipment*
10. *location of equipment and its various parts.*

State the method of obtaining this information:

1. *personal interview*
2. *interview of plaintiff, defendant, others*
3. *depositions of any of the above*
4. *personal investigation*
5. *instruction manuals*
6. *etc.*

None of the things mentioned in this section should be opinion — only facts should be used. For instance, the plaintiff's attorney states that the premise is that something malfunctioned causing the injury. The defense attorney states that the individual removed a protective device and this is why he was injured.

It is your obligation to assume that the condition as described by the retaining attorney is a fact. It is the job of each attorney to present evidence to convince the jury that his facts are the most credible.

The next section should deal with all published material that relates to the incident. This would include all regulations from federal, state, and local codes that relate to the product. Included are any references to manufacturing safety standards, trade standards, published articles, or any publications from recognized sources that develop voluntary safety standards or recommendations.

Following this, there should be a section detailing how the other party did (or did not) comply with either the letter or spirit of the standards, or other printed material.

Point out specifics and relate these to the practical aspects of safety and accident prevention. If there are no standards that mention the type of product by name, but refer to relevant aspects of similar equipment, point this out. In addition, refer to all significant materials that you feel strengthen your contention and detail what the defendant did (or did not) do.

In the final section you should state your opinion — that is, a conclusion based on your professional qualifications that the defendant did (or did not) take reasonable steps to prevent a foreseeable injury. It is important that you state whether you feel that the occurrence was (or was not) foreseeable. This is based on the legal requirement that the manufacturer foresee any possible use, misuse, or action that may be taken by any *reasonably prudent individual*.

In this section you can explain other experiences you have had. Here you are stating what you believe, as a safety professional, is (or is not) an obvious and easily foreseeable occurrence, that could have (or could not have been) prevented by some type of guard or warning. For example, each of us must remember that no one can be expected to be on guard and safety-conscious 100 per cent of the time. It is usually the defendant's responsibility to reduce the potential for injury to the lowest possible economically practical percent.

TESTIMONY

If further work is to be done by the *expert witness* it is usually the giving of a deposition to the opposing attorney. A deposition is a cross examination-style questioning under oath on the facts as they have been presented to you and the opinions and conclusions you have reached. The attorney may spend a part of the time reviewing your qualifications: academic, employment, and related experience. The attorney who has retained you will be present. In addition, there will be a court reporter who will swear you in and then record all discussion.

Prior to being deposed, both you and the attorney should go through "dry runs" of the deposition proceedings. He should attempt to formulate the same type of questions he feels that the deposing attorney will ask. Study your report very carefully and review all the related material, in your file, thoroughly.

When appearing at the location of the deposition, bring all the material that you might have. Let your attorney review the contents of your file.

During the deposition, be absolutely certain you understand each question before you answer. Answer in as few words as possible. If it is necessary to get exact figures or exact wording, simply state that you must refer to the report or a specific book. Since there is a court reporter present say that you are referring to a specific piece of material and identify it as precisely as possible. One point is very important, many of the questions in the deposition will not be specifically related to your report. They will be in the nature of other matters bearing on your qualifications or experience. The answers you give should be *to the best of (your) recollection* at that moment. It would not hurt to say this at some point while you are being deposed. If the attorney asks if you have ever seen a particular piece of equipment, you may answer "No." At some point in the future (hours, days, or weeks), you may remember that, at some time in the past, you have had some experience with this item. During the deposition, you may be asked to liken one thing to another. You might answer that there is no similarity, but on further thought you might alter your opinion. If this should occur, be certain to advise the retaining attorney and let him know the reasons for the change.

Changes in recollection have occurred to me. Try to be as precise as possible. Try to avoid changing your mind and/or your testimony from one occasion to the next. Such changes in testimony should be infrequent. If the case goes to court, remember you are a safety professional and an *Expert*. Not one person in the courtroom knows what you do about the subject. The attorneys, the judge, and above all the jury, are going to be paying attention to every word you, the *Expert*, say. They are going to be impressed with you. Do not destroy this impression. Dress in a conservative manner. This means a dark suit, solid color tie, and dark shoes. You are trying to impress the jury that you are someone who can be relied upon and you would not say anything unless you had thoroughly researched the subject. They must feel that, if necessary, you could document everything you say.

When you are asked a question, once again, be absolutely certain you understand the question. When you answer, speak distinctly. Say it loud enough for all those participating in the trial to hear. When the retaining attorney questions you, direct your answer to the jury. Look directly at them. When you answer the opposing attorney, be courteous, and don't alienate the jury. Speak with conviction.

If you have never appeared in court as an expert witness just remember that there should be no surprises. All evidence, gathered before the trial starts, is shared by all sides. Once you get on that stand you are fair game for every one. There is no one on your side. If the opposing attorney starts working on an area that you feel is irrelevant or makes you uncomfortable — but which the judge says is pertinent, tough luck. Do not look to the judge or the retaining attorney for help. When you are on the stand, you are an independent expert. The opposing attorney will try to discredit you in the eyes of the jury. He may criticize the grades you got in school, the lack of a particular course in engineering, mathematics, etc. He may try to show that you do not have enough practical experience — only theoretical — and the jury may be composed of blue collar workers. He may also attack your credentials, i.e., a P.E. in safety from California but not from the local state, or a CSP by the "grandfather clause" as opposed to a "test." At no time should you lose your composure. Answer the questions as directly and forcefully as possible.

You should even be careful to whom you speak about a pending case, and where. In an effort to discredit an expert safety witness once, the owner of a company which was a defendant in a court case engaged the expert in casual conversation in a corridor during a break in the proceedings. They discussed safety on a job on which the owner was involved. Later, in court, the owner-defendant was introduced and testified that the expert had solicited him for business. The expert had a difficult time convincing the court that his conversation with the defendant had been irrelevant to the pending case.

RECORDKEEPING

It is of the utmost importance that accurate daily records be kept detailing how your time is spent on each case. Keep careful track of expenses. Do not be afraid to put down every minute you spend on the case. This includes time away from your desk. You might discuss the case with others in your office, at lunch, at home, at meetings, etc. This includes phone calls or any other method of communication. You might simply think about the case on the way to and from work. You are entitled to charge for all this time. When you submit your final bill, include documentation of your time calculated to the nearest quarter of an hour.

CONCLUSION

The safety professional can render valuable service as an expert witness, but should be prepared and understand what is expected and how to do a professional job. Remember, you are a safety professional. You are not to give voice to legal conclusions. The expert must keep in mind that he is not a lawyer. The expert witness is a safety professional and as such he is to render an unbiased opinion only on matters that are within his realm of expertise. Doing otherwise not only is unprofessional, it won't work.

Preparation for Your Court Appearance

George A. Peters, J. D.

Editor's Note—As an attorney-safety professional, Mr. Peters has many years of litigation experience in matters relating to occupational safety and health. This article is reprinted by permission from the January 1980 issue of Professional Safety Magazine.

You might be requested by your *employer* to act as an expert witness in the defense of a product liability lawsuit. You could receive a request from an *attorney* to act as an expert witness on behalf of an injured person in your community or as part of an arbitration panel. You might be surprised to receive a *subpoena* that requires your immediate deposition or court testimony, from a plaintiff or from a defendant who has cross-complained against your company or against you personally. Almost any engineer or scientist or manager should expect to become involved, in some manner, in lawsuits, during his occupational career and lifetime. It is usually too late, the week before you are scheduled to testify, to begin to learn and become familiarized with what will be demanded or required in terms of your performance in an alien court arena. There are six basic principles that you should consider, at this time, that might help you when you do face a court appearance.

ADEQUATE PREPARATION

Many attorneys have been unpleasantly surprised, during the trial of an important lawsuit, by a key engineering expert witness who convincingly states his opinion or final conclusion as to the causes of an accident, then has very little in terms of supporting facts to rationally explain the reasons for his opinion and facts that might serve as a substantial foundation for such an important conclusion.

The expert witness may have the best of qualifications in terms of education, experience, professional competency, honors and awards, organizational status and peer approval, patents and publications, and other evidence of special knowledge and standing. But, such qualifications serve only to open the door so that the judge will permit him to testify before the jury and to give the jury a reason to listen. Thus, the expert should be prepared to convince the judge and the jury that he has a reasonable basis for his opinion in terms of his unique or special knowledge of the facts of the accident as they relate to the legal issues that are to be decided by the jury. He may expect to be cross-examined as to the justification for his opinion; including his interpretations of test data as applied to the facts of the case, each step of his engineering analysis, the alternative causal factors, the technical and economic feasibility and costs of various engineering design and manufacturing alternatives, and various challenges to the basic assumptions upon which his opinion and professional beliefs are predicated.

The jurors may elect to disregard or discredit the opinion of any or all expert witnesses and, in many cases, they are justified in doing just that. They should not be overwhelmed by some voice of authority, since that would mean that the scales of justice would be tipped by the more numerous credentials, simplistic beliefs, and personal biases of the authorities mustered for each of the sides to a lawsuit. Instead, the jury must be presented with substantive facts, evidence of reason and logic, and a showing that this expert did his homework.

The attorney should provide certain information to the prospective expert witness, that relates to the technical areas about which he might be questioned; such as, copies of accident reports, test reports, witness statements, maps or diagrams, photographs, portions of written interrogatories and answers, requests for admissions, depositions, advertisements and representations, shop manuals, articles from technical journals, and other selected materials. These are not intended for casual reading and review. They are intended for the specific preparation of the witness and must be diligently committed to memory and logically organized. All too many lawsuits are lost or severely damaged because of sloppy and misdirected preparation by expert witnesses. The depth and scope of preparation is determined by the needs of the lawsuit, not by the personal desires of the witnesses.

Nothing is more important than properly directed preparation of appropriate depth and sufficient scope. Juries do not want their valuable time wasted with dumb, too smart, lengthy, tedious, flippant, or unprepared witnesses. The well prepared witness has gradually simplified his testimony *after* learning all the facts, reviewing areas of uncertainty, and preparing a clear message substantiated by facts rather than beliefs.

Defense experts, if part of a corporate product safety effort, may overcome the appearance of bias that obviously results from employee testimony, by the proper utilization of superior knowledge available within the corporate enterprise. In other words, the witness is so well prepared that he can muster such believable, helpful factual information that the jury will consider him a source of personal real-life knowledge rather than just another representative of a defendant.

The product safety effort, in a company, may be involved in claims and accident investigation so that general causal factors should be fairly well understood, in warranty and reliability efforts so that general failure modes and alternative remedies are understood, in quality and manufacturing discrepancy actions so that probability and decision criteria are understood, and in other areas such as testing, labels, warnings, manuals, advertising, purchasing, training, customer service, etc. With that kind of long term experience, a defense expert should be half-prepared before he even becomes assigned to a particular lawsuit.

Plaintiff experts, however, usually do not have such an initial preparation advantage, nor do they have the time and resources to allot to any one particular lawsuit. They must be quicker learners, more precise in targeting their preparation goals, and must strive harder to be equally prepared. They must use the available months or years for maturation of a broader range of concepts because the plaintiff's affirmative burden of proof in court is greater than that of the defense. At this moment in our history, preparation for court appearances is very uneven and individualistic, based upon what I see being presented as sworn testimony.

UNDERSTANDING THE ISSUES

The expert witness may be so busy with his general familiarization and orientation that he focuses on the wrong issues. On a stuck throttle case, he may focus on the carburetor when the questions revolve around the accelerator linkage. He may run tests on a pressure vessel, when the issues relate to the function of a relief valve. He may not be concerned with whether or not a product feature rendered it "unreasonably dangerous," when the real issue may be whether or not the product failed to perform as safely as an "ordinary consumer would expect" when used in a reasonably foreseeable manner, so he prepares to answer questions as to the reasonableness of a danger rather than the safety expectations of the ordinary consumer. Similarly, the lawsuit might be narrowed at the time of trial, to a "failure to warn" case, so the expert must understand what is a legally adequate and sufficient warning, using common law criteria rather than something that appears in a trade standard or government regulation. For example, what human factors testing of the warning was accomplished or legally required and did the testing meet criteria relating to foreseeable user populations, scientific or experimental research protocols, informed consent requirements, and behavioral modification desired or necessary under the circumstances?

Don't waste the attorney's time, the court's time, the juror's time, and the litigant's money by fooling around with issues that are never going to be heard in a courtroom or that fail to state precisely the law, at the time and in the place of the jurisdiction in which the controversy is to be heard. Obviously, the attorneys will explain the issues, but you must actually understand what is being said by the exact meaning of the words being used. This means that you will have to re-check your understanding of the words, in several different ways, so that you really understand before you act.

The law is relativistic and changing, not a set of invariant and universal rules. It is not your belief and interpretation of what the law should be that is important, it is your ability to deal with the law as it actually is and in terms of the meaning that it gives to the exact issues that are in conflict. Therefore, find out the precise issues about which you may be questioned and cross-examined. Ask for the instructions that might be given to the jury and how your testimony relates to those jury instructions. In other words, understand both your role and what the jury will expect to hear from you relative to the issues upon which they must deliberate and decide.

HONESTY AND IMPARTIALITY

The role of an attorney is that of an advocate attempting to advance the best interests of his client, propounding the arguments most favorable to the party he represents, and countering the arguments adverse to his side of the case. This is not the role of the expert witness. The expert witness should never attempt to be a surrogate advocate, a partisan, or a blindly loyal representative of one side of a controversy. He is expected to be impartial, honest, independent, and factually oriented. When he fails to be impartial, honest, and forthright, the expert may mislead the attorney or even force him to trial in a matter that could have been dismissed or settled at far less cost (based on overall risk or loss management results). If the defense expert fails to be impartial in front of a jury, this may antagonize a jury to the point where they begin to think of verdict amplification or punitive damage. Jurors attempt to do the correct thing for all sides, they attempt to be conscientious and fair, they listen to discern the truth, so they may react against a witness who appears dishonest, biased, or unfair. In fact, they may be given jury instructions, by the judge to disregard *all* of the testimony of a witness that they believe has been untruthful *in any aspect* of his testimony.

The believability and apparent truthfulness of a witness is not helped by verbal fencing with an attorney, becoming defensive or combative, attempting to direct the show in someone else's bailiwick, by an appearance of passive acceptance of the attorney's theories and beliefs, by an expensive "I can't be wrong" ego, or expressions that seem hostile, personal, or foolish.

The expert should set limits on his own testimony and not go beyond his own convictions, areas of personal knowledge, and professional competency. That is, he should avoid being led or voluntarily overextending himself and getting into a weak area in which he can be discredited. This is why the expert is told to avoid "guessing," to say"I don't know," to avoid "volunteering information" when not asked, and, however important his testimony, he is told that his testimony should be recognized as only *one* segment of a larger jig saw puzzle of real-life drama that is being presented to, or unfolded before the jury.

If the expert understands both the pro and con arguments on various issues, he might be in a better position to recognize and avoid pitfalls where his reactions might suggest to the jury that he is a blindly biased advocate, rather than a professionally independent person capable of making his own discretionary impartial decisions based upon adequate knowledge. If the witness cannot be honest and impartial, because of personality problems or psychopathology, the lawyer is in trouble and the lawsuit may not be evaluated on its true merits.

INITIAL INTERACTION

The trial attorney will want to meet and evaluate his prospective witness, to take a measure of the person and determine how such a witness might fit into the context or matrix of his trial presentation, case preparation, or evaluation of the issues. The expert witness should do the same thing with the attorney, to see if he could work with that particular attorney in the role suggested or expected, for the purposes necessary, and given the facts and circumstances of the specific accident, incident, or situation. The expert may be simply a consultant or advisor; may be asked to testify only as to one aspect of his personal knowledge; he may be asked to educate and gain rapport with the jury; to conduct a demonstration in front of a jury; or he may be asked to testify based on a set of given assumptions that lead to a carefully prepared hypothetical question to be answered in front of the jury.

At the initial conference, the expert may underestimate the knowledge and understanding that the lawyer may exhibit, on the technical issues, closer to trial and the depth of understanding that may be exhibited by opposing counsel during the trial of the matter. Incidentally, pre-trial oral depositions should be viewed in the same manner, as an opportunity for the expert witness to evaluate the opposing attorney's style, professionalism, demeanor, habits, traits, logic, persistence, distractability, understanding of the key points, and to discover overlooked areas of inquiry that might loom large during your eventual courtroom appearance.

Thus, the expert should interact with the attorneys, to probe and to understand, abiding by and learning the abritrary roles and rules governing the conduct of each participant in the affair. Don't attempt to suddenly and dramatically redefine the respective roles or rules of the players of the game, just before trial, to meet your personal needs or desires. Any major disharmony or problems with a particular witness as the trial gets underway can wreak havoc with the final outcome. The problem witness may come through unscathed, but serious and irreparable sacrifices and compromises might have to be made elsewhere that might turn a case upside down. Therefore, don't become a problem witness. It is better to get out of a case at the time of the initial interview, than to have others rely upon you to the moment of final decision.

Remember that each claim or lawsuit, regardless of its similarity to prior lawsuits or your past experience, is uniquely different because the facts are never the same, the participants are always different, and the law is probably different. So each case involves a new appraisal, evaluation, and interaction of a personal kind for the expert witness.

DON'T SPECULATE

Witnesses are generally told some things that they find easy to accept; such as dress neatly and conservatively, be on time, be polite and show respect for the court, answer only the question asked, avoid technical terms, don't be condescending in tone or demeanor, don't be a know-it-all, be serious, be sure you understand the question before you answer it, look at the jury or the attorney questioning you rather than at your attorney as if you were seeking signals or approval for your answers, if there is an objection wait for the judge to rule before you answer, take the time necessary to answer the question, ask to explain if you deem it necessary, don't embellish, be responsive to what is actually asked, keep your answers short, and answer "yes" or "no" whenever possible.

There are other areas that seem to cause some trouble. For example, the terms "scientific certainty," "probability," "possibility," and "speculation" may have very different meanings in a court of law than in some engineering and scientific disciplines. The scientist may be trained to be conservative in his conclusions, parsimonius in the application of results, uncertain as to definitive answers, habitually suggesting always more research for more definitive substantiation of research hypotheses. The engineer may be trained in inferential statistics, probability theory, statistical confidence and significance levels, producers vs consumers risk, and areas of the curve that include very small proportions of the population: Thus, he may be thinking in terms of 90%, 95%, 97½% or 99% "certainty." The jury may interpret a refusal to be pinned down as hedging; the normal cautionary reservations, as a lack of knowledge; and statements that absolute certainty is not possible, as foolish evasions! Certainty, in the courtroom, refers to only a 51% probability; that is, the truth of assertation is more likely than not. Many courts will throw out your expert testimony or refuse to allow you to express an opinion if it is merely "speculative" and, in some cases, if it is merely "possible." It should be at least "probable" before a jury should hear it and, generally, your key statements should be "scientifically certain" in the sense of being *more probable than not.*

Too many expert witnesses have been surprised to see their ultimate conclusions discarded or impugned, despite their convincing and otherwise perfect testimony, because of allegations that the witness was engaging in "mere speculations" regarding "remote possibilities," when, in fact, the witness was led into a semantic jungle that he should have avoided or thwarted. Just as the appearance and conduct of a witness may have more actual effect on the jurors than his credentials; so may the clarity and certainty of his assertions have more effect on the jury that the substance of what he is saying. Thus, proper communications may involve using a language appropriate to the rules understood by all who are attempting to honestly resolve a conflict on its merits. Above all, don't "speculate" and be "certain" in the legal sense or meaning of those words, when attempting to communicate in the legal arena.

DON'T ABUSE LEGAL PROCESS

Increasingly, courts are applying sanctions to those who attempt to twist or distort the carefully formulated and balanced legal process. Don't destroy records, alter the physical evidence, deny the existence of facts that you know to be true, "doctor" or "improve" evidence or photographs, clean up or change slightly some facts or evidence, contaminate or switch samples, or deny the obvious. Use common sense and some basic ethics! Don't lose the evidence or a record of the chain-of-possession of evidence. Devious, false, and wrongful conduct may inflame a jury, cause a judge to issue a default, impose procedural or evidentiary restrictions, or invoke a verbal or non-verbal communication to the jury of his displeasure with one side. There have been, and will be more, malpractice or joint tortfeasor actions against engineers or test laboratories for intentional or negligent actions in regard to the handling of vital court evidence. Play it straight! Don't abuse the legal process! By corrupting justice, you dishonor your profession and discredit yourself. The image of your profession, as projected by expert testimony in tens of thousands of cases each year, before numerous lawyers, judges, and juries, has much to do with forming the image, status, respect, and laws governing each profession. Therefore, be a credit and a salesman for your profession.

If you are unfamiliar with expert testimony, ask the trial attorney for help. Perhaps, a dress rehearsal and visits to a courtroom will reduce excessive modesty in stating qualifications, will familiarize the witness with how to give short responsive answers, will uncover gaps such as blind reliance on trade standards, will foster verbal ability relative to the concepts in issue, will permit timely reflection on ethical issues, and may uncover what lawyers might reasonably believe to be an abuse of the legal process before any substantial harm may be done.

CONCLUSION

Different attorneys have different ideas on exactly what the role of the expert witness should be. Obviously, this varies as to whether the lawyer is also an engineer, whether he has had good or bad experiences with experts, what has been recommended to him, his individual style and what has worked for him in the past, the size of the case, the opposing side's experts, the technical complexity of the case, and its stage of preparation. Thus, an expert must remain flexible, adaptive, and "always learning," even if he has already participated in ten, a hundred, or a thousand lawsuits.

Appendices

A–U.S. Occupational Safety and Health Act

Public Law 91-596
91st Congress, S. 2193
December 29, 1970

An Act

To assure safe and healthful working conditions for working men and women; by authorizing enforcement of the standards developed under the Act; by assisting and encouraging the States in their efforts to assure safe and healthful working conditions; by providing for research, information, education, and training in the field of occupational safety and health; and for other purposes.

Be it enacted by the Senate and House of Representatives of the United States of America in Congress assembled, That this Act may be cited as the "Occupational Safety and Health Act of 1970".

CONGRESSIONAL FINDINGS AND PURPOSE

SEC. (2) The Congress finds that personal injuries and illnesses arising out of work situations impose a substantial burden upon, and are a hindrance to, interstate commerce in terms of lost production, wage loss, medical expenses, and disability compensation payments.

(b) The Congress declares it to be its purpose and policy, through the exercise of its powers to regulate commerce among the several States and with foreign nations and to provide for the general welfare, to assure so far as possible every working man and woman in the Nation safe and healthful working conditions and to preserve our human resources—

(1) by encouraging employers and employees in their efforts to reduce the number of occupational safety and health hazards at their places of employment, and to stimulate employers and employees to institute new and to perfect existing programs for providing safe and healthful working conditions;

(2) by providing that employers and employees have separate but dependent responsibilities and rights with respect to achieving safe and healthful working conditions;

(3) by authorizing the Secretary of Labor to set mandatory occupational safety and health standards applicable to businesses affecting interstate commerce, and by creating an Occupational Safety and Health Review Commission for carrying out adjudicatory functions under the Act;

(4) by building upon advances already made through employer and employee initiative for providing safe and healthful working conditions;

(5) by providing for research in the field of occupational safety and health, including the psychological factors involved, and by developing innovative methods, techniques, and approaches for dealing with occupational safety and health problems;

(6) by exploring ways to discover latent diseases, establishing causal connections between diseases and work in environmental conditions, and conducting other research relating to health problems, in recognition of the fact that occupational health standards present problems often different from those involved in occupational safety;

(7) by providing medical criteria which will assure insofar as practicable that no employee will suffer diminished health, functional capacity, or life expectancy as a result of his work experience;

(8) by providing for training programs to increase the number and competence of personnel engaged in the field of occupational safety and health;

(9) by providing for the development and promulgation of occupational safety and health standards;

(10) by providing an effective enforcement program which shall include a prohibition against giving advance notice of any inspection and sanctions for any individual violating this prohibition;

(11) by encouraging the States to assume the fullest responsibility for the administration and enforcement of their occupational safety and health laws by providing grants to the States to assist in identifying their needs and responsibilities in the area of occupational safety and health, to develop plans in accordance with the provisions of this Act, to improve the administration and enforcement of State occupational safety and health laws, and to conduct experimental and demonstration projects in connection therewith;

(12) by providing for appropriate reporting procedures with respect to occupational safety and health which procedures will help achieve the objectives of this Act and accurately describe the nature of the occupational safety and health problem;

(13) by encouraging joint labor-management efforts to reduce injuries and disease arising out of employment.

DEFINITIONS

SEC. 3. For the purposes of this Act—

(1) The term "Secretary" means the Secretary of Labor.

(2) The term "Commission" means the Occupational Safety and Health Review Commission established under this Act.

(3) The term "commerce" means trade, traffic, commerce, transportation, or communication among the several States, or between a State and any place outside thereof, or within the District of Columbia, or a possession of the United States (other than the Trust Territory of the Pacific Islands), or between

points in the same State but through a point outside thereof.

(4) The term "person" means one or more individuals, partnerships, associations, corporations, business trusts, legal representatives, or any organized group of persons.

(5) The term "employer" means a person engaged in a business affecting commerce who has employees, but does not include the United States or any State or political subdivision of a State.

(6) The term "employee" means an employee of an employer who is employed in a business of his employer which affects commerce.

(7) The term "State" includes a State of the United States, the District of Columbia, Puerto Rico, the Virgin Islands, American Samoa, Guam, and the Trust Territory of the Pacific Islands.

(8) The term "occupational safety and health standard" means a standard which requires conditions, or the adoption or use of one or more practices, means, methods, operations, or processes, reasonably necessary or appropriate to provide safe or healthful employment and places of employment.

(9) The term "national consensus standard" means any occupational safety and health standard or modification thereof which (1), has been adopted and promulgated by a nationally recognized standards-producing organization under procedures whereby it can be determined by the Secretary that persons interested and affected by the scope of provisions of the standard have reached substantial agreement on its adoption, (2) was formulated in a manner which afforded an opportunity for diverse views to be considered and (3) has been designated as such a standard by the Secretary, after consultation with other appropriate Federal agencies.

(10) The term "established Federal standard" means any operative occupational safety and health standard established by any agency of the United States and presently in effect, or contained in any Act of Congress in force on the date of enactment of this Act.

(11) The term "Committee" means the National Advisory Committee on Occupational Safety and Health established under this Act.

(12) The term "Director" means the Director of the National Institute for Occupational Safety and Health.

(13) The term "Institute" means the National Institute for Occupational Safety and Health established under this Act.

(14) The term "Workmen's Compensation Commission" means the National Commission on State Workmen's Compensation Laws established under this Act.

APPLICABILITY OF THIS ACT

SEC. 4. (a) This Act shall apply with respect to employment performed in a workplace in a State, the District of Columbia, the Commonwealth of Puerto Rico, the Virgin Islands, American Samoa, Guam, the Trust Territory of the Pacific Islands, Wake Island, Outer Continental Shelf lands defined in the Outer Continental Shelf Lands Act, Johnston Island, and the Canal Zone. The Secretary of the Interior shall, by regulation, provide for judicial enforcement of this Act by the courts established for areas in which there are no United States district courts having jurisdiction.

(b) (1) Nothing in this Act shall apply to working conditions of employees with respect to which other Federal agencies, and State agencies acting under section 274 of the Atomic Energy Act of 1954, as amended (42 U.S.C. 2021), exercise statutory authority to prescribe or enforce standards or regulations affecting occupational safety or health.

(2) The safety and health standards promulgated under the Act of June 30, 1936, commonly known as the Walsh-Healey Act (41 U.S.C. 35 et seq.), the Service Contract Act of 1965 (41 U.S.C. 351 et seq.), Public Law 91-54, Act of August 9, 1969, (40 U.S.C. 333), Public Law 85-742, Act of August 23, 1958 (33 U.S.C. 941), and the National Foundation on Arts and Humanities Act (20 U.S.C. 951 et seq.) are superseded on the effective date of corresponding standards, promulgated under this Act, which are determined by the Secretary to be more effective. Standards issued under the laws listed in this paragraph and in effect on or after the effective date of this Act shall be deemed to be occupational safety and health standards issued under this Act, as well as under such other Acts.

(3) The Secretary shall, within three years after the effective date of this Act, report to the Congress his recommendations for legislation to avoid unnecessary duplication and to achieve coordination between this Act and other Federal laws.

(4) Nothing in this Act shall be construed to supersede or in any manner affect any workmen's compensation law or to enlarge or diminish or affect in any other manner the common law or statutory rights, duties, or liabilities of employers and employees under any law with respect to injuries, diseases, or death of employees arising out of, or in the course of, employment.

DUTIES

SEC. 5. (a) Each employer—

(1) shall furnish to each of his employees employment and a place of employment which are free from recognized hazards that are causing or are likely to cause death or serious physical harm to his employees;

(2) shall comply with occupational safety and health standards promulgated under this Act.

(b) Each employee shall comply with occupational safety and health standards and all rules, regulations, and orders issued pursuant to this Act which are applicable to his own actions and conduct.

OCCUPATIONAL SAFETY AND HEALTH STANDARDS

SEC. 6. (a) Without regard to chapter 5 of title 5, United States Code, or to the other subsections of this section, the Secretary shall, as soon as practicable during the period beginning with the effective date of this Act and ending two years after such date, by rule promulgate as an occupational safety or health standard any national consensus standard, and any established Federal standard, unless he determines that the promulgation of such a standard would not result in improved safety or health for specifically designated employees. In the event of conflict among any such standards, the Secretary shall promulgate the standard which assures the greatest protection of the safety or health of the affected employees.

(b) The Secretary may by rule promulgate, modify, or revoke any occupational safety or health standard in the following manner:

(1) Whenever the Secretary, upon the basis of information submitted to him in writing by an interested person, a representative of any organization of employers or employees, a nationally recognized standards-producing organization, the Secretary of Health, Education, and Welfare, the National Institute for Occupational Safety and Health, or a State or political subdivision, or on the basis of information developed by the Secretary or otherwise available to him, determines that a rule should be promulgated in order to serve the objectives of this Act, the Secretary may request the recommendations of an advisory committee appointed under section 7 of this Act. The Secretary shall provide such an advisory committee with any proposals of his own or of the Secretary of Health, Education, and Welfare, together with all pertinent factual information developed by the Secretary or the Secretary of Health, Education, and Welfare, or otherwise available, including the results of research, demonstrations, and experiments. An advisory committee shall submit to the Secretary its recommendations regarding the rule to be promulgated within ninety days from the date of its appointment or within such longer or shorter period as may be prescribed by the Secretary, but in no event for a period which is longer than two hundred and seventy days.

(2) The Secretary shall publish a proposed rule promul-

gating, modifying, or revoking an occupational safety or health standard in the Federal Register and shall afford interested persons a period of thirty days after publication to submit written data or comments. Where an advisory committee is appointed and the Secretary determines that a rule should be issued, he shall publish the proposed rule within sixty days after the submission of the advisory committee's recommendations or the expiration of the period prescribed by the Secretary for such submission.

(3) On or before the last day of the period provided for the submission of written data or comments under paragraph (2), any interested person may file with the Secretary written objections to the proposed rule, stating the grounds therefor and requesting a public hearing on such objections. Within thirty days after the last day for filing such objections, the Secretary shall publish in the Federal Register a notice specifying the occupational safety or health standard to which objections have been filed and a hearing requested, and specifying a time and place for such hearing.

(4) Within sixty days after the expiration of the period provided for the submission of written data or comments under paragraph (2), or within sixty days after the completion of any hearing held under paragraph (3), the Secretary shall issue a rule promulgating, modifying, or revoking an occupational safety or health standard or make a determination that a rule should not be issued. Such a rule may contain a provision delaying its effective date for such period (not in excess of ninety days) as the Secretary determines may be necessary to insure that affected employers and employees will be informed of the existence of the standard and of its terms and that employers affected are given an opportunity to familiarize themselves and their employees with the existence of the requirements of the standard.

(5) The Secretary, in promulgating standards dealing with toxic materials or harmful physical agents under this subsection, shall set the standard which most adequately assures, to the extent feasible, on the basis of the best available evidence, that no employee will suffer material impairment of health or functional capacity even if such employee has regular exposure to the hazard dealt with by such standard for the period of his working life. Development of standards under this subsection shall be based upon research, demonstrations, experiments, and such other information as may be appropriate. In addition to the attainment of the highest degree of health and safety protection for the employee, other considerations shall be the latest available scientific data in the field, the feasibility of the standards, and experience gained under this and other health and safety laws. Whenever practicable, the standard promulgated shall be expressed in terms of objective criteria and of the performance desired.

(6) (A) Any employer may apply to the Secretary for a temporary order granting a variance from a standard or any provision thereof promulgated under this section. Such temporary order shall be granted only if the employer files an application which meets the requirements of clause (B) and establishes that (i) he is unable to comply with a standard by its effective date because of unavailability of professional or technical personnel or of materials and equipment needed to come into compliance with the standard or because necessary construction or alteration of facilities cannot be completed by the effective date, (ii) he is taking all available steps to safeguard his employees against the hazards covered by the standard, and (iii) he has an effective program for coming into compliance with the standard as quickly as practicable. Any temporary order issued under this paragraph shall prescribe the practices, means, methods, operations, and processes which the employer must adopt and use while the order is in effect and state in detail his program for coming into compliance with the standard. Such a temporary order may be granted only after notice to employees and an opportunity for a hearing: *Provided,* That the Secretary may issue one interim order to be effective until a decision is made on the basis of the hearing. No temporary order may be in effect for longer than the period needed by the employer to achieve compliance with the standard or one year, whichever is shorter, except that such an order may be renewed not more than twice (I) so long as the requirements of this paragraph are met and (II) if an application for renewal is filed at least 90 days prior to the expiration date of the order. No interim renewal of an order may remain in effect for longer than 180 days.

(B) An application for a temporary order under this paragraph (6) shall contain:

(i) a specification of the standard or portion thereof from which the employer seeks a variance,

(ii) a representation by the employer, supported by representations from qualified persons having first-hand knowledge of the facts represented, that he is unable to comply with the standard or portion thereof and a detailed statement of the reasons therefore,

(iii) a statement of the steps he has taken and will take (with specific dates) to protect employees against the hazard covered by the standard,

(iv) a statement of when he expects to be able to comply with the standard and what steps he has taken and what steps he will take (with dates specified) to come into compliance with the standard, and

(v) a certification that he has informed his employees of the application by giving a copy thereof to their authorized representative, posting a statement giving a summary of the application and specifying where a copy may be examined at the place or places where notices to employees are normally posted, and by other appropriate means.

A description of how employees have been informed shall be contained in the certification. The information to employees shall also inform them of their right to petition the Secretary for a hearing.

(C) The Secretary is authorized to grant a variance from any standard or portion thereof whenever he determines, or the Secretary of Health, Education, and Welfare certifies, that such variance is necessary to permit an employer to participate in an experiment approved by him or the Secretary of Health, Education, and Welfare designed to demonstrate or validate new and improved techniques to safeguard the health or safety of workers.

(7) Any standard promulgated under this subsection shall prescribe the use of labels or other appropriate forms of warning as are necessary to insure that employees are apprised of all hazards to which they are exposed, relevant symptoms and appropriate emergency treatment, and proper conditions and precautions of safe use or exposure. Where appropriate, such standard shall also prescribe suitable protective equipment and control or technological procedures to be used in connection with such hazards and shall provide for monitoring or measuring employee exposure at such locations and intervals, and in such manner as may be necessary for the protection of employees. In addition, where appropriate, any such standard shall prescribe the type and frequency of medical examinations or other tests which shall be made available, by the employer or at his cost, to employees exposed to such hazards in order to most effectively determine whether the health of such employees is adversely affected by such exposure. In the event such medical examinations are in the nature of research, as determined by the Secretary of Health, Education, and Welfare, such examinations may be furnished at the expense of the Secretary of Health, Education, and Welfare. The results of such examinations or tests shall be furnished only to the Secretary or the Secretary of Health, Education, and Welfare, and, at the request of the employee, to his physician. The Secretary, in consultation with the Secretary of Health, Education, and Welfare, may by rule promulgated pursuant to section 553 of title 5, United States Code, make appropriate modifications in the foregoing requirements relating to the use of labels or other forms of warning, monitoring or measuring, and medical examinations, as may be warranted by experience, in formation, or medical or technological developments acquired subsequent to the promulgation of the relevant standard.

(8) Whenever a rule promulgated by the Secretary dif-

fers substantially from an existing national consensus standard, the Secretary shall, at the same time, publish in the Federal Register a statement of the reasons why the rule as adopted will better effectuate the purposes of this Act than the national consensus standard.

(c)(1) The Secretary shall provide, without regard to the requirements of chapter 5, title 5, United States Code, for an emergency temporary standard to take immediate effect upon publication in the Federal Register if he determines (A) that employees are exposed to grave danger from exposure to substances or agents determined to be toxic or physically harmful or from new hazards, and (B) that such emergency standard is necessary to protect employees from such danger.

(2) Such standard shall be effective until superseded by a standard promulgated in accordance with the procedures prescribed in paragraph (3) of this subsection.

(3) Upon publication of such standard in the Federal Register the Secretary shall commence a proceeding in accordance with section 6(b) of this Act, and the standard as published shall also serve as a proposed rule for the proceeding. The Secretary shall promulgate a standard under this paragraph no later than six months after publication of the emergency standard as provided in paragraph (2) of this subsection.

(d) Any affected employer may apply to the Secretary for a rule or order for a variance from a standard promulgated under this section. Affected employees shall be given notice of each such application and an opportunity to participate in a hearing. The Secretary shall issue such rule or order if he determines on the record, after opportunity for an inspection where appropriate and a hearing, that the proponent of the variance has demonstrated by a preponderance of the evidence that the conditions, practices, means, methods, operations, or processes used or proposed to be used by an employer will provide employment and places of employment to his employees which are as safe and healthful as those which would prevail if he complied with the standard. The rule or order so issued shall prescribe the conditions the employer must maintain, and the practices, means, methods, operations, and processes which he must adopt and utilize to the extent they differ from the standard in question. Such a rule or order may be modified or revoked upon application by an employer, employees, or by the Secretary on his own motion, in the manner prescribed for its issuance under this subsection at any time after six months from its issuance.

(e) Whenever the Secretary promulgates any standard, makes any rule, order, or decision, grants any exemption or extension of time, or compromises, mitigates, or settles any penalty assessed under this Act, he shall include a statement of the reasons for such action, which shall be published in the Federal Register.

(f) Any person who may be adversely affected by a standard issued under this section may at any time prior to the sixtieth day after such standard is promulgated file a petition challenging the validity of such standard with the United States court of appeals for the circuit wherein such person resides or has his principal place of business, for a judicial review of such standard. A copy of the petition shall be forthwith transmitted by the clerk of the court to the Secretary. The filing of such petition shall not, unless otherwise ordered by the court, operate as a stay of the standard. The determinations of the Secretary shall be conclusive if supported by substantial evidence in the record considered as a whole.

(g) In determining the priority for establishing standards under this section, the Secretary shall give due regard to the urgency of the need for mandatory safety and health standards for particular industries, trades, crafts, occupations, businesses, workplaces or work environments. The Secretary shall also give due regard to the recommendations of the Secretary of Health, Education, and Welfare regarding the need for mandatory standards in determining the priority for establishing such standards.

ADVISORY COMMITTEES; ADMINISTRATION

SEC. 7. (a) (1) There is hereby established a National Advisory Committee on Occupational Safety and Health consisting of twelve members appointed by the Secretary, four of whom are to be designated by the Secretary of Health, Education, and Welfare, without regard to the provisions of title 5, United States Code, governing appointments in the competitive service, and composed of representatives of management, labor, occupational safety and occupational health professions, and of the public. The Secretary shall designate one of the public members as Chairman. The members shall be selected upon the basis of their experience and competence in the field of occupational safety and health.

(2) The Committee shall advise, consult with, and make recommendations to the Secretary and the Secretary of Health, Education, and Welfare on matters relating to the administration of the Act. The Committee shall hold no fewer than two meetings during each calendar year. All meetings of the Committee shall be open to the public and a transcript shall be kept and made available for public inspection.

(3) The members of the Committee shall be compensated in accordance with the provisions of section 3109 of title 5, United States Code.

(4) The Secretary shall furnish to the Committee an executive secretary and such secretarial, clerical, and other services as are deemed necessary to the conduct of its business.

(b) An advisory committee may be appointed by the Secretary to assist him in his standard-setting functions under section 6 of this Act.
Each such committee shall consist of not more than fifteen members and shall include as a member one or more designees of the Secretary of Health, Education, and Welfare, and shall include among its members an equal number of persons qualified by experience and affiliation to present the viewpoint of the employers involved, and of persons similarly qualified to present the viewpoint of the workers involved, as well as one or more representatives of health and safety agencies of the States. An advisory committee may also include such other persons as the Secretary may appoint who are qualified by knowledge and experience to make a useful contribution to the work of such committee, including one or more representatives of professional organizations of technicians or professionals specializing in occupational safety or health, and one or more representatives of nationally recognized standards-producing organizations, but the number of persons so appointed to any such advisory committee shall not exceed the number appointed to such committee as representatives of Federal and State agencies. Persons appointed to advisory committees from private life shall be compensated in the same manner as consultants or experts under section 3109 of title 5, United States Code. The Secretary shall pay to any State which is the employer of a member of such a committee who is a representative of the health or safety agency of that State, reimbursement sufficient to cover the actual cost to the State resulting from such representative's membership on such committee. Any meeting of such committee shall be open to the public and an accurate record shall be kept and made available to the public. No member of such committee (other than representatives of employers and employees) shall have an economic interest in any proposed rule.

(c) In carrying out his responsibilities under this Act, the Secretary is authorized to—

(1) use, with the consent of any Federal agency, the services, facilities, and personnel of such agency, with or without reimbursement, and with the consent of any State or political subdivision thereof, accept and use the services, facilities, and personnel of any agency of such State or subdivision with reimbursement; and

(2) employ experts and consultants or organizations thereof as authorized by section 3109 of title 5, United States Code, except that contracts for such employment may be renewed annually; compensate individuals so employed at rates not in excess of the rate specified at the time of service for grade GS-18

under section 5332 of title 5, United States Code, including traveltime, and allow them while away from their homes or regular places of business, travel expenses (including per diem in lieu of subsistence) as authorized by section 5703 of title 5, United States Code, for persons in the Government service employed intermittently, while so employed.

INSPECTIONS, INVESTIGATIONS, AND RECORDKEEPING

SEC. 8. (a) In order to carry out the purposes of this Act, the Secretary, upon presenting appropriate credentials to the owner, operator, or agent in charge, is authorized—

(1) to enter without delay and at reasonable times any factory, plant, establishment, construction site, or other area, workplace or environment where work is performed by an employee of an employer; and

(2) to inspect and investigate during regular working hours and at other reasonable times, and within reasonable limits and in a reasonable manner, any such place of employment and all pertinent conditions, structures, machines, apparatus, devices, equipment, and materials therein, and to question privately any such employer, owner, operator, agent or employee.

(b) In making his inspections and investigations under this Act the Secretary may require the attendance and testimony of witnesses and the production of evidence under oath. Witnesses shall be paid the same fees and mileage that are paid witnesses in the courts of the United States. In case of a contumacy, failure, or refusal of any person to obey such an order, any district court of the United States or the United States courts of any territory or possession, within the jurisdiction of which such person is found, or resides or transacts business, upon the application by the Secretary, shall have jurisdiction to issue to such person an order requiring such person to appear to produce evidence if, as, and when so ordered, and to give testimony relating to the matter under investigation or in question, and any failure to obey such order of the court may be punished by said court as a contempt thereof.

(c) (1) Each employer shall make, keep and perserve, and make available to the Secretary or the Secretary of Health, Education, and Welfare, such records regarding his activities relating to this Act as the Secretary, in cooperation with the Secretary of Health, Education, and Welfare, may prescribe by regulation as necessary or appropriate for the enforcement of this Act or for developing information regarding the causes and prevention of occupational accidents and illnesses. In order to carry out the provisions of this paragraph such regulations may include provisions requiring employers to conduct periodic inspections. The Secretary shall also issue regulations requiring that employers, through posting of notices or other appropriate means, keep their employees informed of their protections and obligations under this Act, including the provisions of applicable standards.

(2) The Secretary, in cooperation with the Secretary of Health, Education, and Welfare, shall prescribe regulations requiring employers to maintain accurate records of, and to make periodic reports on, work-related deaths, injuries and illnesses other than minor injuries requiring only first aid treatment and which do not involve medical treatment, loss of consciousness, restriction of work or motion, or transfer to another job.

(3) The Secretary, in cooperation with the Secretary of Health, Education, and Welfare, shall issue regulations requiring employers to maintain accurate records of employee exposures to potentially toxic materials or harmful physical agents which are required to be monitored or measured under section 6. Such regulations shall provide employees or their representatives with an opportunity to observe such monitoring or measuring, and to have access to the records thereof. Such regulations shall also make appropriate provision for each employee or former employee to have access to such records as will indicate his own exposure to toxic materials or harmful physical agents. Each employer shall promptly notify any employee who has been or is being exposed to toxic materials or harmful physical agents in concentrations or at levels which exceed those prescribed by an applicable occupational safety and health standard promulgated under section 6, and shall inform any employee who is being thus exposed of the corrective action being taken.

(d) Any information obtained by the Secretary, the Secretary of Health, Education, and Welfare, or a State agency under this Act shall be obtained with a minimum burden upon employers, especially those operating small businesses. Unnecessary duplication of efforts in obtaining information shall be reduced to the maximum extent feasible.

(e) Subject to regulations issued by the Secretary, a representative of the employer and a representative authorized by his employees shall be given an opportunity to accompany the Secretary or his authorized representative during the physical inspection of any workplace under subsection (a) for the purpose of aiding such inspection. Where there is no authorized employee representative, the Secretary or his authorized representative shall consult with a reasonable number of employees concerning matters of health and safety in the workplace.

(f) (1) Any employees or representative of employees who believe that a violation of a safety or health standard exists that threatens physical harm, or that an imminent danger exists, may request an inspection by giving notice to the Secretary or his authorized representative of such violation or danger. Any such notice shall be reduced to writing, shall set forth with reasonable particularity the grounds for the notice, and shall be signed by the employees or representative of employees, and a copy shall be provided the employer or his agent no later than at the time of inspection, except that, upon the request of the person giving such notice, his name and the names of individual employees referred to therein shall not appear in such copy or on any record published, released, or made available pursuant to subsection (g) of this section. If upon receipt of such notification the Secretary determines there are reasonable grounds to believe that such violation or danger exists, he shall make a special inspection in accordance with the provisions of this section as soon as practicable, to determine if such violation or danger exists. If the Secretary determines there are no reasonable grounds to believe that a violation or danger exists he shall notify the employees or representative of the employees in writing of such determination.

(2) Prior to or during any inspection of a workplace, any employees or representative of employees employed in such workplace may notify the Secretary or any representative of the Secretary responsible for conducting the inspection, in writing, of any violation of this Act which they have reason to believe exists in such workplace. The Secretary shall, by regulation, establish procedures for informal review of any refusal by a representative of the Secretary to issue a citation with respect to any such alleged violation and shall furnish the employees or representative of employees requesting such review a written statement of the reasons for the Secretary's final disposition of the case.

(g) (1) The Secretary and Secretary of Health, Education, and Welfare are authorized to compile, analyze, and publish, either in summary or detailed form, all reports or information obtained under this section.

(2) The Secretary and the Secretary of Health, Education, and Welfare shall each prescribe such rules and regulations as he may deem necessary to carry out their responsibilities under this Act, including rules and regulations dealing with the inspection of an employer's establishment.

CITATIONS

SEC. 9. (a) If, upon inspection or investigation, the Secretary or his authorized representative believes that an employer has violated a requirement of section 5 of this Act, of any standard, rule or order promulgated pursuant to section 6 of this Act, or of any regulations prescribed pursuant to this Act, he shall with reasonable promptness issue a citation to the employer. Each citation shall be in writing and shall describe with particularity the nature of the violation, including a reference to the provision of the Act, standard, rule, regulation, or order alleged to have been violated. In addition, the citation shall fix a reasonable time for the abatement of the violation. The Secretary may prescribe procedures for the issuance of a notice in lieu of a citation with respect to de minimis violations which have no direct or immediate relationship to safety or health.

(b) Each citation issued under this section, or a copy or copies thereof, shall be prominently posted, as prescribed in regulations issued by the Secretary, at or near each place a violation referred to in the citation occurred.

(c) No citation may be issued under this section after the expiration of six months following the occurrence of any violation.

PROCEDURE FOR ENFORCEMENT

SEC. 10. (a) If, after an inspection or investigation, the Secretary issues a citation under section 9 (a), he shall, within a reasonable time after the termination of such inspection or investigation, notify the employer by certified mail of the penalty, if any, proposed to be assessed under section 17 and that the employer has fifteen working days within which to notify the Secretary that he wishes to contest the citation or proposed assessment of penalty. If, within fifteen working days from the receipt of the notice issued by the Secretary the employer fails to notify the Secretary that he intends to contest the citation or proposed assessment of penalty, and no notice is filed by any employee or representative of employees under subsection (c) within such time, the citation and the assessment, as proposed, shall be deemed a final order of the Commission and not subject to review by any court or agency.

(b) If the Secretary has reason to believe that an employer has failed to correct a violation for which a citation has been issued within the period permitted for its correction (which period shall not begin to run until the entry of a final order by the Commission in the case of any review proceedings under this section initiated by the employer in good faith and not solely for delay or avoidance of penalties), the Secretary shall notify the employer by certified mail of such failure and of the penalty proposed to be assessed under section 17 by reason of such failure, and that the employer has fifteen working days within which to notify the Secretary that he wishes to contest the Secretary's notification or the proposed assessment of penalty. If, within fifteen working days from the receipt of notification issued by the Secretary, the employer fails to notify the Secretary that he intends to contest the notification or proposed assessment of penalty, the notification and assessment, as proposed, shall be deemed a final order of the Commission and not subject to review by any court or agency.

(c) If an employer notifies the Secretary that he intends to contest a citation issued under section 9(a) or notification issued under subsection (a) or (b) of this section, or if, within fifteen working days of the issuance of a citation under section 9(a), any employee or representative of employees files a notice with the Secretary alleging that the period of time fixed in the citation for the abatement of the violation is unreasonable, the Secretary shall immediately advise the Commission of such notification, and the Commission shall afford an opportunity for a hearing (in accordance with section 554 of title 5, United States Code, but without regard to subsection (a) (3) of such section). The Commission shall thereafter issue an order, based on findings of fact, affirming, modifying, or vacating the Secretary's citation or proposed penalty, or directing other appropriate relief, and such order shall become final thirty days after its issuance. Upon a showing by an employer of a good faith effort to comply with the abatement requirements of a citation, and that abatement has not been completed because of factors beyond his reasonable control, the Secretary, after an opportunity for a hearing as provided in this subsection, shall issue an order affirming or modifying the abatement requirements in such citation. The rules of procedure prescribed by the Commission shall provide affected employees or representatives of affected employees an opportunity to participate as parties to hearings under this subsection.

JUDICIAL REVIEW

SEC. 11. (a) Any person adversely affected or aggrieved by an order of the Commission issued under subsection (c) of section 10 may obtain a review of such order in any United States court of appeals for the circuit in which the violation is alleged to have occurred or where the employer has its principal office, or in the Court of Appeals for the District of Columbia Circuit, by filing in such court within sixty days following the issuance of such order a written petition praying that the order be modified or set aside. A copy of such petition shall be forthwith transmitted by the clerk of the court to the Commission and to the other parties, and thereupon the Commission shall file in the court the record in the proceeding as provided in section 2112 of title 28, United States Code. Upon such filing, the court shall have jurisdiction of the proceeding and of the question determined therein, and shall have power to grant such temporary relief or restraining order as it deems just and proper, and to make and enter upon the pleadings, testimony, and proceedings set forth in such record a decree affirming, modifying, or setting aside in whole or in part, the order of the Commission and enforcing the same to the extent that such order is affirmed or modified. The commencement of proceedings under this subsection shall not, unless ordered by the court, operate as a stay of the order of the Commission. No objection that has not been urged before the Commission shall be considered by the Court, unless the failure or neglect to urge such objection shall be excused because of extraordinary circumstances. The findings of the Commission with respect to questions of fact, if supported by substantial evidence on the record considered as a whole, shall be conclusive. If any party shall apply to the court for leave to adduce additional evidence and shall show to the satisfaction of the court that such additional evidence is material and that there were reasonable grounds for the failure to adduce such evidence in the hearing before the Commission, the court may order such additional evidence to be taken before the Commission and to be made a part of the record. The Commission may modify its findings as to the facts, or make new findings, by reason of additional evidence so taken and filed, and it shall file such modified or new findings, which findings with respect to questions of fact, if supported by substantial evidence on the record considered as a whole, shall be conclusive, and its recommendations, if any, for the modification or setting aside of its original order. Upon the filing of the record with it, the jurisdiction of the court shall be exclusive and its judgment and decree shall be final, except that the same shall be subject to review by the Supreme Court of the United States, as provided in section 1254 of title 28, United States Code. Petitions filed under this subsection shall be heard expeditiously.

(b) The Secretary may also obtain review or enforcement of any final order of the Commission by filing a petition for such relief in the United States court of appeals for the circuit in which the alleged violation occurred or in which the employer has its principal office, and the provisions of subsection (a) shall govern such proceedings to the extent applicable. If no petition for review, as provided in subsection (a), is filed within sixty days after service of the Commission's order, the Commission's findings of fact and order shall be conclusive in connection with any petition for enforcement which is filed by the Secretary after the expiration of such sixty-day period. In any such case, as well as in the case of a noncontested citation or notification by the Secretary which has become a final order of the Commission under subsection (a) or (b) of section 10, the clerk of the court, unless otherwise ordered by the court, shall forthwith enter a decree enforcing the order and shall transmit a copy of such decree to the Secretary and the employer named in the petition. In any contempt proceeding brought to enforce a decree of a court of appeals entered pursuant to this subsection or subsection (a), the court of appeals may assess the penalties provided in section 17, in addition to invoking any other available remedies.

(c) (1) No person shall discharge or in any manner discriminate against any employee because such employee has filed any complaint or instituted or caused to be instituted any proceeding under or related to this Act or has testified or is about to testify in any such proceeding or because of the exercise by such employee on behalf of himself or others of any right afforded by this Act.

(2) Any employee who believes that he has been discharged or otherwise discriminated against by any person in violation of this subsection may, within thirty days after such violation occurs, file a complaint with the Secretary alleging such discrimination. Upon receipt of such complaint, the Secretary shall cause such investigation to be made as he deems appropriate. If upon such investigation, the Secretary determines that the provisions of this subsection have been violated, he shall bring an action in any appropriate United States district court against such person. In any such action the United States district courts shall have jurisdiction, for cause shown to restrain violations of paragraph (1) of this subsection and order all appropriate relief including rehiring or reinstatement of the employee to his former position with back pay.

(3) Within 90 days of the receipt of a complaint filed under this subsection the Secretary shall notify the complainant of his determination under paragraph 2 of this subsection.

THE OCCUPATIONAL SAFETY AND HEALTH REVIEW COMMISSION

SEC. 12. (a) The Occupational Safety and Health Review Commission is hereby established. The Commission shall be composed of three members who shall be appointed by the President, by and with the advice and consent of the Senate, from among persons who by reason of training, education, or experience are qualified to carry out the functions of the Commission under this Act. The President shall designate one of the members of the Commission to serve as Chairman.

(b) The terms of members of the Commission shall be six years except that (1) the members of the Commission first taking office shall serve, as designated by the President at the time of appointment, one for a term of two years, one for a term of four years, and one for a term of six years, and (2) a vacancy caused by the death, resignation, or removal of a member prior to the expiration of the term for which he was appointed shall be filled only for the remainder of such unexpired term. A member of the Commission may be removed by the President for inefficiency, neglect of duty, or malfeasance in office.

(c) (1) Section 5314 of title 5, United States Code, is amended by adding at the end thereof the following new paragraph:

"(57) Chairman, Occupational Safety and Health Review Commission."

(2) Section 5315 of title 5, United States Code, is amended by adding at the end thereof the following new paragraph:

"(94) Members, Occupational Safety and Health Review Commission."

(d) The principal office of the Commission shall be in the District of Columbia. Whenever the Commission deems that the convenience of the public or of the parties may be promoted, or delay or expense may be minimized, it may hold hearings or conduct other proceedings at any other place.

(e) The Chairman shall be responsible on behalf of the Commission for the administrative operations of the Commission and shall appoint such hearing examiners and other employees as he deems necessary to assist in the performance of the Commission's functions and to fix their compensation in accordance with the provisions of chapter 51 and subchapter III of chapter 53 of title 5, United States Code, relating to classification and General Schedule pay rates: *Provided,* That assignment, removal and compensation of hearing examiners shall be in accordance with sections 3105, 3344, 5362, and 7521 of title 5, United States Code.

(f) For the purpose of carrying out its functions under this Act, two members of the Commission shall constitute a quorum and official action can be taken only on the affirmative vote of at least two members.

(g) Every official act of the Commission shall be entered of record, and its hearings and records shall be open to the public. The Commission is authorized to make such rules as are necessary for the orderly transaction of its proceedings. Unless the Commission has adopted a different rule, its proceedings shall be in accordance with the Federal Rules of Civil Procedure.

(h) The Commission may order testimony to be taken by deposition in any proceedings pending before it at any state of such proceeding. Any person may be compelled to appear and depose, and to produce books, papers, or documents, in the same manner as witnesses may be compelled to appear and testify and produce like documentary evidence before the Commission. Witnesses whose depositions are taken under this subsection, and the persons taking such depositions, shall be entitled to the same fees as are paid for like services in the courts of the United States.

(i) For the purpose of any proceeding before the Commission, the provisions of section 11 of the National Labor Relations Act (29 U.S.C. 161) are hereby made applicable to the jurisdiction and powers of the Commission.

(j) A hearing examiner appointed by the Commission shall hear, and make a determination upon, any proceeding instituted before the Commission and any motion in connection therewith, assigned to such hearing examiner by the Chairman of the Commission, and shall make a report of any such determination which constitutes his final disposition of the proceedings. The report of the hearing examiner shall become the final order of the Commission within thirty days after such report by the hearing examiner, unless within such period any Commission member has directed that such report shall be reviewed by the Commission.

(k) Except as otherwise provided in this Act, the hearing examiners shall be subject to the laws governing employees in the classified civil service, except that appointments shall be made without regard to section 5108 of title 5, United States Code. Each hearing examiner shall receive compensation at a rate not less than that prescribed for GS-16 under section 5332 of title 5, United States Code.

PROCEDURES TO COUNTERACT IMMINENT DANGERS

SEC. 13. (a) The United States district courts shall have jurisdiction, upon petition of the Secretary, to restrain any conditions or practices in any place of employment which are such that a danger exists which could reasonably be expected to cause death or serious physical harm immediately or before the imminence of such danger can be eliminated through the enforcement procedures otherwise provided by this Act. Any order issued under this section may require such steps to be taken as may be necessary to avoid, correct, or remove such imminent danger and prohibit the employment or presence of any individual in locations or under conditions where such imminent danger exists, except individuals whose presence is necessary to avoid, correct, or remove such imminent danger or to maintain the capacity of a continuous process operation to resume normal operations without a complete cessation of operations, or where a cessation of operations is necessary, to permit such to be accomplished in a safe and orderly manner.

(b) Upon the filing of any such petition the district court shall have jurisdiction to grant such injunctive relief or temporary restraining order pending the outcome of an enforcement proceeding pursuant to this Act. The proceeding shall be as provided by Rule 65 of the Federal Rules, Civil Procedure, except that no temporary restraining order issued without notice shall be effective for a period longer than five days.

(c) Whenever and as soon as an inspector concludes that conditions or practices described in subsection (a) exist in any place of employment, he shall inform the affected employees and employers of the danger and that he is recommending to the Secretary that relief be sought.

(d) If the Secretary arbitrarily or capriciously fails to seek relief under this section, any employee who may be injured by reason of such failure, or the representative of such employees, might bring an action against the Secretary in the United States district court for the district in which the imminent danger is alleged to exist or the employer has its principal office, or for the District of Columbia, for a writ of mandamus to compel the Secretary to seek such an order and for such further relief as may be appropriate.

REPRESENTATION IN CIVIL LITIGATION

SEC. 14. Except as provided in section 518(a) of title 28, United States Code, relating to litigation before the Supreme Court, the Solicitor of Labor may appear for and represent the Secretary in any civil litigation brought under this Act but all such litigation shall be subject to the direction and control of the Attorney General.

CONFIDENTIALITY OF TRADE SECRETS

SEC. 15. All information reported to or otherwise obtained by the Secretary or his representative in connection with any inspection or proceeding under this Act which contains or which might reveal a trade secret referred to in section 1905 of title 18 of the United States Code shall be considered confidential for the purpose of that section, except that such information may be disclosed to other officers or employees concerned with carrying out this Act or when relevant in any proceeding under this Act. In any such proceeding the Secretary, the Commission, or the court shall issue such orders as may be appropriate to protect the confidentiality of trade secrets.

VARIATIONS, TOLERANCES, AND EXEMPTIONS

SEC. 16. The Secretary, on the record, after notice and opportunity for a hearing may provide such reasonable limitations and may make such rules and regulations allowing reasonable variations, tolerances, and exemptions to and from any or all provisions of this Act as he may find necessary and proper to avoid serious impairment of the national defense. Such action shall not be in effect for more than six months without notification to affected employees and an opportunity being afforded for a hearing.

PENALTIES

SEC. 17. (a) Any employer who willfully or repeatedly violates the requirements of section 5 of this Act, any standard, rule, or order promulgated pursuant to section 6 of this Act, or regulations prescribed pursuant to this Act, may be assessed a civil penalty of not more than $10,000 for each violation.

(b) Any employer who has received a citation for a serious violation of the requirements of section 5 of this Act, of any standard, rule, or order promulgated pursuant to section 6 of this Act, or of any regulations prescribed pursuant to this Act, shall be assessed a civil penalty of up to $1,000 for each such violation.

(c) Any employer who has received a citation for a violation of the requirements of section 5 of this Act, of any standard, rule, or order promulgated pursuant to section 6 of this Act, or of regulations prescribed pursuant to this Act, and such violation is specifically determined not to be of a serious nature, may be assessed a civil penalty of up to $1,000 for each such violation.

(d) Any employer who fails to correct a violation for which a citation has been issued under section 9(a) within the period permitted for its correction (which period shall not begin to run until the date of the final order of the Commission in the case of any review proceeding under section 10 initiated by the employer in good faith and not solely for delay or avoidance of penalties), may be assessed a civil penalty of not more than $1,000 for each day during which such failure or violation continues.

(e) Any employer who willfully violates any standard, rule, or order promulgated pursuant to section 6 of this Act, or of any regulations prescribed pursuant to this Act, and that violation caused death to any employee, shall, upon conviction, be punished by a fine of not more than $10,000 or by imprisonment for not more than six months, or by both; except that if the conviction is for a violation committed after a first conviction of such person, punishment shall be by a fine of not more than $20,000 or by imprisonment for not more than one year, or by both.

(f) Any person who gives advance notice of any inspection to be conducted under this Act, without authority from the Secretary or his designees, shall, upon conviction, be punished by a fine of not more than $1,000 or by imprisonment for not more than six months, or by both.

(g) Whoever knowingly makes any false statement, representation, or certification in any application, record, report, plan, or other document filed or required to be maintained pursuant to this Act shall, upon conviction, be punished by a fine of not more than $10,000, or by imprisonment for not more than six months, or by both.

(h) (1) Section 1114 of title 18, United States Code, is hereby amended by striking out "designated by the Secretary of Health, Education, and Welfare to conduct investigations, or inspections under the Federal Food, Drug, and Cosmetic Act" and inserting in lieu thereof "or of the Department of Labor assigned to perform investigative, inspection, or law enforcement functions".

(2) Notwithstanding the provisions of sections 1111 and 1114 of title 18, United States Code, whoever, in violation of the provisions of section 1114 of such title, kills a person while engaged in or on account of the performance of investigative, inspection, or law enforcement functions added to such section 1114 by paragraph (1) of this subsection, and who would otherwise be subject to the penalty provisions of such section 1111, shall be punished by imprisonment for any term of years or for life.

(i) Any employer who violates any of the posting requirements, as prescribed under the provisions of this Act, shall be assessed a civil penalty of up to $1,000 for each violation.

(j) The Commission shall have authority to assess all civil penalties provided in this section, giving due consideration to the appropriateness of the penalty with respect to the size of the business of the employer being charged, the gravity of the violation, the good faith of the employer, and the history of previous violations.

(k) For purposes of this section, a serious violation shall be deemed to exist in a place of employment if there is a substantial probability that death or serious physical harm could result from a condition which exists, or from one or more practices, means, methods, operations, or processes which have been adopted or are in use, in such place of employment unless the employer did not, and could not with the exercise of reasonable diligence, know of the presence of the violation.

(l) Civil penalties owed under this Act shall be paid to the Secretary for deposit into the Treasury of the United States and shall accrue to the United States and may be recovered in a civil action in the name of the United States brought in the United States district court for the district where the violation is alleged to have occurred or where the employer has its principal office.

STATE JURISDICTION AND STATE PLANS

SEC. 18. (a) Nothing in this Act shall prevent any State agency or court from asserting jurisdiction under State law over any occupational safety or health issue with respect to which no standard is in effect under section 6.

(b) Any State which, at any time, desires to assume responsibility for development and enforcement therein of occupational safety and health standards relating to any occupational safety or health issue with respect to which a Federal standard has been promulgated under section 6 shall submit a State plan for the development of such standards and their enforcement.

(c) The Secretary shall approve the plan submitted by a State under subsection (b), or any modification thereof, if such plan in his judgment—

(1) designates a State agency or agencies as the agency or agencies responsible for administering the plan throughout the State,

(2) provides for the development and enforcement of safety and health standards relating to one or more safety or health issues, which standards (and the enforcement of which standards) are or will be at least as effective in providing safe and healthful employment and places of employment as the standards promulgated under section 6 which relate to the same issues, and which standards, when applicable to products

which are distributed or used in interstate commerce, are required by compelling local conditions and do not unduly burden interstate commerce,

(3) provides for a right of entry and inspection of all workplaces subject to the Act which is at least as effective as that provided in section 8, and includes a prohibition on advance notice of inspections,

(4) contains satisfactory assurances that such agency or agencies have or will have the legal authority and qualified personnel necessary for the enforcement of such standards,

(5) gives satisfactory assurances that such State will devote adequate funds to the administration and enforcement of such standards,

(6) contains satisfactory assurances that such State will, to the extent permitted by its law, establish and maintain an effective and comprehensive occupational safety and health program applicable to all employees of public agencies of the State and its political subdivisions, which program is as effective as the standards contained in an approved plan,

(7) requires employers in the State to make reports to the Secretary in the same manner and to the same extent as if the plan were not in effect, and

(8) provides that the State agency will make such reports to the Secretary in such form and containing such information, as the Secretary shall from time to time require.

(d) If the Secretary rejects a plan submitted under subsection (b), he shall afford the State submitting the plan due notice and opportunity for a hearing before so doing.

(e) After the Secretary approves a State plan submitted under subsection (b), he may, but shall not be required to, exercise his authority under sections 8, 9, 10, 13, and 17 with respect to comparable standards promulgated under section 6, for the period specified in the next sentence. The Secretary may exercise the authority referred to above until he determines, on the basis of actual operations under the State plan, that the criteria set forth in subsection (c) are being applied, but he shall not make such determination for at least three years after the plan's approval under subsection (c). Upon making the determination referred to in the preceding sentence, the provisions of sections 5(a) (2), 8 (except for the purpose of carrying out subsection (f) of this section), 9, 10, 13, and 17, and standards promulgated under section 6 of this Act, shall not apply with respect to any occupational safety or health issues covered under the plan, but the Secretary may retain jurisdiction under the above provisions in any proceeding commenced under section 9 or 10 before the date of determination.

(f) The Secretary shall, on the basis of reports submitted by the State agency and his own inspections make a continuing evaluation of the manner in which each State having a plan approved under this section is carrying out such plan. Whenever the Secretary finds, after affording due notice and opportunity for a hearing, that in the administration of the State plan there is a failure to comply substantially with any provision of the State plan (or any assurance contained therein), he shall notify the State agency of his withdrawal of approval of such plan and upon receipt of such notice such plan shall cease to be in effect, but the State may retain jurisdiction in any case commenced before the withdrawal of the plan in order to enforce standards under the plan whenever the issues involved do not relate to the reasons for the withdrawal of the plan.

(g) The State may obtain a review of a decision of the Secretary withdrawing approval of or rejecting its plan by the United States court of appeals for the circuit in which the State is located by filing in such court within thirty days following receipt of notice of such decision a petition to modify or set aside in whole or in part the action of the Secretary. A copy of such petition shall forthwith be served upon the Secretary, and thereupon the Secretary shall certify and file in the court the record upon which the decision complained of was issued as provided in section 2112 of title 28, United States Code. Unless the court finds that the Secretary's decision in rejecting a proposed State plan or withdrawing his approval of such a plan is not supported by substantial evidence the court shall affirm the Secretary's decision. The judgment of the court shall be subject to review by the Supreme Court of the United States upon certiorari or certification as provided in section 1254 of title 28, United States Code.

(h) The Secretary may enter into an agreement with a State under which the State will be permitted to continue to enforce one or more occupational health and safety standards in effect in such State until final action is taken by the Secretary with respect to a plan submitted by a State under subsection (b) of this section, or two years from the date of enactment of this Act, whichever is earlier.

FEDERAL AGENCY SAFETY PROGRAMS AND RESPONSIBILITIES

SEC. 19. (a) It shall be the responsibility of the head of each Federal agency to establish and maintain an effective and comprehensive occupational safety and health program which is consistent with the standards promulgated under section 6. The head of each agency shall (after consultation with representatives of the employees thereof)—

(1) provide safe and healthful places and conditions of employment, consistent with the standards set under section 6;

(2) acquire, maintain, and require the use of safety equipment, personal protective equipment, and devices reasonably necessary to protect employees;

(3) keep adequate records of all occupational accidents and illnesses for proper evaluation and necessary corrective action;

(4) consult with the Secretary with regard to the adequacy as to form and content of records kept pursuant to subsection (a) (3) of this section; and

(5) make an annual report to the Secretary with respect to occupational accidents and injuries and the agency's program under this section. Such report shall include any report submitted under section 7902(e) (2) of title 5, United States Code.

(b) The Secretary shall report to the President a summary or digest of reports submitted to him under subsection (a) (5) of this section, together with his evaluations of and recommendations derived from such reports. The President shall transmit annually to the Senate and the House of Representatives a report of the activities of Federal agencies under this section.

(c) Section 7902(c) (1) of title 5, United States Code, is amended by inserting after "agencies" the following: "and of labor organizations representing employees".

(d) The Secretary shall have access to records and reports kept and filed by Federal agencies pursuant to subsections (a) (3) and (5) of this section unless those records and reports are specifically required by Executive order to be kept secret in the interest of the national defense or foreign policy, in which case the Secretary shall have access to such information as will not jeopardize national defense or foreign policy.

RESEARCH AND RELATED ACTIVITIES

SEC. 20. (a) (1) The Secretary of Health, Education, and Welfare, after consultation with the Secretary and with other appropriate Federal departments or agencies, shall conduct (directly or by grants or contracts) research, experiments, and demonstrations relating to occupational safety and health, including studies of psychological factors involved, and relating to innovative methods, techniques, and approaches for dealing with occupational safety and health problems.

(2) The Secretary of Health, Education, and Welfare shall from time to time consult with the Secretary in order to develop specific plans for such research, demonstrations, and experiments as are necessary to produce criteria, including criteria identifying toxic substances, enabling the Secretary to meet his responsibility for the formulation of safety and health standards under this Act; and the Secretary of Health, Education, and Welfare, on the basis of such research, demonstrations, and experiments and any other information available to him, shall develop and publish at least annually such criteria as will effectuate the purposes of this Act.

(3) The Secretary of Health, Education, and Welfare, on the basis of such research, demonstrations, and experiments, and any other information available to him, shall develop criteria dealing with toxic materials and harmful physical agents and substances which will describe exposure levels that are safe for various periods of employment, including but not limited to the exposure levels at which no employee will suffer impaired health or functional capacities or diminished life expectancy as a result of his work experience.

(4) The Secretary of Health, Education, and Welfare shall also conduct special research, experiments, and demonstrations relating to occupational safety and health as are necessary to explore new problems, including those created by new technology in occupational safety and health, which may require ameliorative action beyond that which is otherwise provided for in the operating provisions of this Act. The Secretary of Health, Education, and Welfare shall also conduct research into the motivational and behavioral factors relating to the field of occupational safety and health.

(5) The Secretary of Health, Education, and Welfare, in order to comply with his responsibilties under paragraph (2), and in order to develop needed information regarding potentially toxic substances or harmful physical agents, may prescribe regulations requiring employers to measure, record, and make reports on the exposure of employees to substances or physical agents which the Secretary of Health, Education, and Welfare reasonably believes may endanger the health or safety of employees. The Secretary of Health, Education, and Welfare also is authorized to establish such programs of medical examinations and tests as may be necessary for determining the incidence of occupational illnesses and the susceptibility of employees to such illnesses. Nothing in this or any other provision of this Act shall be deemed to authorize or require medical examination, immunization, or treatment for those who object thereto on religious grounds, except where such is necessary for the protection of the health or safety of others. Upon the request of any employer who is required to measure and record exposure of employees to substances or physical agents as provided under this subsection, the Secretary of Health, Education, and Welfare shall furnish full financial or other assistance to such employer for the purpose of defraying any additional expense incurred by him in carrying out the measuring and recording as provided in this subsection.

(6) The Secretary of Health, Education, and Welfare shall publish within six months of enactment of this Act and thereafter as needed but at least annually a list of all known toxic substances by generic family or other useful grouping, and the concentrations at which such toxicity is known to occur. He shall determine following a written request by any employer or authorized representative of employees, specifying with reasonable particularity the grounds on which the request is made, whether any substance normally found in the place of employment has potentially toxic effects in such concentrations as used or found; and shall submit such determination both to employers and affected employees as soon as possible. If the Secretary of Health, Education, and Welfare determines that any substance is potentially toxic at the concentrations in which it is used or found in a place of employment, and such substance is not covered by an occupational safety or health standard promulgated under section 6, the Secretary of Health, Education, and Welfare shall immediately submit such determination to the Secretary, together with all pertinent criteria.

(7) Within two years of enactment of this Act, and annually thereafter the Secretary of Health, Education, and Welfare shall conduct and publish industrywide studies of the effect of chronic or low-level exposure to industrial materials, processes, and stresses on the potential for illness, disease, or loss of functional capacity in aging adults.

(b) The Secretary of Health, Education, and Welfare is authorized to make inspections and question employers and employees as provided in section 8 of this Act in order to carry out his functions and responsibilities under this section.

(c) The Secretary is authorized to enter into contracts, agreements, or other arrangements with appropriate public agencies or private organizations for the purpose of conducting studies relating to his responsibilities under this Act. In carrying out his responsibilities under this subsection, the Secretary shall cooperate with the Secretary of Health, Education, and Welfare in order to avoid any duplication of efforts under this section.

(d) Information obtained by the Secretary and the Secretary of Health, Education, and Welfare under this section shall be disseminated by the Secretary to employers and employees and organizations thereof.

(e) The functions of the Secretary of Health, Education, and Welfare under this Act shall, to the extent feasible, be delegated to the Director of the National Institute for Occupational Safety and Health established by section 22 of this Act.

TRAINING AND EMPLOYEE EDUCATION

SEC. 21. (a) The Secretary of Health, Education, and Welfare, after consultation with the Secretary and with other appropriate Federal departments and agencies, shall conduct, directly or by grants or contracts (1) education programs to provide an adequate supply of qualified personnel to carry out the purposes of this Act, and (2) informational programs on the importance of and proper use of adequate safety and health equipment.

(b) The Secretary is also authorized to conduct, directly or by grants or contracts, short-term training of personnel engaged in work related to his responsibilities under this Act.

(c) The Secretary, in consultation with the Secretary of Health, Education, and Welfare, shall (1) provide for the establishment and supervision of programs for the education and training of employers and employees in the recognition, avoidance, and prevention of unsafe or unhealthful working conditions in employments covered by this Act, and (2) consult with and advise employers and employees, and organizations representing employers and employees as to effective means of preventing occupational injuries and illnesses.

NATIONAL INSTITUTE FOR OCCUPATIONAL SAFETY AND HEALTH

SEC. 22. (a) It is the purpose of this section to establish a National Institute for Occupational Safety and Health in the Department of Health, Education, and Welfare in order to carry out the policy set forth in section 2 of this Act and to perform the functions of the Secretary of Health, Education, and Welfare under sections 20 and 21 of this Act.

(b) There is hereby established in the Department of Health, Education, and Welfare a National Institute for Occupational Safety and Health. The Institute shall be headed by a Director who shall be appointed by the Secretary of Health, Education, and Welfare, and who shall serve for a term of six years unless previously removed by the Secretary of Health, Education, and Welfare.

(c) The Institute is authorized to—

(1) develop and establish recommended occupational safety and health standards; and

(2) perform all functions of the Secretary of Health, Education, and Welfare under sections 20 and 21 of this Act.

(d) Upon his own initiative, or upon the request of the Secretary or the Secretary of Health, Education, and Welfare, the Director is authorized (1) to conduct such research and experimental programs as he determines are necessary for the development of criteria for new and improved occupational safety and health standards, and (2) after consideration of the results of such research and experimental programs make recommendations concerning new or improved occupational safety and health standards. Any occupational safety and health standard recommended pursuant to this section shall immediately be forwarded to the Secretary of Labor, and to the Secretary of Health, Education, and Welfare.

(e) In addition to any authority vested in the Institute by other provisions of this section, the Director, in carrying out the functions of the Institute, is authorized to—

(1) prescribe such regulations as he deems necessary governing the manner in which its functions shall be carried out;

(2) receive money and other property donated, bequeathed, or devised, without condition or restriction other than that it be used for the purposes of the Institute and to use, sell, or otherwise dispose of such property for the purpose of carrying out its functions;

(3) receive (and use, sell, or otherwise dispose of, in accordance with paragraph (2)), money and other property donated, bequeathed, or devised to the Institute with a condition or restriction, including a condition that the Institute use other funds of the Institute for the purposes of the gift;

(4) in accordance with the civil service laws, appoint and fix the compensation of such personnel as may be necessary to carry out the provisions of this section;

(5) obtain the services of experts and consultants in accordance with the provisions of section 3109 of title 5, United States Code;

(6) accept and utilize the services of voluntary and noncompensated personnel and reimburse them for travel expenses, including per diem, as authorized by section 5703 of title 5, United States Code;

(7) enter into contracts, grants or other arrangements, or modifications thereof to carry out the provisions of this section, and such contracts or modifications thereof may be entered into without performance or other bonds, and without regard to section 3709 of the Revised Statutes, as amended (41 U.S.C. 5), or any other provision of law relating to competitive bidding;

(8) make advance, progress, and other payments which the Director deems necessary under this title without regard to the provisions of section 3648 of the Revised Statutes, as amended (31 U.S.C. 529); and

(9) make other necessary expenditures.

(f) The Director shall submit to the Secretary of Health, Education, and Welfare, to the President, and to the Congress an annual report of the operations of the Institute under this Act, which shall include a detailed statement of all private and public funds received and expended by it, and such recommendations as he deems appropriate.

GRANTS TO THE STATES

SEC. 23. (a) The Secretary is authorized, during the fiscal year ending June 30, 1971, and the two succeeding fiscal years, to make grants to the States which have designated a State agency under section 18 to assist them—

(1) in identifying their needs and responsibilities in the area of occupational safety and health,

(2) in developing State plans under section 18, or

(3) in developing plans for—

(A) establishing systems for the collection of information concerning the nature and frequency of occupational injuries and diseases;

(B) increasing the expertise and enforcement capabilities of their personnel engaged in occupational safety and health programs; or

(C) otherwise improving the administration and enforcement of State occupational safety and health laws, including standards thereunder, consistent with the objectives of this Act.

(b) The Secretary is authorized, during the fiscal year ending June 30, 1971, and the two succeeding fiscal years, to make grants to the States for experimental and demonstration projects consistent with the objectives set forth in subsection (a) of this section.

(c) The Governor of the State shall designate the appropriate State agency for receipt of any grant made by the Secretary under this section.

(d) Any State agency designated by the Governor of the State desiring a grant under this section shall submit an application therefor to the Secretary.

(e) The Secretary shall review the application, and shall, after consultation with the Secretary of Health, Education, and Welfare, approve or reject such application.

(f) The Federal share for each State grant under subsection (a) or (b) of this section may not exceed 90 per centum of the total cost of the application. In the event the Federal share for all States under either such subsection is not the same, the differences among the States shall be established on the basis of objective criteria.

(g) The Secretary is authorized to make grants to the States to assist them in administering and enforcing programs for occupational safety and health contained in State plans approved by the Secretary pursuant to section 18 of this Act. The Federal share for each State grant under this subsection may not exceed 50 per centum of the total cost to the State of such a program. The last sentence of subsection (f) shall be applicable in determining the Federal share under this subsection.

(h) Prior to June 30, 1973, The Secretary shall, after consultation with the Secretary of Health, Education, and Welfare, transmit a report to the President and to the Congress, describing the experience under the grant programs authorized by this section and making any recommendations he may deem appropriate.

STATISTICS

SEC. 24. (a) In order to further the purposes of this Act, the Secretary, in consultation with the Secretary of Health, Education, and Welfare, shall develop and maintain an effective program of collection, compilation, and analysis of occupational safety and health statistics. Such program may cover all employments whether or not subject to any other provisions of this Act but shall not cover employments excluded by section 4 of the Act. The Secretary shall compile accurate statistics on work injuries and illnesses which shall include all disabling, serious, or significant injuries and illnesses, whether or not involving loss of time from work, other than minor injuries requiring only first aid treatment and which do not involve medical treatment, loss of consciousness, restriction of work or motion, or transfer to another job.

(b) To carry out his duties under subsection (a) of this section, the Secretary may—

(1) promote, encourage, or directly engage in programs of studies, information and communication concerning occupational safety and health statistics;

(2) make grants to States or political subdivisions thereof in order to assist them in developing and administering programs dealing with occupational safety and health statistics; and

(3) arrange, through grants or contracts, for the conduct of such research and investigations as give promise of furthering the objectives of this section.

(c) The Federal share for each grant under subsection (b) of this section may be up to 50 per centum of the State's total cost.

(d) The Secretary may, with the consent of any State or political subdivision thereof, accept and use the services, facilities, and employees of the agencies of such State or political subdivision, with or without reimbursement, in order to assist him in carrying out his functions under this section.

(e) One the basis of the records made and kept pursuant to section 8 (c) of this Act, employers shall file such reports with the Secretary as he shall prescribe by regulation, as necessary to carry out his functions under this Act.

(f) Agreements between the Department of Labor and States pertaining to the collection of occupational safety and health statistics already in effect on the effective date of this Act shall remain in effect until superseded by grants or contracts made under this Act.

AUDITS

SEC. 25. (a) Each recipient of a grant under this Act shall keep such records as the Secretary or the Secretary of Health, Education, and Welfare shall prescribe, including records which fully disclose the amount and disposition by such recipient of the proceeds of such grant, the total cost of the project or undertaking in connection with which such grant is made or used, and the amount of that portion of the cost of the project or undertaking supplied by other sources, and such other records as will facilitate an effective audit.

(b) The Secretary or the Secretary of Health, Education, and Welfare, and the Comptroller General of the United States, or any of their duly authorized representatives, shall have access for the purpose of audit and examination to any books, documents, papers, and records of the recipients of any grant under this Act that are pertinent to any such grant.

ANNUAL REPORT

SEC. 26. Within one hundred and twenty days following the convening of each regular session of each Congress, the Secretary and the Secretary of Health, Education, and Welfare shall each prepare and submit to the President for transmittal to the Congress a report upon the subject matter of this Act, the progress toward achievement of the purpose of this Act, the needs and requirements in the field of occupational safety and health, and any other relevant information. Such reports shall include information regarding occupational safety and health standards, and criteria for such standards, developed during the preceding year; evaluation of standards and criteria previously developed under this Act, defining areas of emphasis for new criteria and standards; an evaluation of the degree of observance of applicable occupational safety and health standards, and a summary of inspection and enforcement activity undertaken; analysis and evaluation of research activities for which results have been obtained under governmental and nongovernmental sponsorship; an analysis of major occupational diseases; evaluation of available control and measurement technology for hazards for which standards or criteria have been developed during the preceding year; description of cooperative efforts undertaken between Government agencies and other interested parties in the implementation of this Act during the preceding year; a progress report on the development of an adequate supply of trained manpower in the field of occupational safety and health, including estimates of future needs and the efforts being made by Government and others to meet those needs; listing of all toxic substances in industrial usage for which labeling requirements, criteria, or standards have not yet been established; and such recommendations for additional legislation as are deemed necessary to protect the safety and health of the worker and improve the administration of this Act.

NATIONAL COMMISSION ON STATE WORKMEN'S COMPENSATION LAWS

SEC. 27. (a) (1) The Congress hereby finds and declares that—

(A) the vast majority of American workers, and their families, are dependent on workmen's compensation for their basic economic security in the event such workers suffer disabling injury or death in the course of their employment; and that the full protection of American workers from job-related injury or death requires an adequate, prompt, and equitable system of workmen's compensation as well as an effective program of occupational health and safety regulation; and

(B) in recent years serious questions have been raised concerning the fairness and adequacy of present workmen's compensation laws in the light of the growth of the economy, the changing nature of the labor force, increases in medical knowledge, changes in the hazards associated with various types of employment, new technology creating new risks to health and safety, and increases in the general level of wages and the cost of living.

(2) The purpose of this section is to authorize an effective study and objective evaluation of State workmen's compensation laws in order to determine if such laws provide an adequate, prompt, and equitable system of compensation for injury or death arising out of or in the course of employment.

(b) There is hereby established a National Commission on State Workmen's Compensation Laws.

(c) (1) The Workmen's Compensation Commission shall be composed of fifteen members to be appointed by the President from among members of State workmen's compensation boards, representatives of insurance carriers, business, labor, members of the medical profession having experience in industrial medicine or in workmen's compensation cases, educators having special expertise in the field of workmen's compensation, and representatives of the general public. The Secretary, the Secretary of Commerce, and the Secretary of Health, Education, and Welfare shall be ex officio members of the Workmen's Compensation Commission:

(2) Any vacancy in the Workmen's Compensation Commission shall not affect its powers.

(3) The President shall designate one of the members to serve as Chairman and one to serve as Vice Chairman of the Workmen's Compensation Commission.

(4) Eight members of the Workmen's Compensation Commission shall constitute a quorum.

(d) (1) The Workmen's Compensation Commission shall undertake a comprehensive study and evaluation of State workmen's compensation laws in order to determine if such laws provide an adequate, prompt, and equitable system of compensation. Such study and evaluation shall include, without being limited to, the following subjects: (A) the amount and duration of permanent and temporary disability benefits and the criteria for determining the maximum limitations thereon, (B) the amount and duration of medical benefits and provisions insuring adequate medical care and free choice of physician, (C) the extent of coverage of workers, including exemptions based on numbers or type of employment, (D) standards for determining which injuries or diseases should be deemed compensable, (E) rehabilitation, (F) coverage under second or subsequent injury funds, (G) time limits on filing claims, (H) waiting periods, (I) compulsory or elective coverage, (J) administration, (K) legal expenses, (L) the feasibility and desirability of a uniform system of reporting information concerning job-related injuries and diseases and the operation of workmen's compensation laws, (M) the resolution of conflict of laws, extraterritoriality and similar problems arising from claims with multistate aspects, (N) the extent to which private insurance carriers are excluded from supplying workmen's compensation coverage and the desirability of such exclusionary practices, to the extent they are found to exist, (O) the relationship between workmen's compensation on the one hand, and old-age, disability, and survivors insurance and other types of insurance, public or private, on the other hand, (P) methods of implementing the recommendations of the Commission.

(2) The Workmen's Compensation Commission shall transmit to the President and to the Congress not later than July 31, 1972, a final report containing a detailed statement of the findings and conclusions of the Commission, together with such recommendations as it deems advisable.

(e) (1) The Workmen's Compensation Commission or, on the authorization of the Workmen's Compensation Commission, any subcommittee or members thereof, may, for the purpose of carrying out the provisions of this title, hold such hearings, take such testimony, and sit and act at such times and places as the Workmen's Compensation Commission deems advisable. Any member authorized by the Workmen's Compensation Commission may administer oaths or affirmations to witnesses appearing before the Workmen's Compensation Commission or any subcommittee or members thereof.

(2) Each department, agency, and instrumentality of the executive branch of the Government, including independent agencies, is authorized and directed to furnish to the Workmen's Compensation Commission, upon request made by the Chairman or Vice Chairman, such information as the Workmen's Compensation Commission deems necessary to carry out its functions under this section.

(f) Subject to such rules and regulations as may be adopted by the Workmen's Compensation Commission, the Chairman shall have the power to—

(1) appoint and fix the compensation of an execu-

tive director, and such additional staff personnel as he deems necessary, without regard to the provisions of title 5, United States Code, governing appointments in the competitive service, and without regard to the provisions of chapter 51 and subchapter III of chapter 53 of such title relating to classification and General Schedule pay rates, but at rates not in excess of the maximum rate for GS-18 of the General Schedule under section 5332 of such title, and

(2) procure temporary and intermittent services to the same extent as is authorized by section 3109 of title 5, United States Code.

(g) The Workmen's Compensation Commission is authorized to enter into contracts with Federal or State agencies, private firms, institutions, and individuals for the conduct of research or surveys, the preparation of reports, and other activities necessary to the discharge of its duties.

(h) Members of the Workmen's Compensation Commission shall receive compensation for each day they are engaged in the performance of their duties as members of the Workmen's Compensation Commission at the daily rate prescribed for GS-18 under section 5332 of title 5, United States Code, and shall be entitled to reimbursement for travel, subsistence, and other necessary expenses incurred by them in the performance of their duties as members of the Workmen's Compensation Commission.

(i) There are hereby authorized to be appropriated such sums as may be necessary to carry out the provisions of this section.

(j) On the ninetieth day after the date of submission of its final report to the President, the Workmen's Compensation Commission shall cease to exist.

ECONOMIC ASSISTANCE TO SMALL BUSINESSES

SEC. 28. (a) Section 7 (b) of the Small Business Act, as amended, is amended—

(1) by striking out the period at the end of "paragraph (5)" and inserting in lieu thereof "; and"; and

(2) by adding after paragraph (5) a new paragraph as follows:

"(6) to make such loans (either directly or in cooperation with banks or other lending institutions through agreements to participate on an immediate or deferred basis) as the Administration may determine to be necessary or appropriate to assist any small business concern in effecting additions to or alterations in the equipment, facilities, or methods of operation of such business in order to comply with the applicable standards promulgated pursuant to section 6 of the Occupational Safety and Health Act of 1970 or standards adopted by a State pursuant to a plan approved under section 18 of the Occupational Safety and Health Act of 1970, if the Administration determines that such concern is likely to suffer substantial economic injury without assistance under this paragraph."

(b) The third sentence of section 7(b) of the Small Business Act, as amended, is amended by striking out "or (5)" after "paragraph (3)" and inserting a comma followed by "(5) or (6)".

(c) Section 4(c) (1) of the Small Business Act, as amended, is amended by inserting "7(b) (6)," after "7(b) (5),".

(d) Loans may also be made or guaranteed for the purposes set forth in section 7(b) (6) of the Small Business Act, as amended, pursuant to the provisions of section 202 of the Public Works and Economic Development Act of 1965, as amended.

ADDITIONAL ASSISTANT SECRETARY OF LABOR

SEC. 29. (a) Section 2 of the Act of April 17, 1946 (60 Stat. 91) as amended (29 U.S.C. 553) is amended by—

(1) striking out "four" in the first sentence of such section and inserting in lieu thereof "five"; and

(2) adding at the end thereof the following new sentence, "One of such Assistant Secretaries shall be an Assistant Secretary of Labor for Occupational Safety and Health."

(b) Paragraph (20) of section 5315 of title 5, United States Code, is amended by striking out "(4)" and inserting in lieu thereof "(5)".

ADDITIONAL POSITIONS

SEC. 30. Section 5108(c) of title 5, United States Code, is amended by—

(1) striking out the word "and" at the end of paragraph (8);

(2) striking out the period at the end of paragraph (9) and inserting in lieu thereof a semicolon and the word "and"; and

(3) by adding immediately after paragraph (9) the following new paragraph:

"(10) (A) the Secretary of Labor, subject to the standards and procedures prescribed by this chapter, may place an additional twenty-five positions in the Department of Labor in GS-16, 17, and 18 for the purposes of carrying out his responsibilities under the Occupational Safety and Health Act of 1970;

"(B) the Occupational Safety and Health Review Commission, subject to the standards and procedures prescribed by this chapter, may place ten positions in GS-16, 17, and 18 in carrying out its functions under the Occupational Safety and Health Act of 1970."

EMERGENCY LOCATOR BEACONS

SEC. 31. Section 601 of the Federal Aviation Act of 1958 is amended by inserting at the end thereof a new subsection as follows:

"EMERGENCY LOCATOR BEACONS

"(d) (1) Except with respect to aircraft described in paragraph (2) of this subsection, minimum standards pursuant to this section shall include a requirement that emergency locator beacons shall be installed—

"(A) on any fixed-wing, powered aircraft for use in air commerce the manufacture of which is completed, or which is imported into the United States, after one year following the date of enactment of this subsection; and

"(B) on any fixed-wing, powered aircraft used in air commerce after three years following such date.

"(2) The provisions of this subsection shall not apply to jet-powered aircraft; aircraft used in air transportation (other than air taxis and charter aircraft); military aircraft; aircraft used solely for training purposes not involving flights more than twenty miles from its base; and aircraft used for the aerial application of chemicals."

SEPARABILITY

SEC. 32. If any provision of this Act, or the application of such provision to any person or circumstance, shall be held invalid, the remainder of this Act, or the application of such provision to persons or circumstances other than those as to which it is held invalid, shall not be affected thereby.

APPROPRIATIONS

SEC. 33. There are authorized to be appropriated to carry out this Act for each fiscal year sums as the Congress shall deem necessary.

EFFECTIVE DATE

SEC. 34. This Act shall take effect one hundred and twenty days after the date of its enactment.

Approved December 29, 1970.

LEGISLATIVE HISTORY:

HOUSE REPORTS: No. 91-1291 accompanying H.R. 16785 (Comm. on Education and Labor) and No. 91-1765 (Comm. of Conference).

SENATE REPORT No. 91-1282 (Comm. on Labor and Public Welfare).

CONGRESSIONAL RECORD, Vol. 116 (1970):

Oct. 13, Nov. 16, 17, considered and passed Senate.

Nov. 23, 24, considered and passed House, amended, in lieu of H.R. 16785.

Dec. 16, Senate agreed to conference report.

Dec. 17, House agreed to conference report.

B — British Law and Court Cases

(This appendix lists the most pertinent programs of HASAWA only).

Occupational Health and Safety Cases reprinted by permission from the ROSPA Bulletin, monthly publication of Royal Society for the Prevention of Accidents, Birmingham, England. Volume 11, No. 1, pp. 2–4. ***(See p. 33)***

ELIZABETH II
Health and Safety at Work etc. Act 1974

An Act to make further provision for securing the health, safety and welfare of persons at work, for protecting others against risk to health or safety in connection with the activities of persons at work, for controlling the keeping and use and preventing the unlawful acquisition, possession and use of dangerous substances, and for controlling certain emissions into the atmosphere; to make further provision with respect to the employment medical advisory service; to amend the law relating to medical advisory service; to amend the law relating to building regulations, and the Building (Scotland) Act 1959; and for connected purposes. [31st July 1974]

BE IT ENACTED by the Queen's most Excellent Majesty, by and with the advice and consent of the Lords Spiritual and Temporal, and Commons, in this present Parliament assembled, and by the authority of the same, as follows:—

PART I
HEALTH, SAFETY AND WELFARE IN CONNECTION WITH WORK,
AND CONTROL OF DANGEROUS SUBSTANCES AND CERTAIN
EMISSIONS INTO THE ATMOSPHERE

Preliminary

1.—(1) The provisions of this Part shall have effect with a view to—

(*a*) securing the health, safety and welfare of persons at work;
(*b*) protecting persons other than persons at work against risks to health or safety arising out of or in connection with the activities of persons at work;
(*c*) controlling the keeping and use of explosive or highly flammable or otherwise dangerous substances, and generally preventing the unlawful acquisition, possession and use of such substances; and
(*d*) controlling the emission into the atmosphere of noxious or offensive substances from premises of any class prescribed for the purposes of this paragraph.

(2) The provisions of this Part relating to the making of health and safety regulations and agricultural health and safety regulations and the preparation and approval of codes of practice shall in particular have effect with a view to enabling the enactments specified in the third column of Schedule 1 and the regulations, orders and other instruments in force under those enactments to be progressively replaced by a system of regulations and approved codes of practice operating in combination with the other provisions of this Part and designed to maintain or improve the standards of health, safety and welfare established by or under those enactments.

(3) For the purposes of this Part risks arising out of or in connection with the activities of persons at work shall be treated as including risks attributable to the manner of conducting an undertaking, the plant or substances used for the purposes of an undertaking and the condition of premises so used or any part of them.

(4) References in this Part to the general purposes of this Part are references to the purposes mentioned in subsection (1) above.

General Duties

2.—(1) It shall be the duty of every employer to ensure, so far as is reasonably practicable, the health, safety and welfare at work of all his employees.

(2) Without prejudice to the generality of an employer's duty under the preceding subsection, the matters to which that duty extends include in particular—

(*a*) the provision and maintenance of plant and systems of work that are, so far as is reasonably practicable, safe and without risks to health;
(*b*) arrangements for ensuring, so far as is reasonably practicable, safety and absence of risks to health in connection with the use, handling, storage and transport or articles and substances;
(*c*) the provision of such information, instruction, training and supervision as is necessary to ensure, so far as is reasonably practicable, the health and safety at work of his employees;
(*d*) so far as is reasonably practicable as regards any place of work under the employer's control, the maintenance of it in a condition that is safe and without risks to health and the provision and maintenance of means of access to and egress from it that are safe and without such risks;
(*e*) the provision and maintenance of a working environment for his employees that is, so far as is reasonably practicable, safe, without risks to health, and adequate as regards facilities and arrangements for their welfare at work.

(3) Except in such cases as may be prescribed, it shall be the duty of every employer to prepare and as often as may be appropriate revise a written statement of his general policy with respect to the health and safety at work of his employees and the organisation and arrangements for the time being in force for carrying out that policy, and to bring the

statement and any revision of it to the notice of all of his employees.

(4) Regulations made by the Secretary of State may provide for the appointment in prescribed cases by recognised trade unions (within the meaning of the regulations) of safety representatives from amongst the employees, and those representatives shall represent the employees in consultations with the employers under subsection (6) below and shall have such other functions as may be prescribed.

(6) It shall be the duty of every employer to consult any such representatives with a view to the making and maintenance of arrangements which will enable him and his employees to cooperate effectively in promoting and developing measures to ensure the health and safety at work of the employees, and in checking the effectiveness of such measures.

(7) In such cases as may be prescribed it shall be the duty of every employer, if requested to do so by the safety representatives mentioned in subsections (4) and (5) above, to establish, in accordance with regulations made by the Secretary of State, a safety committee having the function of keeping under review the measures taken to ensure the health and safety at work of his employees and such other functions as may be prescribed.

3.—(1) It shall be the duty of every employer to conduct his undertaking in such a way as to ensure, so far as is reasonably practicable, that persons not in his employment who may be affected thereby are not thereby exposed to risks to their health or safety.

(2) It shall be the duty of every self-employed person to conduct his undertaking in such a way as to ensure, so far as is reasonably practicable, that he and other persons (not being his employees) who may be affected thereby are not thereby exposed to risks to their health or safety.

(3) In such cases as may be prescribed, it shall be the duty of every employer and every self-employed person, in the prescribed circumstances and in the prescribed manner, to give to persons (not being his employees) who may be affected by the way in which he conducts his undertaking the prescribed information about such aspects of the way in which he conducts his undertaking as might affect their health or safety.

4.—(1) This section has effect for imposing on persons duties in relation to those who—

(*a*) are not their employees; but

(*b*) used non-domestic premises made available to them as a place of work or as a place where they may use plant or substances provided for their use there,

and applies to premises so made available and other non-domestic premises used in connection with them.

(2) It shall be the duty of each person who has, to any extent, control of premises to which this section applies or of the means of access thereto or egress therefrom or of any plant or substance in such premises to take such measures as it is reasonable for a person in his position to take to ensure, so far as is reasonably practicable, that the premises, all means of access thereto or egress therefrom available for use by persons using the premises, and any plant or substance in the premises or, as the case may be, provided for use there, is or are safe and without risks to health.

(3) Where a person has, by virtue of any contract or tenancy, an obligation of any extent in relation to—

(*a*) the maintenance or repair of any premises to which this section applies or any means of access thereto or egress therefrom; or

(*b*) the safety of or the absence of risks to health arising from plant or substances in any such premises;

that person shall be treated, for the purposes of subsection (2) above, as being a person who has control of the matters to which his obligation extends.

(4) Any reference in this section to a person having control of any premises or matter is a reference to a person having control of the premises or matter in connection with the carrying on by him of a trade, business or other undertaking (whether for profit or not).

5.—(1) It shall be the duty of the person having control of any premises of a class prescribed for the purposes of section 1(1)(*d*) to use the best practicable means for preventing the emission into the atmosphere from the premises of noxious or offensive substances and for rendering harmless and inoffensive such substances as may be so emitted.

(2) The reference in subsection (1) above to the means to be used for the purposes there mentioned includes a reference to the manner in which the plant provided for those purposes is used and to the supervision of any operation involving the emission of the substances to which that subsection applies.

(3) Any substance or a substance of any description prescribed for the purposes of subsection (1) above as noxious or offensive shall be a noxious or, as the case may be, an offensive substance for those purposes whether or not it would be so apart from this subsection.

(4) Any reference in this section to a person having control of any premises is a reference to a person having control of the premises in connection with the carrying on by him of a trade, business or other undertaking (whether for profit or not) and any duty imposed on any such person by this section shall extend only to matters within his control.

6.—(1) It shall be the duty of any person who designs, manufactures, imports or supplies any article for use at work—

(*a*) to ensure, so far as is reasonably practicable, that the article is so designed and constructed as to be safe and without risks to health when properly used;

(*b*) to carry our or arrange for the carrying out of such testing and examination as may be necessary for the performance of the duty imposed on him by the preceding paragraph;

(*c*) to take such steps as are necessary to secure that there will be available in connection with the use of the article at work adequate information about the use for which it is designed and has been tested, and about any conditions necessary to ensure that, when put to that use, it will be safe and without risks to health.

(2) It shall be the duty of any person who undertakes the design or manufacture of any article for use at work to carry out or arrange for the carrying out of any necessary research with a view to the discovery and, so far as is reasonably practicable, the elimination or minimisation of any risks to health or safety to which the design or article may give rise.

(3) It shall be the duty of any person who erects or installs any article for use at work in any premises where that article is to be used by persons at work to ensure, so far as is reasonably practicable, that nothing about the way in which it is erected or installed makes it unsafe or a risk to health when properly used.

(4) It shall be the duty of any person who manufactures, imports or supplies any substance for use at work—

(*a*) to ensure, so far as is reasonably practicable, that the substance is safe and without risks to health when properly used;

(*b*) to carry out or arrange for the carrying out of such testing and examination as may be necessary for the performance of the duty imposed on him by the preceding paragraph;

(*c*) to take such steps as are necessary to secure that there will be available in connection with the use of the substance at work adequate information about the results of any relevant tests which have been carried out on or in connection with the substance and about any conditions necessary to ensure that it will be safe and without risks to health when properly used.

(5) It shall be the duty of any peson who undertakes the manufacture of any substance for use at work to carry out or arrange for the carrying out of any necessary research with a view to the discovery and, so far as is reasonably practicable, the elimination of minimisation of any risks to health or safety to which the substance may give rise.

(6) Nothing in the preceding provisions of this section shall be taken to require a person to repeat any testing, examination or research which has been carried out otherwise than by him or at his instance, in so far as it is reasonable for him to rely on the results thereof for the purposes of those provisions.

(7) Any duty imposed on any person by any of the preceding provisions of this section shall extend only to things done in the course of a trade, business or other undertaking carried on by him (whether for profit or not) and to matters within his control.

(8) Where a person designs, manufactures, imports or supplies an article for or to another on the basis of a written undertaking by that other to take specified steps sufficient to ensure, so far as is reasonably practicable, that the article will be safe and without risks to health when properly used, the undertaking shall have the effect of relieving the first-mentioned person from the duty imposed by subsection (1)(*a*) above to such extent as is reasonable having regard to the terms of the undertaking.

(9) Where a person ("the ostensible supplier") supplies any article for use at work or substance for use at work to another ("the customer") under a hire-purchase agreement, conditional sale agreement or credit-sale agreement, and the ostensible supplier—

(*a*) carries on the business of financing the acquisition of goods by others by means of such agreements; and

(*b*) in the course of that business acquired his interest in the article or substance supplied to the customer as a means of financing its acquisition by the customer from a third person ("the effective supplier").

the effective supplier and not the ostensible supplier shall be treated for the purposes of his section as supplying the article or substance to the customer, and any duty imposed by the preceding provisions of this section on suppliers shall accordingly fall on the effective supplier and not on the ostensible supplier.

(10) For the purposes of this section an article or substance is not to be regarded as properly used where it is used without regard to any relevant information or advice relating to its use which has been made available by a person by whom it was designed, manufactured, imported or supplied.

7. It shall be the duty of every employee while at work—

(*a*) to take reasonable care for the health and safety of himself and of other persons who may be affected by his acts or omissions at work; and

(*b*) as regards any duty or requirement imposed on his employer or any other person by or under any of the relevant statutory provisions, to co-operate with him so far as is necessary to enable that duty or requirement to be performed or complied with.

8. No person shall intentionally or recklessly interfere with or misuse anything provided in the interests of health, safety or welfare in pursuance of any of the relevant statutory provisions.

9. No employer shall levy or permit to be levied on any employee of his any charge in respect to anything done or provided in pursuance of any specific requirement of the relevant statutory provisions.

The Health and Safety Commission and the Health and Safety Executive

10.—(1) There shall be two bodies corporate to be called the Health and Safety Commission and the Health and Safety Executive which shall be constituted in accordance with the following provisions of this section.

(*b*) at the end of paragraph (*b*) there shall be added the words "and

(*c*) section 23(2) of the Summary

Jurisdiction (Scotland) Act 1954 (date of commencement of proceedings) shall have effect as it has effect for the purposes of that section.".

35. An offence under any of the relevant statutory provisions committed in connection with any plant or substance may, if necessary for the purpose of bringing the offence within the field of responsibility of any enforcing authority or conferring jurisdiction on any court to entertain proceedings for the offence, be treated as having been committed at the place where that plant or substance is for the time being.

36.—(1) Where the commission by any person of an offence under any of the relevant statutory provisions is due to the act or default of some other person, that other person shall be guilty of the offence, and a person may be charged with and convicted of the offence by virtue of this subsection whether or not proceedings are taken against the first-mentioned person.

(2) Where there would be or have been the commission of an offence under section 33 by the Crown but for the circumstance that that section does not bind the Crown, and that fact is due to the act or default of a person other than the Crown, that person shall be guilty of the offence which, but for that circumstance, the Crown would be committing or would have committed, and may be charged with and convicted of that offence accordingly.

(3) The preceding provisions of this section are subject to any provision made by virtue of section 15(6).

37.—(1) Where an offence under any of the relevant statutory provisions committed by a body corporate is proved to have been committed with the consent or connivance of, or to have been attributable to any neglect on the part of, any director, manager, secretary or other similar officer of the body corporate or a person who was purporting to act in any such capacity, he as well as the body corporate shall be guilty of that offence and shall be liable to be proceeded against and punished accordingly.

(2) Where the affairs of a body corporate are managed by its members, the preceding subsection shall apply in relation to the acts and defaults of a member in connection with his functions of management as if he were a director of the body corporate.

38. Proceedings for an offence under any of the relevant statutory provisions shall not, in England and Wales, be instituted except by an inspector or by or with the consent of the Director of Public Prosecutions.

39.—(1) An inspector, if authorised in that behalf by the enforcing authority which appointed him, may, although not of counsel or a solicitor, prosecute before a magistrates' court proceedings for an offence under any of the relevant statutory provisions.

(2) This section shall not apply to Scotland.

40. In any proceedings for an offence under any of the relevant statutory provisions consisting of a failure to comply with a duty or requirement to do something so far as is practicable or so far as is reasonably practicable, or to use the best practicable means to do something, it shall be for the accused to prove (as the case may be) that it was not practicable or not reasonably practicable to do more than was in fact done to satisfy the duty or requirement, or that there was no better practicable means than was in fact used to satisfy the duty or requirement.

41.—(1) Where an entry is required by any of the relevant statutory provisions to be made in any register or other record, the entry, if made, shall, as against the person by or on whose behalf it was made, be admissible as evidence or in Scotland sufficient evidence of the facts stated therein.

(2) Where an entry which is so required to be so made with respect to the observance of any of the relevant statutory provisions has not been made, that fact shall be admissible as evidence or in Scotland sufficient evidence that that provision has not been observed.

42.—(1) Where a person is convicted of an offence under any of the relevant statutory provisions in respect of any matters which appear to the court to be matters which it is in his power to remedy, the court may, in addition to or instead of imposing any punishment, order him, within such time as may be fixed by the order, to take such steps as may be specified in the order for remedying the said matters.

(2) The time fixed by an order under subsection (1) above may be extended or further extended by order of the court on an application made before the end of that time as originally fixed or as extended under this subsection, as the case may be.

(3) Where a person is ordered under subsection (1) above to remedy any matters, that person shall not be liable under any of the relevant statutory provisions in respect of those matters in so far as they continue during the time fixed by the order or any further time allowed under subsection (2) above.

(4) Subject to the following subsection, the court by or before which a person is convicted of an offence such as is mentioned in section 33(4)(*c*) in respect of any such explosive article or substance as is there mentioned may order the article or substance in question to be forfeited and either destroyed or dealt with in such other manner as the court may order.

(5) The court shall not order anything to be forfeited under the preceding subsection where a person claiming to be the owner of or otherwise interested in it applies to be heard by the court, unless an opportunity has been given to him to show cause why the order should not be made.

Financial provisions

43.—(1) It shall be the duty of the Secretary of State to pay to the Commission such sums as are approved by the Treasury and as he considers appropriate for the purpose of enabling the Commission to perform its functions; and it shall be the duty of the Commission to pay to the Executive such sums as the Commission considers appropriate for the purpose of enabling the Executive to perform its functions.

(2) Regulations may provide for such fees as

may be fixed by or determined under the regulations to be payable for or in connection with the performance by or on behalf of any authority to which this subsection applies of any function conferred on that authority by or under any of the relevant statutory provisions.

(3) Subsection (2) above applies to the following authorites, namely the Commission, the Executive, the Secretary of State, the Minister of Agriculture, Fisheries and Food, every enforcing authority, and any other person on whom any function is conferred by or under any of the relevant statutory provisions.

(4) Regulations under this section may specify the person by whom any fee payable under the regulations is to be paid; but no such fee shall be made payable by a person in any of the following capacities, namely an employee, a person seeking employment, a person training for employment, and a person seeking training for employment.

(5) Without prejudice to section 82(3), regulations under this section may fix or provide for the determination of different fees in relation to different functions, or in relation to the same function in different circumstances.

(6) The power to make regulations under this section shall be exercisable—

(*a*) as regards functions with respect to matters not relating exclusively to agricultural operations, by the Secretary of State;

(*b*) as regards functions with respect to matters relating exclusively to the relevant agricultural purposes, by the appropriate agricultural authority.

(7) Regulations under this section as regards functions falling within subsection (6)(*b*) above may be either regulations applying to Great Britain and made by the Minister of Agriculture, Fisheries and Food and the Secretary of State acting jointly, or regulations applying to England and Wales only and made by the said Minister, or regulations applying to Scotland only and made by the Secretary of State; and in subsection (6)(*b*) above "the appropriate agricultural authority" shall be construed accordingly.

(8) In subsection (4) above the references to a person training for employment and a person seeking training for employment shall include respectively a person attending an industrial rehabilitation course provided by virtue of the Employment and Training Act 1973 and a person seeking to attend such a course.

Court Cases—U.K.

Amputated thumb

A supervisor at a pharmaceuticals company was operating a mixing machine when the flow of powder being mixed suddenly stopped. The man put his right arm up the outlet duct to see if there was a blockage but the machine was still running and the top of his thumb was immediately amputated by the rotating blade.

A factory inspector told the magistrates' court that when the machine was bought it had been fitted with a guard but this had been removed because it impeded the emptying of the mixer.

Although the company said in their defence that it was unreasonable to say that they were wholly responsible for the accident since the supervisor was an experienced man, familiar with the machine and in a position to have known better, the magistrates disagreed and fined the firm £300 under Section 2 of HASAWA.

Flash burns

An engineering firm was found guilty of failing to ensure the safety, supervision and instruction of its employees following a near fatal accident to one of the fitters — even though the man was under the direct control of another firm at the time.

The man was one of a group of men sub-contracted to a machinery company removing surplus steel at a rolling mill. The workers had started by removing cables leading to the mill by sawing through them. The work was being carried out in a manhole under the floor.

The men had been assured that the power had been isolated but, in fact, three of the seventeen cables led to adjacent premises and were still live.

According to one of the men: "there was a blue flash and a bang and a cloud of smoke." He continued by explaining that one of his colleagues had sawed through one of the live 400 volt cables and "came out of the hole with his hands in the air saying 'My eyes, my eyes'."

An Electrical Inspector of Factories told the court that the man was lucky to have only received flash burns to his eyes and hair — he could easily have died. He said that steel armoured cable — the type in question — could emit plasma at temperature up to 10,000 degrees C when sawn through and, he added 'you can imagine what that can do to human flesh.'

The firm was fined £500 under Section 2 of HASAWA.

Acid fountain

A firm used concentrated cyanide solutions in the production of wire for the motor tyre industry. The solutions were pumped through a factory pipe circuit.

It became necessary to shut down one of the pumps and by-pass it by opening up two of the lines carrying the liquid. The circuit was shut down by closing valves and two men were given the all clear to commence work on the pump.

But when they did so some liquid started to trickle out of one pipe and then a sudden fountain of caustic solution estimated at being between 20 to 30 feet high shot out over the men who were the employees of a sub contractor.

One man received a severe eye injury which may require a corneal graft.

A factory inspector told a magistrates' court that if either man had swallowed any of the liquid it would almost certainly have been fatal. He said that the precautions taken were totally inadequate in that the circuit should have been adequately isolated and not protected by a simple valve. The two men should also have been wearing proper eye protection.

In their defence the firm said that the injured man was an employee of specialist contractors who had been called in specifically because of the nature of the work.

Nevertheless, the firm was fined £200 under Section 3(1) of HASAWA.

Fall through roof

A firm of glass merchants and glaziers admitted failing to ensure the safety of their workmen and failing to prepare a written health and safety policy when they were taken to court following an accident to one of their employees.

The injured man fell through an asbestos roof after trying to help two men clean out gutterings and gulleys. In order to do so they had to walk over the roof which they reached by ladder. While they were up there, they called to the other man to bring up a box and some pieces of wood.

The man went up the ladder with the material but fell through the roof and dropped 11 feet to the floor below. He received severe spinal injuries and, the magistrates' court was told, was now attending a rehabilitation centre.

The prosecuting counsel told the court that no clear instructions had been given to employees as to what safety practices they should have followed. There were no warning notices on the approaches to the roof and the dangers were not made apparent.

In their defence, the firm said that it was the first time in their 100-year history that anything of this nature had happened. The two men who were first sent on the roof were experienced and had authority to work there. The injured man had no such authority and he was not told by his colleagues to walk on a plank. The firm was fined £350.

Shocking conditions

An electroplating firm employing about 50 people was taken to court by the Factory Inspectorate following incidents which occurred during an inspector's routine visit.

The factory, housed in premises underneath railway arches, had been the subject of worry to the Inspectorate for about two years following reports of nasal perforations and chrome ulceration. Inspectors were also concerned at the general poor condition of the factory and the bad quality of the electrical installations.

During one visit, an inspector saw an employee putting his hand into a switchboard in order to manually depress a live 400 volt contractor which was not operating properly. On one electroplating *line he found that there were connector block joints on electrical conductors and an uninsulated joint of twisted wire on a motor that was within reach of employees.*

The inspector had just started to take statements when a worker on another line complained of having received a mild electric shock when he touched one of the centrifugal drying machines. A senior electrical inspector was called in and he found serious electrical faults on all the drying machines.

The senior inspector then saw another employee sitting on a beam on top of the drum transporting mechanism over cyanide baths used for removing anodes. There was no barrier to prevent him falling from the 12cm wide beam into the bath and he was ordered down immediately. A prohibition notice was served there and then.

The firm was taken to court for 5 offences under the Electricity (Factories Act) Special Regulations 1908 and 1944 — two under Reg 1 concerning the drying machines; one under Reg 6 in relation to the twisted wire joint; one under Reg 15 for the open live switchboard; and one under Reg 21 for faulty earthing. A case was also taken under Section 2(1), HASWA for the lack of a safe system of work for removing the anodes.

The company was fined a total of £2,800 but although it had pleaded guilty to the charges, it appealed to the Crown Court against the sentence.

In the firm's defence it was stated that the firm had a previous good record and that it was currently in a loss-making financial situation. They felt the severity of the fine was too harsh for a first offence. The judge, however, unheld the fine saying that the case related to a number of offences which involved a very real risk of injury to employees.

Drop of bubbly?

A night shift employee in a food factory put some cleaning fluid into a cup. He did not realise that the fluid contained caustic soda when he told a fellow worker that the cup contained cider. His workmate drank some of the solution and was taken ill.

Magistrates were told that an investigation was held and it was found that the employers fulfilled their duties in respect of devising safe systems of work by providing special containers for the dispensing of cleaning solutions. The bulk storage drum was also found to have been labelled with a warning that its contents were harmful if swallowed.

Local police, who carried out the initial investigation, would have proceeded against the man who put the solution in the cup under the Offences Against the Persons Act but they were obliged to drop the proposed action because they would have needed to prove an intent to harm. The man maintained that he thought the drum contained a harmless detergent and insisted that he had not invited his workmate to drink the substance — he had merely told him it was cider.

However, the HSE took the case to court under Section 7(a) of the HASWA in which they showed that the man had failed to take reasonable care for the safety of other employees.

Although the defence argued that the defendant had not intended any harm, that the injured man had not taken reasonable care of himself and that the employer's system of work was defective, magistrates fined the man £50.

C — Notes and References, R. Ben Hogan, Negligent OSHA Inspections (See p. 69).

[1] 29 U.S.C. § 651 et seq. (1970).

[2] OSHA at § 657(a) gives authority to the Secretary of Labor to "inspect and investigate during working hours and at other reasonable times" most employments in the United States. The OSH Administration has developed and promulgated regulations governing these inspections, and many court decisions have interpreted the scope and limits of authority of the OSH Administration to conduct these inspections. The authority for, and procedures of, OSHA inspections are beyond the scope of this article. See generally, R. Hogan & R. Hogan, OSHA, New York: Matthew Bender, 1977, with Annual Update.

[3] Taylor v. Brighton Corp., 616 F.2d 256 (6th Cir. 1980), BNA 8 OSHC 1010 (declining to find private right of action on behalf of employees wrongfully discharged for reporting OSHA violations); Russell v. Bartley, 494 F.2d 334 (6th Cir. 1974), BNA 1 OSHC 1589 (refusing to find private right of action on behalf of employees injured by OSHA safety violations); Jeter v. St. Regis Paper Co., 507 F.2d 973 (5th Cir. 1975), BNA 2 OSHC 1591 (no private cause of action can be based on OSHA); Horn v. Osborn Contracting Co., 591 F.2d 318 (5th Cir. 1979), BNA 7 OSHC 1256 (OSHA by its terms not applicable to non-employees except in cases, as here, where construction contract incorporates OSHA regulations by reference); Federal Employees for Non-Smokers Rights v. United States, 598 F.2d 310 (D.C. Cir. 1979), BNA 7 OSHC 1634 (no independent right exists for private organizations to enforce OSHA regulations, aff'g. 446 F.Supp. 181 (D.C.D.C. 1978), BNA 6 OSHC 1407); Byrd v. Fieldcrest Mills, Inc., 496 F.2d 1323 (4th Cir. 1974), BNA 1 OSHC 1743 (no private right right of action for wrongful death created by OSHA); Skidmore v. Travels Insurance Co., 483 F.2d 67 (5th Cir. 1973), BNA 1 OSHC 1294 (nothing in OSHA permits private right of action by employees against exeuctive officers of company, aff'g. 356 F. Supp. 670 (E.D. La. 1973), BNA 1 OSHC 1173); Koll v. Manatt's Transportation Co., 253 N.W. 2d 265 (Iowa 1977), BNA 5 OSHC 1398 (OSHA regulations no basis for independent cause of action, but can be evidence of negligence or negligence per se); Knight v. Burns, Kirkley & Williams Construction Co., 331 So. 2d 651 (Ala. 1976), BNA 4 OHSC 1271 (OSHA no basis for independent cause of action, but regulations admissible on issue of negligence).

[4] E.g., Dunn Roofing Co. v. Brimer, 537 S.W. 2d 164 (Ark. 1976), BNA 4 OSHC 1501; Knight v. Burns, Kirkley & Williams Construction Co., supra note 3; DiSabatino Brothers Inc. v. Dominick Baio, 366 A.2d 508 (Del. 1976), BNA 4 OSHC 1855; Buhler v. Marriott Hotels, Inc., 390 F.Supp. 999 (E.D. La. 1974), BNA 3 OSHC 1199; Johnson v. Niagara Machine & Tool Works, 666 F.2d 1223 (8th Cir. 1981)(OSHA regulations admissible on issue of comparative negligence of non-party employer); Melerine v. Avondale Shipyards, Inc., 659 F.2d 706 (5th Cir. 1981), BNA 10 OSHC 1075 (while OSHA regulations evidence of the standard of care, they do not establish negligence per se for third parties or create an implied cause of action); Koll v. Manatt's Transportation Co., id. (OSHA regulations evidence of negligence as to all persons likely to be exposed to injury as a result of the violation, and evidence of negligence per se as to employees); Kelley v. Howard Wright Construction Co., 582 P.2d 500 (Wash. 1978), BNA 6 OSHC 1934 (OSHA regulations evidence of negligence per se against general contractor in favor of employee of subcontractor).

[5] 28 U.S.C § 1346(b).

[6] In the last few years the OSH Administration has experienced a cutback in enforcement funding, which has required a reordering of priorities. At present there are relatively few unannounced OSHA inspections of industrial workplaces. Enforcement has centered by necessity on employee complaints, investigations of fatalities, and so-called "target" industries with unusually high rates of work-related injuries or illnesses.

[7] The Bureau of National Affairs, Inc., for instance, publishes the Occupational Safety & Health Reporter, which contains all OSHA regulations and procedures. Write to BNA at 1231 25th Street, N.W., Washington, DC 20037.

[8] The act at § 654(a) requires each employer to "furnish to each of his employees employment and a place of employment which are free from recognized hazards that are causing or are likely to cause death or serious physical harm to his employees" and to "comply with [OSHA] standards...." The legislative history of OSHA makes it clear that this was intended to be a restatement of the common law duty of employers to furnish employees a safe place to work. S.Rep. No. 1282, 91st Cong., 2d Sess., reprinted in U.S. CODE CONG. & ADMIN. NEWS (1970) at 5177, 5186.

[9] Blessing v. United States, 447 F.Supp. 1160, 1196 (E.D. Pa. 1978).

[10] E.g., Beasley v. MacDonald Engineering Co., 287 Ala. 189, 249 So. 2d 844 (1971)(negligent inspection by a workers compensation insurance carrier); United States Fidelity And Guaranty Co. v. Jones, 356 So. 2d 596 (Ala. 1978)(negligent insurance inspection); Corson v. Liberty Mutual Insurance Co., 110 N.H. 210, 265 A.2d 315 (1970)(negligent safety inspection); Evans v. Liberty Mutual Insurance Co., 398 F.2d 665 (3d Cir. [Pa.] 1968)(negligent safety inspection).

[11] Davis v. Liberty Mutual Insurance Co., 525 F.2d 1204 (5th Cir. 1976)(no liabilty under § 324A for a workers compensation inspection where the defendant did not undertake to perform a duty owed by employer); Tillman v. Travelers Indemnity Co., 506 F.2d 917, 921 (5th Cir.

1975)(insurer undertook safety inspections but no liability under § 324A(b) where the record was void of any indication that the employer had delegated to the insurer "any part of its direct and primary duty to discover unsafe conditions").

[12] *Hill v. James Walker Memorial Hospital, 407 F.2d 1036 (4th Cir. 1969)(liability under § 324A(b) on inspecting independent contractor (exterminating company) at a hospital); United States Fidelity and Guaranty Co. v. Jones, 356 So. 2d 596, 598 (Ala. 1978)("The law, simply stated, is that one who volunteers to act, though under no duty to do so, is thereafter charged with the duty of acting with due care.").*

[13] *28 U.S.C. § 1346(b).*

[14] *Plaintiffs may not base FTCA claims on alleged breaches of duty arising soley out of federal law when there is no corresponding duty under state law. Baker v. F&F Investment Co., 489 F.2d 829 (7th Cir. 1973); Devlin Lumber & Supply Corp. v. United States, 488 F.2d 88 (4th Cir. 1973). In any event there is no duty arising out of OSHA itself because of § 653 (b)(4).*

[15] *United States v. Yellow Cab Co., 340 U.S. 543 (1951); Dalehite v. United States, 346 U.S. 15 (1953).*

[16] *As a condition to bringing suit, the plaintiff must show that he or she has filed a Form 95 (administrative claim) with the applicable governmental department, and that said claim has either been denied or had no action taken with respect to it for six months.*

[17] *The government cannot be liable, for instance, for claims "arising out of the loss, miscarriage or negligent transmission of letters" (§ 2680(b)); or for "damages caused by the imposition or establishment of a quarantine" (§ 2680(f)); or for fraud, deceit, or misrepresentation (§ 2860(h)); or for damages caused by the "fiscal operations of the Treasury..." (§ 2680(i)), as well as others.*

[18] *Dalehite v. United States, 346 U.S. 15 (1953).*

[19] *Id., at 42.*

[20] *ID., at 35. Other cases discussing the discretionary function exception include Indian Towing Co. v. United States, 350 U.S. 61 (1955); Hatahley v. United States, 351 U.S. 173 (1956); United States v. Muniz, 374 U.S. 150 (1963).*

[21] *500 F.2d 1059 (3rd Cir. 1974).*

[22] *418 F.2d 774 (2d Cir. 1969).*

[23] *Id., at 783.*

[24] *Id., at 774.*

[25] *United States v. DeCamp, 478 F.2d 1188 (9th Cir. 1973)("The decision...was not predicated upon consideration of public policy but upon general standards of safety. Accordingly, state tort law can capably measure the reasonableness of the engineers judgment in applying professional standards of safety.") 478 F.2d at 1192.*

[26] *Fair v. United States, 234 F.2d 288 (5th Cir. 1956); United States v. Gray, 199 F.2d 239 (10th Cir. 1952).*

[27] *Eastern Airlines, Inc. v. Union Trust Co., 221 F.2d 62 (D.C. Cir.), aff'd. per curiam, United States v. Union Trust Co., 350 U.S. 907 (1955); Ingham v. Eastern Airlines, Inc., 373 F.2d 227 (7th Cir. 1967); Hartz v. United States, 387 F.2d 870 (5th Cir. 1968).*

[28] *J.H. Rutter Rex Mfg. Co. v. United States. 515 F.2d 97, 99 (5th Cir. 1975), cert. denied, 424 U.S. 954 (1976).*

[29] *Blessing v. United States, 447 F.Supp. 1160 (E.D. Pa. 1978); Irving v. United States, _____ F.Supp. _____(No. 81-501, D.C. N.H. 1982), BNA 10 OSHC 1353 (citing Blessing).*

[30] *See generally, W. Prosser, Handbook of the Law of Torts, § 56 (4th ed. 1971) at 343-348, which describes the rule that one who undertakes, whether gratuitously or for consideratioon, to render services to another may be held liable for negligent rendering of those services if the negligence causes injury either to the person on whose behalf the services are being performed or to a foreseeable third party. As discussed earlier, the rule is articulated in Restatement (Second) of torts §§ 323 and 324A (1965).*

[31] *E.g., Indian Towing Co. v. United States, supra note 20; Ingham v. Eastern Airlines, Inc., supra note 27; Armiger v. United States, 339 F.2d 625, 168 Ct. Cl. 379 (1964).*

[32] *Blessing v. United States, supra note 29 (allegations of negligent OSHA inspection state viable FTCA claim under Pennsylvania law); Caldwell v. United States, _____F. Supp. _____ (No. 75-1005) (D.C. D.C. 1978), BNA 6 OSHC 1410 (allegations of negligent OSHA inspection state no viable FTCA claim under District of Columbia law); Irving v. United States, surpa note 29 (allegations of negligent OSHA inspection state viable FTCA claim under New Hampshire law); Davis v. United States, 758 (8th Cir. Neb. 1976), BNA 4 OSHC 1417 (no FTCA wrongful death action conferred by Nebraska law against federal OSHA inspector for negligent inspection).*

[33] *Blessing, id.*

[34] *Irving v. United States, (citing Blessing, id.).*

[35] *Blessing, id., at 1197, n. 53.*

[36] *Id. at 1198, citing inter alia, Evans v. Liberty Mutual Ins. Co., 398 F.2d 665 (3rd Cir 1968); Clemente v. United States, 567 F.2d 1140 (1st Cir. 1977). See also, Davis v. Liberty Mutual Ins. Co., supra note 11; "Tillman v. Travelers Indemnity Co., supra note 11; Stacy v. Aetna Casualty & Surety Co., 484 F.2d 289, 293, 294 (5th Cir. 1973).*

[37] *Blessing v. United States, supra note 29, at 1186-1187, n. 37.*

D — References, Harry M. Philo, New Dimensions in the Tortious Failure to Warn (See p. 95)

1. *National Machine Tool Builders Association. Bulletin no. 69-4 (Jan. 15, 1969)*
2. *American National Standards Institute (ANSI) Standards*
   - *Z35.1 (1972) Specifications for Accident Prevention Signs*
   - *Z35.2 (1968) R 1974 Specifications for Accident Prevention Tags*
   - *Z35.4 (1973) Specifications for Informational Signs*
   - *D6.1 (1978) Manual on Uniform Traffic Control Devices for Streets and Highways*
   - *B14.1 (1971) Slow Moving Vehicle Identification Emblem (This is the same as ASAE S276.2 (1968) and SAE J 943)*
   - *N2.3 (1967) Immediate Evaluation Signal for Use in Industrial Installations Where Radiation Exposure May Occur*
   - *Z53.1 (1971) Safety Color Code for Marking Physical Hazards*
   - *A13.1 (1956) Scheme for the Identification of Piping Systems*
   - *Z129.1 (1976) Precautionary Labeling of Hazardous Industrial Chemicals*
3. *Encycopedia of Chemical Labeling. Chemical Publishing Co., Inc., 1961*
4. *Safety Signs for Agricultural, Earthmoving and Forestry Machines.*
5. *API Bulletin on Precautionary Labeling. Bulletin no. 2511, third edition, August 1969. American Petroleum Institute.*
6. *Guide to Precautionary Labeling of Hazardous Chemicals: Manual L-1, Seventh edition, 1970. (Superseded by ANSI Z129.1 1976). Manufacturing Chemists Association*
7. *Warnings and Human Behavior: Implications for the Design of Product Warnings. Alan L. Dorris and Jerry L. Purswell.* Journal of Products Liability *v 1, n 4, 1977, pp 257–263*
8. *How to Label Hazardous Products. H. H. McIntyre.* A Modern Packaging *Special Report. 1968*
9. *Product Liability Portfolio: Section on Warnings and Recalls. Business Research Publications, 87 Terminal Drive, Plainview, N.Y. (formerly published by Man and Manager) 1975*
10. *Labeling Hazardous Products: paper by Harry McIntyre delivered at National Safety Congress, September 20, 1976. National Safety Council.*
11. *Duty to Warn. Defense Research Institute Monograph No. 2, 1980*
12. *Legal and Practical Considerations for the Creation of Warning Labels and Instruction Books. Kenneth Ross.* Journal of Products Liability *v 4, 1981, pp 29–45.*
13. *The Danger Never Was Obvious. Philo and Rine.* Journal of Products Liability *vl, n 1 1977 pp 12–19.*
14. *Products Liability: A Trilogy of Duty-To-Warn Cases. Thomas F. Lambert, Jr. 36* ALTA L. J. *pp 1–19, 1976*
15. *How John Deere Deals with Safety.* National Safety News, *December 1970. See also John Deere Design Manual #4, Safety, Instructional and Miscellaneous Signs and Standard Letters and Numerals.*
16. *A Guide to Signalling Requirements of OSHA: Federal Sign and Signal Corp. Monograph.*
17. *Product Safety and Liability Loss Control Handbook: see pages on labeling. Alliance of American Insurers, 1979*
18. *New Dimensions of Tortious Failure to Warn. Harry M. Philo.* Trial *v 18, n 4 November 1981*
19. *Labeling and Warning Systems: Proceedings of a Topical Symposium; November 1977, Washington, D.C. American Conference of Governmental Industrial Hygienists (ACGIH,) 1978*
20. *Product Safety Sign and Label System, 3rd. edition: January 1980. FMC Corporation, 1980*
21. *The Hazard Association Values of Accident Prevention Signs. Thomas F. Bresnahan and Joseph Bryk.* Professional Safety. *January 1975, pp 17–25.*
22. *NIOSH Proposed System for Employee Warning of Hazardous Materials.* Professional Safety *May 1975, pp 25–27*
23. *Labeling Hazardous Materials Can be Complex-a Practical Approach. John C. Henning.* Professional Safety, *November 1975, pp 36–40*
24. *Warning: Signs are Changing.* National Safety News. *March 1978, pp 113–114*
25. *ANSI Standard: Simple, Direct, Flexible. Warren H. Jones.* Occupational Health & Safety. *March/April 1978. pp 29–30*
26. *Effective Safety Signs and Posters. Edward D. Dionne.* National Safety News. *October 1979, pp 48–52*
27. *Psychologically Effective Warnings. Robert Jesse Cunitz.* Hazard Prevention. *v 17, n 3 May/June 1981, pp 5–7*
28. *Warnings Label Design. Michael W. Riley, David S. Cochran and John E. Deacy.* Professional Safety. *October 1981, pp 44–46*
29. *FMC's Systematic Approach to Product Safety Warning Labels. Sam Rosenberg.* Agricultural Engineering. *v 62 n 10 October 1981, pp 22–24*
30. *How to Make Signs and Labels for*

Safety....a Guidepost. National Safety News. *March 1982, pp 43–44*

31. *Product Safety Signs and Labels. Bowen H. Tucker, F.M.C. Corporation. ASAE Paper no. 78–1559*

See also the catalogues of the warning sign suppliers listed below:

1. *W. H. Brady*
   Facilities Identification Products Division
   727 W. Glendale Avenue
   P.O. Box 571
   Milwaukee, Wisconsin 53201
2. *Doculum*
   P.O. Box 18338
   Memphis, TN 38118
3. *Eastern Metal of Elmira, Inc.*
   Industrial Park
   1430 Sullivan Street
   Elmira, N.Y. 14901
4. *Emed Company*
   Box 369
   330 Greene Street
   Buffalo, N.Y. 14240
5. *Glas-Tex*
   P.O. Box 368
   Baldwin Park, CA 91706
6. *HCL Company*
   P.O. Box 359
   Menlo Park, CA 94025
7. *Hazard Controls, Inc.*
   Woodland and Yale Avenues
   Cherry Hill, N.J. 08034
8. *Identification Service Corp.*
   25 W. 26th Street
   New York, N.Y. 10010
9. *Legible Signs, Inc.*
   2221 Nimitz Road
   Rockford, IL 61111
10. *Litho/Color Inc.*
    840 W. Baltimore
    Detroit, Michigan 48202
11. *Lyle Signs, Inc.*
    7379 Washington Avenue South
    Minneapolis, Minnesota 55435
12. *Marzetta Signs, Inc.*
    1356 South 50th Street
    Richmond, CA, 94804
13. *National Marker Corporation*
    P.O. Box 1659
    100 Dexter Street
    Pawtucket, R.I. 02862
14. *Nutheme Illustrated Safety*
    2020 Lunt Avenue
    Elk Grove Village, IL 60007
15. *Self Powered Lighting, Inc.*
    8 Weschester Plaza
    Elmsford, N.Y. 10523
16. *Seton Name Plate Corporation*
    P.O. Drawer BG-1331
    New Haven, CT 06505
17. *Stonehouse Signs, Inc.*
    P.O. Box 546
    Arvada, Colorado 80001
18. *T & B/Westline*
    Div. of Thomas and Betts Co.
    220 South Rose Street
    Los Angeles, CA 90012

E — Access to Records Standard and Commentary (See p. 61)

Access to Employee Exposure and Medical Records

On May 21, 1980, OSHA issued a final standard requiring the preservation of and access to "employer maintained exposure and medical records" relevant to employees exposed to toxic substances and harmful physical agents, 29 CFR 1910.20 Access is also provided to "analyses" using exposure and medical records. Absent judicial action on the challenges which have been filed, the standard became effective on August 21, 1980. An analysis of the principal requirements of the standard follows:

I. Scope of the Standard

The standard applies to each general industry, maritime and construction employer of employees exposed (both past and present exposure) to toxic substances or harmful physical agents. 29 C.F.R. 1910.20 (b) (1). There is no exemption for small businesses or employers with multiple or transient work sites or transient work forces. The standard applies to *all* employee exposure and medical records and analyses, *whether or not* the records are related to specific occupational safety and health standards and whether or not exposure exceeds permissible limits imposed by OSHA. Moreover, it applies to records and analyses created both before and after the effective date of the rule. The standard applies to records generated or maintained by contractors of the employer as well as by in-house employees of the employer. The right of access is provided not only for current employees but also for former employees and legal representatives of deceased and incapacitated employees. Current employers and also former employers and successor employers must provide access to the covered records.

II. Description of Records Covered

Subject to access under the standard are employee *medical* records, employee *exposure* records and *analyses* using exposure or medical records. The standard defines the term "employee exposure record" to mean a record of monitoring or measuring which contains qualitative or quantitative information indicative of employee exposures to toxic materials and harmful physical agents. Generally, this includes all data which in any way characterizes the environment in which employees are working, eg. material safety data sheets; environmental monitoring, measuring or sampling; biological monitoring results which assess the absorption of a substance or agent by body systems such as urinary analysis and pulmonary function tests; or in the absence of the above, any other record which reveals the identity of a toxic substance or harmful physical agent. An example of this latter kind of exposure record would be a detailed manual concerning toxic substances which some employers develop for the benefit of their employees.

"Employee medical records" means those records concerning the health status of employees which are *made or maintained* by a physician, nurse or other health care personnel or technician. Inclusion of "technicians" within the standard is meant to cover those situations in which, for example, health questionnaires, monitoring tests (pulmonary function) or audiometric tests are conducted by persons who, strictly speaking, are not considered health care personnel. The use of the word "made" was intended to assure access in situations where medical information is held by non-medical departments such as personnel or industrial relations. Examples of records which would be considered to be included within the definition of medical records are: medical and employment questionnaires or histories (including job descriptions and occupational exposures but excluding other information peripherally related to an employee's health status which have never been included in an employee's medical file nor created by health care personnel); results of medical examinations and laboratory tests; medical opinions, diagnoses, descriptions of treatment and prescriptions; and employee medical complaints. Specifically excluded from the definition of an employee medical record are physical specimens which are routinely discarded as part of medical practice; records concerning health insurance claims if maintained separately from the employer's medical records; and records concerning voluntary employee assistance programs, such as alcohol, drug abuse and personal counselling, if maintained separately from the employer's medical program and its records. The definition of medical records makes no distinction between occupational and non-occupational information.

An "analysis" using exposure or medical records is defined as any compilation of data, or any research, statistical or other study based in part on information collected from individual employee exposure or medical records or information collected from health insurance claims records.

III. Access to Records

Upon request, access to employee exposure records and analyses must be provided to employees, designated representatives of employees and OSHA. An employee or his designated representative has the right of access to exposure records relevant to the employee, similarly situated employees, and the workplace in which the employee works or to which he will be transferred. OSHA and any recognized or certified collective bargaining agent have an automatic right of access to employee exposure records regardless of whether the employee has authorized such access. This means that collective bargaining agents and OSHA have automatic rights of access to exposure records and analyses without employee consent. Moreover, a collective bargaining agent's ability to obtain a copy of records to use on behalf of employees is not encumbered by the fact that a copy of the record was previously provided to a specific employee.

With respect to medical records, each employer must provide to the employee upon request, direct access to *his own* medical records, subject to one exception applicable to potentially harmful information involving terminal illness or psychiatric conditions. Access to medical records by a designated representative of the employee is only permitted where the employee has given the designated representative specific written consent. Absent this written consent, designated representatives (including collective bargaining agents) have no right of access to employee medical records. The standard contains a sample form which may be used by employees to authorize specific written consent for access to their medical records.

OSHA access to employee medical records is *not* conditioned on employee consent. However, whenever OSHA seeks access to employee medical records containing personally identifiable medical information, OSHA must first seek and present to the employer a written access order approved by the Assistant Secretary of Labor for Occupational Safety and Health. In order to inform employees of the contents of this order, the employer is required to post a copy of the access order and its cover letter for at least 15 working days. Regulations pertaining to OSHA access orders are contained in 29 CFR 1913.10.

Employers must provide access to the records covered by the standard in a reasonable time, place and manner within 15 days after a request for access is received. Access is defined as the right and opportunity to examine and copy the records. When a copy of the record is requested, the employer must either provide one without cost, make available copying facilities, again without cost, or loan the record for a reasonable time for copying elsewhere. The standard permits employers to establish orderly procedures for providing access so that work schedules are not unduly disrupted and employees not unduly inconvenienced. For example, an employer need not pay employees during the time a requested record is being reviewed if the record is made available before or after the employees' normal working hours. Moreover, it is permissable to store records in several locations or in a central area, and thus not immediately accessible at the place of employment, hence the 15-day retrieval period.

Whenever a record has once been provided without cost to an employee or designated representative, the employer may thereafter charge reasonable administrative costs for a request for additional copies of the record. Finally, it must be remembered, the standard specifically provides that nothing is intended to preclude employees and collective bargaining agents from collectively bargaining to obtain access to information in addition to that available under the rule.

IV. Preservation of Records

The standard requires that once created by an employer, for whatever reason, records must be preserved and made available for access by employees, designated representatives and OSHA. The standard does not however require the creation of new records or reports, or require an employer to monitor or measure employee exposure or provide medical surveillance or examinations. It does, however, require the preservation of those records that are created.

Employee exposure records and analyses must generally be preserved and maintained for at least 30 years while employee medical records must be retained for at least the duration of employment plus 30 years. However, if another specific standard sets a retention period for exposure and medical records different from that set forth in this standard, the specific provisions of the standard will control (*e.g.*, cotton dust, lead, alpha-naphthylamine, bis-chloromethyl ether, coke oven emissions, asbestos).

V. Employee Information

The standard provides that employers must inform employees of the existence, location and availability of records covered by the rule, the person responsible for obtaining and providing access to the records, and each employee's rights of access to these records. This instruction must be completed within sixty days of this part of the standard's effective date (October 21, 1980) for current employees and *annually* thereafter. Employers may use any method which will effectively apprise employees of their rights under the standard, including bulletin board posting, group discussions or individual notification. For example, if posting is used, the employer must inform the employee of his rights and must also make available to the employee a copy of the standard and its appendices plus any informational, training or educational materials concerning the standard which are made available to the employer by OSHA.

VI. Transfer of Records and Trade Secrets

The standard requires that an employer who is going out of business in situations where there is no successor employer must notify its employees of their access rights at least three months in advance of ceasing to do business. If a successor is taking over, the employer is required to transfer all records to the successor employer. In certain situations records must be given to NIOSH.

With respect to trade secrets, the standard provides that nothing precludes an employer from deleting trade secret data from the records which have been requested by an employee or designated representative. If such deletion impairs the evaluation of the place where or the time when exposure to a toxic substance or harmful physical agent occurred, the employer must provide alternative information sufficient to permit the employee to identify where and when exposure occurred.

VII. Commentary

The standard may require internal procedural or policy changes on the part of employers in order to comply with its requirements. The following is a list of suggested areas which employers may wish to explore in attempts to comply with the standard:

(1) Identify those records which meet the definition of medical records, employee exposure records or analyses and then ascertain, especially with respect to analyses, if there is personally

identifiable medical information contained therein. Examples of records which should be checked include pre-employment physicals, employment applications, post-employment histories, medical leaves of absence, and workers compensation and insurance claims.

(2) Ascertain which OSHA standards, if any, are applicable to the employer's place of business and which have record retention requirements different from those set forth in this standard. Those standards which may have different record retention requirements include those dealing with commercial diving operations, asbestos, benzidene, arsenic, vinyl chloride, lead, benzene, coke oven emissions, cotton dust and acrylonite.

(3) Determine if there are toxic substances and harmful physical agents in use in the workplace, and identify the specific work areas where they are used.

(4) Develop an employee authorization (written consent) form for use in the release of employee medical information to designated representatives. The authorization form should indicate who is authorized to disclose the information, who may have access to the information for what purpose, for what period of time and the general nature of the information to be disclosed.

(5) Designate a specific person(s) who is to be responsible for coordinating access to medical and exposure records and analyses, and inform employees when, where and how access to these records is to be obtained. Resolve conflicts with state laws which may limit disclosure of medical records or which may conflict with the new OSHA requirements.

(6) The substantive content of medical and exposure records may at times be relevant to: (i) the type of enforcement action OSHA intiates against an employer; (ii) proof of the appropriateness of an enforcement action; or (iii) compliance with recordkeeping requirements. Review of and access to these records should be considered from this perspective.

(7) Consultation with counsel is strongly recommended prior to implementing any personnel, procedural or policy changes to comply with the standard, in view of the significant impact that the standard may have upon privacy rights, equal employment opportunity, and labor relations matters.